Mending Broken Families

Mending Broken Families

SOCIAL POLICIES FOR DIVORCED FAMILIES: HOW EFFECTIVE ARE THEY?

Emily M. Douglas

ROWMAN & LITTLEFIELD PUBLISHERS, INC.
Lanham • Boulder • New York • Toronto • Oxford

ROWMAN & LITTLEFIELD PUBLISHERS, INC.

Published in the United States of America
by Rowman & Littlefield Publishers, Inc.
A wholly owned subsidiary of The Rowman & Littlefield Publishing Group, Inc.
4501 Forbes Boulevard, Suite 200, Lanham, Maryland 20706
www.rowmanlittlefield.com

PO Box 317
Oxford
OX2 9RU, UK

Copyright © 2006 by Rowman & Littlefield Publishers, Inc.

All rights reserved. No part of this publication may be reproduced, stored in a retrieval system, or transmitted in any form or by any means, electronic, mechanical, photocopying, recording, or otherwise, without the prior permission of the publisher.

British Library Cataloguing in Publication Information Available

Library of Congress Cataloging-in-Publication Data

Douglas, Emily M., 1973-
  Mending broken families : social policies for divorced families : how effective are they? / Emily M. Douglas.
    p. cm.
  Includes bibliographical references and index.
  ISBN-13: 978-0-7425-4276-1 (cloth : alk. paper)
  ISBN-10: 0-7425-4276-9 (cloth : alk. paper)
  ISBN-13: 978-0-7425-4277-8 (pbk. : alk. paper)
  ISBN-10: 0-7425-4277-7 (pbk. : alk. paper)
  1. Divorce—United States. 2. Family mediation—United States. 3. Custody of children—United States. 4. Family policy—United States. 5. Broken homes—United States. I. Title.
  HQ834.D68 2006
  306.89—dc22   2006005687

Printed in the United States of America

∞™ The paper used in this publication meets the minimum requirements of American National Standard for Information Sciences—Permanence of Paper for Printed Library Materials, ANSI/NISO Z39.48-1992.

For Dorothy

Contents

Preface	ix
Acknowledgments	xi
1 Introduction	1
2 Mediation	15
3 Divorce Education Programs	39
4 Parenting Plans	65
5 Joint Custody	91
6 Declaring a Rebuttable Presumption in Child-custody Statutes	117
7 Emerging Trends: Difficult Cases and Efforts Toward Prevention	143
8 Conclusions and Recommendations	169
Appendix: Joint-custody Statutes Nationwide	191
Index	203
About the Author	211

Preface

I began this book on social policies for families of divorce as a pessimist, believing that most, if not all, social policies for this target population were ineffective. Somewhere along the way, however, I became a cautious optimist, a careful enthusiast who believes that social policies and programming for families of divorce *do* bring about changes for children and families—modest as they may be.

My change of heart was brought about through two means. First, my reviews of the literature revealed true changes in parental behavior and family functioning. This alone might have been enough, but I also encountered comments made by seasoned, social-behavioral scholars—far wiser than I—at conferences and among my colleagues at the Family Research Laboratory and Crimes against Children Research Center at the University of New Hampshire. These scholars argued that a change in behavior for a minority of a sample does not spell failure, but it is, in fact, a success that *some* behavioral changes were made. As a conference attendee at the Association for Public Policy and Management, I heard scholars argue that rather than finding a single blanket policy solution for all families, a network of social policies and programs is necessary to target and change behaviors for the majority of a population. Another scholar questioned, tongue in cheek, "If years of therapy don't result in change, why would we expect that a few hours of mediation would be the end-all and be-all for divorcing couples?" Finally, I was urged by my colleagues at the University of New Hampshire to relinquish my pessimism in favor of more optimistic conclusions.

In truth, it took much convincing; for a long time I remained a pessimist—a condition that is in direct contrast to my true nature. But one day, after working on a particularly difficult chapter in preparation for a presentation of my work-in-progress, I stepped back from my work and was struck by my pessimism having turned into optimism. I saw that small behavioral changes from short interventions are in fact indications of success and should point the way for greater improvements. Moreover, I concluded that even if one-time interventions only improve two out of ten indicators of family functioning, then this is success, as opposed to failure. In short, the literature and my colleagues convinced me of the importance of celebrating small successes and, more important, of seeing small successes in the social sciences as worthy of attention by our federal and state legislatures.

Emily M. Douglas

Acknowledgments

There are many people who helped to make this book possible. First, I would like to acknowledge my dissertation committee at the University of Massachusetts, Boston. This book is the result of a question that I received during my dissertation defense, which focused on the effectiveness of a presumption for joint legal custody in the state of New Hampshire. If a presumption didn't seem to make a difference, then what *did* make a difference in the lives of divorced families?

I owe an endless debt of gratitude to my Friday Seminar colleagues at the Family Research Laboratory and the Crimes against Children Research Center at the University of New Hampshire. They provided critical reviews of most of the chapters in this book, as well as constant support and enthusiasm for my developing scholarly work. Drs. Murray Straus and David Finkelhor were especially encouraging of my writing and reviews of the literature, and for this I am forever grateful. I also extend a sincere thank you to Jen Douglas for her diligent and speedy assistance with the proofs of this book, and to Zachary Lowell for tracking down numerous requests for articles and references.

As always, many friends and family members have provided me with support throughout my writing process in the ways that are most important—by providing a sympathetic ear and opportunities for rest and pleasure. But, most of all, I am especially thankful to my husband, who, for over a year, performed endless household tasks and single-handedly took care of all of life's necessities without a single complaint—so that I could write this book.

1

Introduction

Divorce is known to have significant and largely negative effects on children. Most research has documented that children of divorce are more likely than children of intact families to have academic problems, to display anger and aggression toward peers and family members, to develop problems with depression and anxiety, and to feel torn between their parents [1–6]. There is also evidence that the consequences of growing up in a divorced family continue into adulthood, when adult children of divorced families are faced with choosing intimate partners and starting families of their own [7], although not all research finds that these consequences are negative [8]. In an effort to minimize the detrimental effects of divorce on children and parents, state legislatures have developed and passed legislation that is intended to simultaneously promote family-friendly divorce procedures and healthier outcomes for families of divorce. This book will review five such social policies and their outcomes for children and families: (1) mediation, (2) divorce education programs, (3) parenting plans, (4) voluntary joint custody, and (5) a presumption for joint custody. First, however, allow us to step back a couple hundred years so that the efforts of today's legislators can be placed in the proper context.

HISTORY OF DIVORCE LAW IN THE UNITED STATES

The Early Years

Although uncommon in eighteenth-century America, some marriages ended in divorce. In such circumstances, all family property, including children, were awarded to the husband. This action arose from the fact that women could not own property and at this time in history, children were considered property because of their future economic potential [9]. Women who pursued divorce risked losing all contact with their children, as noncustodial parents were not guaranteed "child contact" rights. This reality forced many women to stay in unhappy and sometimes unhealthy marriages to ensure a life with their children [10].

Also in the era of the eighteenth century, children were viewed as "little adults" whose needs did not differ from those of actual adults. In the nineteenth century an expanded view of children came into being that recognized that children have unique needs that deserve special attention. Building on the Victorian reverence for women, often called the "Cult of True Womanhood" [11], mothers were eventually judged as the only persons who could truly provide this special attention, especially for children of "tender years, or children in early childhood." The first legal case to use the "tender-years doctrine," as it was later to be called, occurred in Philadelphia in 1840. The attorneys argued that a child of tender years needed the special care that only a mother could provide [12].

This emphasis on maternal care was a growing theme in the United States, as evidenced by books on parenting directed at mothers but not at fathers, advertisements for children's products that were specifically aimed at mothers, and the clear division of labor within the household as men moved from farms to factories [13]. The ideological change in family roles fueled the tender-years doctrine, and it quickly spread throughout the nation. As a result, women increasingly became the sole custodian of their children when their marriages dissolved. Despite efforts as late as 1898 to maintain paternal control through legislation stating that fathers would receive sole custody, the Census Bureau figures reported that between 1887 and 1906, women received custody at a three-to-one ratio to men [10].

In the twentieth century, the use of another doctrine eventually came to prevail in child custody cases. This doctrine—"the best interests of the child"—was introduced through a child-custody suit in 1925. This high legal standard seeks to answer the question, "What would be in the best interests of a child?" In 1925, the answer to this question was that custody of children should be granted to mothers and that contact with noncustodial parents was permissible [14]. The answer to this question today is not usually this straightforward, and a number of different factors can be used to decide what is in a child's best interest. Despite the early introduction of this standard, the legal presumption of the tender-years doctrine prevailed well into the 1970s before courts turned their attention to the best interests of the child standard.

The No-fault Movement

The end of the active civil rights movement and the beginning of the women's rights movement coincided with an era that brought substantial change to American families [15]. These changes, which mostly involved alterations in family formation, began in the early 1970s, when couples wanted to obtain divorces because of "irreconcilable differences." Before this time, couples that wanted to divorce had to substantiate a reason for divorce, such as infidelity, cruelty, or substance abuse problems. At a time when social customs were routinely being questioned, the American public challenged the restrictive conditions under which marriages could legally be terminated [16].

This challenge resulted in "no-fault" divorce legislation, which stated that couples could obtain a divorce because of dissatisfaction or unhappiness, without declaring that one party was "at fault" [17]. No-fault divorce legislation swept across the county, and a record number of couples throughout the nation began divorcing [18]—even in states that had not officially adopted no-fault legislation [19–21]. Many of these newly divorced couples began to question the "status quo" for the handling of divorced families. These questions eventually led to significant changes within the laws that regulate divorce, many of which are addressed in this book. Although there is some overlap in the sequence of divorce laws, a pattern emerges and shows trends in the legislation that swept across the country; thus the book's organization and discussion of policies reflect these historical trends.

Gender-neutral Policies

Shortly after the rise in the divorce rate, there was a wave of legislation that targeted divorcing couples with children. As previously stated, the tender-years doctrine prevailed well into the early 1970s. This meant that in a preponderance of cases mothers received custody of children when families divorced. The sexual revolution that both preceded and accompanied the move to no-fault divorces resulted in more fathers being involved with their children. Moreover, the traditional division of labor within the home was blurred as more women worked outside of the home, and men engaged in more parenting responsibilities [22, 23]. When couples divorced, many men wished to continue this increased parenting role—a circumstance that was difficult to accomplish when most children lived with their mothers [24, 25]. Divorced fathers challenged the tender-years doctrine and successfully argued that dogmatically giving custody to women was a form of sex discrimination against men. This argument led to the implementation of gender-neutral child-custody statutes, which declare that the gender of a parent cannot be a deciding factor in contested child-custody cases [26]. Such laws exist in about half of the states in the country today, but the spirit of the law is widely practiced throughout the nation. Despite gender-neutral laws, women obtain custody in the majority of uncontested child custody cases [27, 28], not because of a statutory preference, but primarily because of social custom.

Best Interests of the Child

About 90 percent of divorcing couples walk into the courtroom with a divorce agreement. That means that only one out of every ten cases is contested [28, 29]. In such instances, courts need guidance in how to divide family assets, and most important, how to award custody of children [30, 31]. Today, every state in the nation relies on the best interests of the child standard [32, 33]. This overarching set of guidelines for making child-custody decisions originated with the 1970 Uniform Marriage and Divorce Act, which was drafted by the National Conference of Commissioners on Uniform State Laws [34, 35]. This act, or a version of this act, was adopted by every state and is the foundation for divorce laws today. Although each state is permitted to define what is considered to be in a child's best interests and how to decide custody cases, there are common themes across states. The following is a partial list of considerations that states include as criteria for how to decide child-custody cases.

- The wishes of the child's parent or parents as to his custody (recommended by the National Conference of Commissioners on Uniform State Laws)
- The desires of children if they are old enough to responsibly voice a preference (such as in Georgia, O.C.G.A. § 19-9-1)
- The child's adjustment to home, school, and community (such as in Montana, MCA § 40-4-212)
- The love, affection, and other emotional ties existing between the parties involved and the child (such as in Michigan, MCL § 722.23)
- The ability and disposition of each parent to foster a positive relationship and frequent and continuing contact with the other parent, including physical contact, except where contact will result in harm to the child or to a parent (such as in Vermont, 15 V.S.A. § 665)

Summary

The middle of the twentieth century brought marked changes to families, the family law profession, and state statutes. The tender-years doctrine was abandoned, no-fault divorces and an increase in divorce spread across the country, child-custody decisions could no longer be based on the gender of the parent, and a new standard for determining child custody—the best interests of the child—was put into place. This revolution occurred primarily during the 1970s. The new laws did not, however, prepare the court, the states, or the public to address many of the social ills that inherently follow divorce: parental conflict, triangulating behaviors between parents and children (placing children in the middle of parental arguments), increases in poverty, and general questions about the well-being of children from families of divorce. State-level social policies that were first implemented in the 1980s and continue today sought to address these social problems, and they are the subject of this book.

OUTLINE OF THE BOOK

This brief historical review brings us to the early 1980s—the time when social policies to assist families of divorce were first implemented. This book discusses the most prominent social policies that have been implemented as potential "solutions" for the problems of children (and parents) who live in divorced families. These social policies are:

- Mediation (chapter 2): Primarily implemented in the 1980s, these laws either recommend or mandate that parents seek services from a mediator to help resolve their divorce-related disputes.
- Divorce Education Programs (chapter 3): The availability of these programs exploded during the 1990s. Social policies either recommend or mandate that divorcing parents attend an educational seminar or course that instructs them on how to better meet the needs of their children in divorced families.
- Parenting Plans (chapter 4): Legislation pertaining to parenting plans took off during the 1990s and will likely continue to be implemented in many states throughout the early decades of the twenty-first century. In the best of circumstances, parenting plans replace traditional divorce decrees and encourage parents to plan for most aspects of their co-parental postdivorce life.
- Joint Custody (chapter 5): Legislation concerning joint custody has been on the policy table since the late 1970s and, unless there are any significant changes in families and the legal system, will continue to be addressed and tinkered with by feminist groups, fathers' rights activists, and children's advocates. Social policies that address shared-parenting arrangements can address joint decision making or joint living arrangements.
- Declaring a Rebuttable Presumption (chapter 6): Legislative bills that declare a rebuttable presumption, or a mandate, for joint custodial arrangements rarely pass, or are watered down to statutes that

encourage joint parenting arrangements. Nonetheless, some do survive and ultimately legally mandate that all families of divorce adopt a particular custodial arrangement.
- Emerging Trends (chapter 7): This chapter focuses on new innovations, challenges, and trends within family law and their potential effects on children and families of divorce.
- Conclusions and Recommendations (chapter 8): This chapter draws conclusions from the policies that are reviewed in this book and provides recommendations to policymakers, researchers, and practitioners working with families of divorce.

As noted, chapters 2 through 6 will be dedicated to the review of individual social policies. The outline for each of these chapters is:

- What is the social policy solution?
- The history of the social policy
- The prevalence and use of the social policy today in statutes across the country [40]
- What are the outcomes for children and families who use or are subjected to this social policy?

The chapters will also follow the life of the Barnes family, a fictitious but realistic divorcing family. The profile of this family and the problems that they face are established at the end of this introductory chapter. I will use this family to demonstrate application of each social policy that is explored and how the presence of each policy would alter the legal, and possibly social, ramifications for the family.

CHILD CUSTODY AND TERMINOLOGY

The legal and sociall terminology used throughout this book should be explained up front. The most frequently occurring problem with terminology in this field concerns the different terms used to discuss the custody of children. The public and professionals alike are often confused about these terms and their exact definitions. Tables 1.1 and 1.2 summarize custodial types and different custodial arrangements. *Physical custody*, sometimes also called *residential custody*, concerns where children live. A parent can have *sole physical custody* of his or her children, which means that the children live only with him or her. This parent is usually called the *custodial parent*. The parent *without physical custodial rights*, usually called the *noncustodial parent*, may have *access rights* (also called *visitation*) to his or her children. Parents can have *joint physical custody*, or *shared residential custody*, which means that the children di-

Table 1.1. Types and Definitions of Custodial Arrangements

Type of Custody	Definition
Physical custody	This type of custody concerns with whom the child lives. Other commonly used terms include: residential custody, residential parent. Examples: • *Sole physical custody*: The circumstances under which a child lives primarily with one parent and when that parent's home is declared as the child's legal address (often called the "custodial parent") • *Joint physical custody*: An arrangement in which a child shares living time between the homes of two parents; one parent may still be declared as having the primary physical address • *No physical custody*: An arrangement in which a parent does not have any physical custody rights to his or her child; this parent is usually granted "access" rights to the child, but not always (often called the "noncustodial" parent)
Legal custody	This type of custody concerns who makes decisions about the major events in a child's life, such as education, religious training, medical attention, etc. Other commonly used terms: parental rights and responsibilities; decision-making responsibilities. Examples: • *Sole legal custody*: Wherein one parent is granted the right to make all decisions about the child's life • *Joint legal custody*: Wherein the parents share in the decision-making responsibilities about a child's life; sometimes the decision-making responsibilities will be split between the two parents • *No legal custody*: Wherein a parent has no right to make decisions about his or her child

vide their living time between their parents. Having an arrangement of joint physical custody does not always mean that children split their time between their mothers and fathers 50–50; parents could split their parenting time a variety of different ways, such as 70–30 or 60–40. Thus, the focus on joint physical custody does not always concentrate on the percentage of shared time, just that it is shared. Most often in joint physical-custody arrangements children move between their parents' homes; however, in highly cooperative postdivorce families, the children may live in one home and the parents may move in and out of the home as stated in their divorce agreement. The most common physical custodial arrangement is for mothers to have sole physical custody and fathers to have access rights to the children. Most often this has meant that fathers see their children once a week for dinner and every other

Table 1.2. Possible Custodial Arrangements

Type of Custodial Arrangement	Explanation
Sole legal and physical custody awarded to mother	*Decision making*: • Child's mother makes all decisions • Child's father has no legal right to make decisions *Living Arrangement*: • Child resides with mother • Child most likely permitted to have access to father, as stated by divorce decree/parenting plan
Sole legal and physical custody awarded to father	*Decision making*: • Child's father makes all decisions • Child's mother has no legal right to make decisions *Living Arrangement*: • Child resides with father • Child most likely permitted to have access to mother, as stated by divorce decree/parenting plan
Joint legal custody, physical custody awarded to mother	*Decision making*: • Child's mother and father make decisions about child *Living Arrangement*: • Child resides with mother • Child most likely permitted to have access to father, as stated by divorce decree/parenting plan
Joint legal custody, physical custody awarded to father	*Decision making*: • Child's mother and father make decisions about child *Living Arrangement*: • Child resides with father • Child most likely permitted to have access to mother, as stated by divorce decree/parenting plan
Joint legal and physical custody	*Decision making*: • Child's mother and father make decisions about child *Living Arrangement*: • Child resides with both mother and father on an alternating schedule as stated by divorce decree/parenting plan

weekend. When legal professionals and laypersons use the terms *custodial parent* and *noncustodial parent*, they are usually referring to physical-custody arrangements.

Legal custody, sometimes termed *parental rights and responsibilities*, concerns decision making about major events in children's lives, such as education, religion, and medical treatment. Parents can be assigned *sole legal custody* or *joint legal custody*. In the former case, one parent is assigned sole legal custody of the children, granting him or her the full legal authority to make all decisions about the children's lives. In cases of joint legal custody, the parents share in the decision making about the major events in their children's lives. Parents with no legal custody are not permitted to make decisions about their children's lives. Since children usually live most of the time with their mothers, this usually means that mothers make decisions concerning the day-to-day events about the children (such as manners, extracurricular events, bedtimes, etc.) and that fathers participate in decisions about major events (such as religious training, changes in schools, seeking psychotherapy, etc.). Very few states keep records of legal custodial arrangements. There is some evidence, however, to support the idea that a joint agreement may be the most common form of legal custody today [26, 36].

A final type of custodial arrangement that is not often used is called *split custody*. In this type of arrangement one parent is awarded sole physical custody of one (or more) of the children and the other parent is awarded sole physical custody of the other child (or children). In such instances legal custody would likely be shared between the parents. Split custody arrangements are not commonly used.

There are several different terms that are used to describe the contact that children have with their noncustodial or nonresidential parent. The traditional term is "visitation." This came from the idea that children would live with one parent and visit the other parent. Such terminology has often been the center of criticism, with noncustodial parents stating the desire to be more than "visitors" in their children's lives [37–39]. As a result of these concerns the language that is used to describe this relationship has changed. Some states refer to visitation as "parenting time," "access rights," or the "child contact schedule." You will find that I use these more neutral terms when referring to the time that children spend with their nonresidential parents.

MEET THE BARNES FAMILY

Joanne and Mark Barnes, ages thirty-three and thirty-five, respectively, have been married for eight years. They have two children, April, age six, and Nathan, age four. They live in a three-bedroom house in a suburb of a large metropolitan area. Mark works full-time for the federal government and has a twenty-five-minute commute to work. Joanne works twenty hours per week as a bank teller and has a fifteen-minute commute to work. April is in first grade and Nathan attends preschool on the days and times that Joanne works at the bank. Although Joanne and Mark maintain close contact with their own parents, they live approximately one hour from both sets of parents.

Joanne and Mark have been having marital problems for about two years. They argue frequently about money, the children, and how much time they spend or do not spend together. They sought help from a marital counselor, but ceased treatment after a few weeks when they became dissatisfied with what they perceived to be their lack of progress. Shortly thereafter, Joanne hired an attorney and filed for divorce. Mark is unhappy that Joanne has chosen to take legal action, but he confesses that he does not see much opportunity for improvement in the marriage. Moreover, the children are exhibiting signs of stress, such as bed-wetting and fear of abandonment. Thus Mark, too, is becoming resigned to the fact that divorce may be the only way to bring peace to everyone's lives.

Mark hires an attorney to handle his "side" of the divorce. He has heard about "joint custody," and because he does not want to lose touch with his children, he declares that he wants to arrange for joint custody, even though he is confident that Joanne will fight against adopting such an arrangement. Mark's attorney tries to convince him that custody is most often granted to mothers, that it is very expensive to fight for joint custody, and that it is in his children's best interests if they live with one parent. Mark does not accept this advice and reports to both his attorney and Joanne that he is determined to fight for joint custody.

Mark and Joanne, together, search for an apartment for Mark, and within a month of hiring his own attorney, Mark has moved into a two-bedroom apartment that is approximately fifteen minutes from Joanne and the children. The children are unhappy that Mark has left home, and they are unsure of the reasons for his move. Because of their ages, they frequently inquire if their behavior is in some way responsible for the changes in their household composition. Joanne and Mark took sincere steps to make the children feel comfortable at their father's new residence, but the children complain that it doesn't feel like "home." When they spend the night with their father, they have to share a bedroom, they don't have as many toys at his apartment, and there is no yard in which they can play. The children want to bring their dog to Mark's home, but animals are not permitted in the apartment. The children and Mark truly enjoy spending time together, but Mark feels that his relationship with them has become significantly strained. He doesn't know how they are doing in school; the names of new classmates; or the ever-changing preferences in clothing, toys, and food. He refrains from asking Joanne because even seemingly neutral topics usually result in conflict.

Joanne and the children remain in the house, and she increases her workweek from fifteen to thirty-five hours per week. This change in Joanne's schedule necessitates additional child care and changes in schedules for both of the children. Joanne is concerned that Mark will "take the children" away from her, and she is worried about how frequent moves between her home and Mark's apartment will affect the children. She has already noticed that the children seem tired more often, that they are fearful when she leaves them with another caregiver, and that they are more challenging to parent when they are transitioning to or away from seeing their father. She is concerned about the amount of time they spend in child *care and considers asking Mark is take the children on evenings when she is at the bank, but she fears that any further interaction with him will result in a quarrel; moreover, she disapproves of some of his parenting behavior and thinks that the children do not receive a good supper when they are with their father.*

Joanne and Mark cannot come to an agreement regarding custody of their children and a few other details concerning the termination of their joint households. Mark's attorney writes a proposed agreement and sends it to Joanne's attorney, who in turn rejects the proposal and submits Joanne's proposed agreement. This routine lasts for the better part of six months, and because of it, Joanne and Mark become so furious with one another that they stop communicating about everything, including the children. Nonetheless, Mark maintains his desire for joint custody of the children, and a trial date is set for many months later. As the date approaches, his relationships with his children and Joanne become more strained, and with his legal debt mounting, Mark agrees to settle outside of court. Approximately eighteen months after filing for divorce, Joanne is granted full physical and legal custody of the children. Joanne will live in the house with the children and will increase her workweek to forty hours per week. Mark will see the children every other weekend and one night a week for dinner. He will continue to work full-time, and he will give Joanne 27 percent of his income in the form of child support.

April and Nathan are displeased with their family's new living arrangements. They maintain a strong and often-voiced desire that their parents should reconcile their relationship so that the family can live together again. Their parents do not generally speak to one another, and as a result April has become the correspondent between her parents—carrying messages that often make one or both of her parents angry. On the occasions when Mark and Joanne do speak with one another about a matter concerning the children, such as a pick-up or drop-off time, one of them explodes into anger and the children are distressed by the open hostility between their parents. Mark and Joanne frequently speak negatively about each other in front of the children, which causes April and Nathan to feel trapped and unsure which parent they should believe. Finally, their parents have different rules about such things as the number of hours that they may watch television, the completion of homework, spending time with friends, and chores around the house. The inconsistency between their parents' homes and the open hostility between their parents leave April and Nathan feeling overwrought and conflicted about the changes in their family.

The case scenario of the Barnes family details the standard process that many divorces follow in the United States. This process is described as the "traditional adversarial method" of the family court system. There have been many efforts to reform the process of divorce and to make it less adversarial, especially when children are involved. Throughout the course of this book I will revisit the Barnes family and explore how their marital dissolution would have been handled differently had they lived in a state or district with more family-friendly programs and policies for families of divorce.

REFERENCES

1. Amato, P. R., and B. Keith. Parental divorce and the well-being of children: A meta-analysis. *Psychological Bulletin*, 1991, 110(1): pp. 26–46.
2. Amato, P. R. Children of divorce in the 1990s: An update of the Amato and Keith (1991) meta-analysis. *Journal of Family Psychology*, 2001, 15(3): pp. 355–70.
3. Buchanan, C. M., E. E. Maccoby, and S. M. Dornbush. *Adolescents after divorce*. 1996, Cambridge, MA: Harvard University Press.
4. Peterson, J. L., and N. Zill. Marital disruption, parent-child relationships and behavior problems in children. *Journal of Marriage and the Family*, 1986, 48(May): pp. 295–307.
5. Wallerstein, J. Children after divorce: Wounds that don't heal. *Perspectives in Psychiatric Care*, 1987, 24(3-4): pp. 107–13.
6. Lowery, C., and S. Settle. Effects of divorce on children: Differential impact of custody and visitation patterns. *Family Relations*, 1985, 34(4): pp. 455–63.
7. Wallerstein, J. *The unexpected legacy of divorce: The 25-year landmark study*. 2000, New York: Hyperion Books.
8. Sprecher, S., R. Cate, and L. Levin. Parental divorce and young adults' beliefs about love. *Journal of Divorce and Remarriage*, 1998, 28(3/4): pp. 107–20.
9. Chused, R. H. *Private acts in public places: A social history of divorce in the formative era of American family law*. 1994, Philadelphia: University of Pennsylvania Press.
10. Riley, G. *Divorce: An American tradition*. 1991, New York: Oxford University Press.
11. Coontz, S. *The way we never were: American families and the nostalgia trap*. 1992, New York: Basic Books.
12. Woodhouse, B. B. Child custody in the age of children's rights: The search for a just and workable standard. *Family Law Quarterly*, 1999, 33(3): pp. 815–32.
13. Stearns, P. N. Fatherhood in historical perspective: The role of social change. In *Fatherhood and families in cultural context: Focus on men*, ed. S. M. H. Hanson, pp. 28–52. 1991, New York: Springer.
14. Halem, L. C. *Divorce reform: Changing legal and social perspectives*. 1980, New York: Free Press.
15. Glick, P. C. Fifty years of family demography: A record of social change. *Journal of Marriage and Family*, 1988, 50(4): pp. 861–73.
16. D. B. New trends in family law. *Social Work*, 1979, 24(4): pp. 266–67.
17. Kay, H. H. An appraisal of California's no-fault divorce law. *California Law Review*, 1987, 75(29): pp. 291–319.
18. Glick, P. C. A demographer looks at American families. *Journal of Marriage and Family*, 1975, 37(1): pp. 15–26.

19. Wright, G. C., and D. M. Stetson. The impact of no-fault divorce law reform on divorce in American states. *Journal of Marriage and Family*, 1978, 40(3): p. 575.

20. Mazur-Hart, S. F., and J. J. Berman. Changing from fault to no-fault divorce: An interrupted time series analysis. *Journal of Applied Social Psychology*, 1977, 7(4): pp. 300–312.

21. Marvell, T. B. Divorce rates and the fault requirement. *Law and Society Review*, 1989, 23(4): pp. 543–67.

22. Rotundo, E. A. American fatherhood: A historical perspective. *American Behavioral Scientist*, 1985, 29: pp. 7–25.

23. Lamb, M. E. The changing role of fathers. In *Becoming a father*, ed. M. Greenberg, pp. 18–35. 1995, New York: Springer Publishing Company, Inc.

24. Roman, M., and W. Haddad. *The disposable parent: The case for joint custody.* 1978, New York: Holt.

25. Green, M. *Fathering.* 1976, New York: McGraw-Hill Company.

26. Kelly, J. B. The determination of child custody. *Future of Children*, 1994, 4(1): pp. 121–42.

27. Kuhn, D. R. Shared parenting ranges from 19% to 25.8% of divorced families in the U.S. *Speak Out for Children*, 2003, (Winter): pp. 19–21.

28. Maccoby, E. E., and R. H. Mnookin. *Dividing the child: Social and legal dilemmas of custody.* 1992, Cambridge, MA: Harvard University Press.

29. Hastings, H. *The New Hampshire divorce handbook.* 1999, Amherst, NH: Amoskeag Press.

30. Wald, M. S. Legal policies affecting children: A lawyer's request for aid. *Child Development* 1976, 47(1): pp. 1–5.

31. Child custody debate finds no easy road. *ABA Journal*, 1978, p. 1336.

32. Weiner, B. A. An overview of child custody laws. *Hospital and Community Psychiatry*, 1985, 36(8): pp. 838–43.

33. Howell, R. J., and K. E. Toepke. Summary of the child custody laws for the fifty states. *American Journal of Family Therapy*, 1984, 12: pp. 56–60.

34. Musetto, A. P. Standards for deciding contested child custody. *Journal of Clinical Child Psychology*, 1981, 10(1): pp. 51–55.

35. Creswell, R. W. The proposed Tennessee Family Law Act in context. *Tennessee Law Review*, 1974, 41: pp. 463–501.

36. Douglas, E. M. The influence of public policies on human behavior: Is there an effect of a New Hampshire law stating a presumption for joint legal custody on father involvement in divorced families? Public Policy Program, 2002, Boston: University of Massachusetts, p. 354.

37. Foster, C. Plea for fathers' rights: divorced but still a dad. *Christian Science Monitor*, July 6, 1982: p. 2.

38. Young, C. Equal access to children after a divorce. *Boston Globe*, October 16, 2004.

39. Lee, P. Reinventing fatherhood. *Ottawa Citizen*, March 3, 2001. p. B1.

40. The reader should note that upon publication, a book which documents social policies, is likely out-of-date. This is because legislation is proposed and bills are passed every day across the county. The legal research for this book was conducted in 2004 and 2005, thus some of the statutes could have changed in the time between preparation of the manuscript and publication of the book.

2

Mediation

Mediation is one of the most popular policy solutions for working with divorcing couples with disputes. An often-used conflict-resolution tool, this technique is frequently implemented to help parents find a common solution to their divorce-related disagreements. First mandated and popularized by the state of California in the early 1980s, the mediation movement spread quickly across the country and is widely used in the family court system today.

WHAT IS MEDIATION?

Mediation is a conflict-resolution technique that is offered for and used by parents who are divorcing or parents who are divorced and have continuing postdivorce conflict. If couples are unable to decide on the terms of their divorce, often they will seek or be referred to mediation. Such services are intended to be an alternative to traditional, adversarial litigation that identifies "winners" and "losers" of the legal system [1] and that can inflame existing hostile feelings between divorcing couples. Starting in the 1970s, members of the legal profession, as well as members of the "helping" professions (such as the psychotherapeutic, medical, and child welfare professions) began to seek ways to improve the divorce and postdivorce experiences of families [2]. The presence of children in a divorce necessitates an ongoing postdivorce relationship between parents, and a positive postdivorce relationship, which is often predicated on a positive divorcing experience, makes for better adjustment among children from divorced families [3]. Thus, mediation is intended to neutralize the inherently adversarial nature of the legal system and to bring parents together to find common solutions to their impending postdivorce lives. In fact, there is evidence to support the notion that, theoretically, mediation changes the "winner-loser" approach that results from traditional, adversarial divorces. R. E. Emery and his colleagues [46] found a negative correlation in mothers' and fathers' attitudes about the divorce settlement among couples who litigated using the adversarial system and a positive correlation among couples who used mediation services. In other words, among couples who litigated, when mothers reported that they had "won" their case, fathers were more likely to report having "lost" their case, and vice versa. Couples who used mediation services were more likely to have parallel responses. The more mothers felt that they had won their case, the more fathers did, too.

Mediation has been described as a time-limited, goal-focused, and solution-oriented intervention [4]. Parents meet with a trained, yet unbiased, mediator, typically for hour-long sessions over the course of several weeks or months. Mediated resolutions are usually obtained within an average of six to nine hours [5], and some mediators advocate for a limited number of sessions in order to force participants into working cooperatively with one another [6]. Trained divorce mediators include professionals who have backgrounds in psychotherapy, counseling, conflict resolution, or law. Also, mediators usually have an understanding of family processes and conflict and have skills in how to bring about resolution between two warring sides [2]. Although most mediation sessions take place between a divorcing (or divorced) couple and a mediator, other forms of conflict resolution include providing mediation services to a group of couples who face similar obstacles to resolution [7]. Another model for mediation that is often proposed is to include children in mediation sessions, either during direct negotiations, such as with older children, or bringing children into later sessions to explain the outcome of the resolution [1, 4, 8]. Other mediators have argued for the importance of incorporating psychological evaluations of children into the mediation work so that the postdivorce plan can be tailored to meet the individual needs of each child and family [9]. Finally, another model concerns the use of two mediators rather than one [10]. This model has been proposed to be more effective because ideas are generated by the multiple participants; it is said to promote perceptions of unbiased mediators, and it is hypothesized that this type of mediation would take less time and thus cost less money.

The issues on which most divorcing or divorced couples cannot agree—usually the children, property, and finances [6]—are designated as the focus of the mediated intervention. During the sessions the couple, under the direction of the mediator, explore possible different solutions in order to look for one that will be acceptable to both parties [11]. For example, if a couple cannot decide on a child-contact schedule, a mediator might encourage each parent to propose several schedules that would be acceptable and to then explore what common ground might exist between the two parents' proposals. Mediators with mental-health training might also provide some education for couples about the effects of divorce on children and also explore what factors might impede the resolution of their divorce. For example, if one member of a couple desires reconciliation, he or she might refuse to settle negotiations in an attempt to keep the marriage together [7]. If couples cannot come to a resolution during mediation, their case is brought to court, where a judge decides what is in the best interest of the children or what is legally the best, or most fair, solution to the problem.

One of the most striking aspects of mediation is that it is case specific. Unlike other social policy solutions, such as divorce education (see chapter 3) or a presumption for joint custody (see chapter 6), the methods and outcomes of mediation are determined by couple-specific family needs and conflicts. This is because what is deemed a solution by one couple might be deemed a disaster by another. Couples together decide what is best for their children or what is suitable in terms of a financial arrangement. In many ways, mediation is intended to lay the groundwork for compromise and the co-parenting relationship that should exist after marital dissolution. The notion behind mediation is that when both parties feel that they have won, it promotes a cooperative atmosphere that, with luck, transfers over into the postdivorce period.

Mediation in Application: The Barnes Family

The Barnes family would have been ideal candidates for mediation services. As readers may recall, Mark and Joanne were unable to come to an agreement about the custody of their children and a child-contact schedule. Mark wanted joint physical custody and Joanne did not. If Joanne and Mark had lived in a state that mandates mediation, they would have been required to attend mediation services before moving their case toward a trial. This means that the Barnes family would not have been permitted to appear before a judge for resolution to their conflict until they had sought assistance from a court-approved mediator. If Mark and Joanne still had not been able to resolve their conflict with a mediator, then their case would have moved to trial, where a judge, perhaps in conjunction with a guardian *ad litem*, someone appointed to be a voice for children, and the "eyes and ears" of the court, would have made a decision regarding custody and parent-child contact.

Although in the end Mark settled out of court, he did so because he felt that the trial and legal costs were placing considerable strain on his life and the lives of his family members. Moreover, Mark felt that he had "lost," that he had relented to a family schedule that he did not think was best for his children or for him. Mediation provides an opportunity for divorcing parents to discuss their differences and to come to conclusions about custody and child-contact schedules together. While it may not be successful for all families, it provides an opportunity for cooperation that is absent from the traditional adversarial system.

THE HISTORY OF MEDIATION

By the late 1970s, divorce rates were skyrocketing and many members of the helping professions were seeking new ways to assist families of divorce. No-fault divorce legislation that was passed in the early 1970s [12] opened a floodgate to couples wanting to get divorced who could not have done so under the old law [13]. Furthermore, no-fault legislation meant no one was to blame for the breakup of the marriage. Thus, with the introduction of these new laws, divorcing couples essentially had equal claim to all of the family assets, including the children [14].

A Call for a New Profession

The increase in the number of couples who were divorced resulted in new, or an increase of existing, social problems. There was a rise in the number of women and children who were living in poverty [15] (although there is some debate about extent of this problem—see [16]), as well as a rise in the number of children who were suffering from the psychological pain that is inherent in family dissolution [17]. An article written in 1978 for the journal *Social Work*, responded to these growing changes in American life. Haynes [18] outlined a new role for professionals with social work training—the role of mediator for divorcing families. The article discussed the many challenges that families of divorce face, such as issues of family finances and child custody—issues well-known to the majority of the public today but not well documented in the late 1970s. The author encouraged social workers to respond to the increasing divorce rate by using their knowledge of families and relationships to become trained mediators.

Mediation Legislation

This call for professionals to specialize in mediation was coupled with small, county-based, demonstration programs dotted across the country, such as in Cumberland County, Maine; Dade County, Wisconsin; Ramsey County, Minnesota [2]; and Los Angeles County, California [19]. This unorganized national trend was closely followed by a 1980 mandate for California residents to use mediation during contested divorce proceedings [20] and by 1981, nineteen states had passed legislation supporting some type of court-connected mediation services [19]. The mediation movement quickly took hold during the decade of the 1980s as the most effective way to handle divorce-related conflict, and by the early 1990s many states had passed legislation that addressed, either through endorsement or mandate, the use of mediation. As of the year 2000, thirty-eight states had legislation that regulated mediation services for families of divorce, and among the states that have not passed statutes, mediation is often regulated by local or county code [21].

Current Trends of Mediation

The United States is not alone in experiencing high rates of divorce. This trend has also been repeated across other parts of the developed world (as cited in [22]). Not surprisingly, the use of mediation services for divorcing couples has become part of an international movement and is a commonly used technique in many developed nations such as England [23], Sweden [24], Israel [25], China [26], Canada, and New Zealand [27].

As American families have changed and become more complex, mediators have been forced to meet the new demands that divorcing couples bring to the table. For example, many couples who seek mediation today, unlike when the field of divorce mediation was born, are likely to be on their second or third divorce, and children from prior marriages may be part of the negotiations [28]. (There is actually some evidence that having been through a divorce before makes couples more willing to negotiate and to come to a quicker resolution in mediation [29].)

Who Are Mediators?

According to the Association for Conflict Resolution, mediators have a variety of backgrounds including law, social work, human resources, psychology, education, and ministry [30]. Most often, family-law mediators come from the family-law or mental-health professions. There are no national training requirements for becoming a mediator, and only a handful of states have accreditation programs. Even without national regulation, most states have some type of licensing requirements. One can become a mediator by attending a basic forty-hour training session or by completing a degree/certification program in conflict resolution [30].

CAUTIONS ABOUT USING MEDIATION

So far, I have discussed the widespread use of mediation services. There is a considerable body of literature, however, that explores what types of parents might be ill fitted for mediation services. For example, some mediators argue that couples who have been married for fewer than five years [2] or childless couples [29, 31] will not likely have enough emotional attachment to be invested in a mediated process of resolution. Likewise, spouses who are very angry, who engage in battles over trivial matters, who resist taking responsibility for the breakdown of the marriage, or who are unable to communicate with one another are not likely to be successful candidates for mediation services [25].

Mediation and Family Violence

The mediation literature consistently cautions against using mediation with a family that presents with a history of family violence [6, 25, 32, 33]. In fact, most states won't permit a referral to mediation services if intimate partner violence has been present during the marriage [21]. Advocates for female victims of partner violence argue that there is an inherent conflict between the ideology of mediation and the culture of battering. Mediators stress the importance of focusing on the future, as opposed to the past, and also emphasize the importance of both parties being willing to negotiate. Refusing to focus on, or to even acknowledge, the past may deny victims the validation they may seek and need, not to mention place them at risk if proper protection is not established for their postdivorce life. It may be psychologically impossible for victims to negotiate with their abusers, increasing the likelihood that victims may agree to a settlement out of fear of retribution [34].

While many practitioners and researchers screen out couples with a history of partner violence, others argue that violent couples can successfully participate in mediation as long as appropriate precautions are taken, such as using a male and a female mediator together, meeting with the victim separately at first, building in a safety plan for the pre- and postdivorce period, and assessing the success of their agreement after several months of implementation [35]. Hahn and Kleist [36] stress that families with violence are not unidimensional; partner violence varies in duration, severity, and frequency, and oftentimes violence is mutual between couples [37]. For example, some couples experiencing minor and mutual violence, often called "common couple" violence, do not experience problems with power and manipulation related to the violence. Therefore, the presence of violence in and of itself should not be the sole deciding factor about the use of mediation services. As J. B. Kelly argues, additional factors about the violence should also be considered, such as the severity of the violence, the risks that it poses to one or both of the parties, and whether the mediators can alter their services to match the needs of violent couples.

Mediation and Gender

On a related note, some practitioners and scholars have expressed concern that women are at a significant disadvantage in mediation sessions because women have not been socialized to be negotiators with men, and that there are inherent power imbalances between men and women in our society that will be replicated during mediation. Although there was a significant response to this concern, such as recommendations for how mediators can promote equal empowerment for and entitlements for women [38], the research does not support these concerns. Kelly and Duryee [39] found almost no differences between groups of men and women who had participated in mediation and those who had used the adversarial system, with regard to issues of process and empowerment, satisfaction with divorce agreement, anger at spouse, or reported co-parental cooperation. Similarly, another study found that mothers' and fathers' styles in mediation are quite similar. Men and women did not greatly differ with regard to the use of a negative or positive tone while in mediation sessions, the use of questions or statements, the proportion of self-disclosing statements that were made, and how often they proposed a solution to their disagreements [40]. In their review of the literature, Beck and Sales [41] conclude that gender-based responses to mediation have yet to be fully investigated, but there is little reason to currently believe that women suffer when they participate in mediation services.

Additional Concerns

There are additional instances when mediation services are sometimes not recommended. For example, the state of North Carolina does not recommend the use of mediation when one of the parents has a substance abuse problem [21]; this is also the case in some regions of Ohio [33].

There is also reason to believe that in instances when a child is refusing to see one of his or her parents, that the parent without contact may be at a disadvantage for fair negotiations [42].

MEDIATION: STYLES AND CONTENT

There are different approaches to using mediation and different beliefs about the core goals of mediation services for divorcing families. Vanderkooi and Pearson [43] outline some of the different techniques that are used by mediators. Some mediators generate explicit rules during mediation sessions. In such instances, couples might not be permitted to speak negatively about one another or accuse each other of wrongdoings. Other mediators might have more passive styles in which there are few limits placed on participants' expressions.

These same researchers [43] state that there are generally five issues that need to be resolved during mediation: custody of the children, contact between children and each of their parents, division of spousal property, financial support of children, and financial support of spouses postdivorce—if necessary. These issues address the concrete structures of divorce that are focused around legal considerations. Kelly [44] argues that the major issues in divorce mediation focus on relationship dynamics and how these dynamics can be shaped for successful resolution and postdivorce living. The four key dynamics are (1) helping parents to see the patterns in their conflict and how potentially harmful they are to their children, (2) planning for the couple's postdivorce relationship together and how much and what type of contact they want to have with one another, (3) how and about what parents will communicate with one another, and (4) how to achieve effective postdivorce co-parenting.

MEDIATION IN PUBLIC POLICY TODAY

Most states in the country have legislation that regulates or directs the use of mediation for divorcing families [21]. Today, forty states have such legislation. Within the remaining ten states, some counties or cities also regulate the implementation of mediation for couples that are deemed in need. For states that regulate its use, mediation is most frequently employed at the discretion of the court and is not mandated. Most often, parties are responsible for payment of the services, and usually the court appoints qualified mediators, although in some states couples are permitted to find their own mediators. Table 2.1 illustrates the existing mediation statutes nationwide.

Table 2.1. Mediation Statutes, by State

State	Statute?	Code	Compulsory
Alabama	Yes	§ 6-6-20*	Yes (by request of any party)
Alaska	Yes	Alaska Stat. § 25.20.080	No
Arizona	Yes	A.R.S. § 25-413 to 414	No
Arkansas	Yes	A.C.A. § 9-12-322	No
California	Yes	Cal Fam Code § 3170	Yes (contested issues)
Colorado	Yes	Colo. Rev. Stat. Ann. § 13-22-311	No
Connecticut	Yes	Con. Gen. Stat. Ann. § 46b-53a	No
Delaware	Yes	Del. Fam. CT. R. 16(b)(1)	Yes
District of Columbia	Yes	D.C. Code § 16-914	No
Florida	Yes	FLA. Stat. Ann. § 44.102(6)	Yes
Georgia	No		
Hawaii	Yes	HRS § 580-41.5	No
Idaho	Yes	Idaho Rules for Civ. Proc. Rule 16(j)**	Yes
Illinois	Yes	750 ILCS 5/607.1	No
Indiana	Yes	Burns Ind. Code Ann. § 31-12-2-6	No
Iowa	Yes	Iowa Codes § 598.7A	No
Kansas	Yes	Kan. Stat. Ann.§ 23-701	No
Kentucky	Yes	KRS § 403.036	No
Louisiana	Yes	La. R.S. §9:332	No
Maine	Yes	ME. Rev. Ann. Tit. 19-A § 251.2	Yes (child custody disputes)
Maryland	Yes	MD. Code Ann., Fam. Law § 9-205	No
Massachusetts	No		
Michigan	Yes	MCL § 552.513	No
Minnesota	Yes	Minn. Stat. § 518.619	No
Mississippi	Yes		
Missouri	No	Title 32 § 487.100 R.S.Mo.	No
Montana	Yes	Mont. Code Ann. § 40-4-301, 302, 305	No
Nebraska	Yes	Neb. Rev. Stat. § 43-2906 to 2910	No
Nevada	Yes	NRS § 3.475, 3.500	Yes, in certain counties
New Hampshire	Yes	N.H. Rev. Stat. Ann. § 461-A:7	No
New Jersey	Yes	N.J. Court Rules, 1969 R. 1:40-5**	No
New Mexico	Yes	N.M. Stat. Ann. § 40-12-5	No
New York	No		
North Carolina	Yes	N.C. Gen. Stat. § 50-13.1	Yes (child custody disputes)
North Dakota	Yes	N.D. Cent. Code, § 14-09.1-02	No

(*continues*)

Table 2.1. (*continued*)

State	Statute?	Code	Compulsory
Ohio	Yes	ORC Ann. § 3109.052	No
Oklahoma	Yes	43 Okl. St. § 107.3	No
Oregon	Yes	OR. Rev. Stat. § 107.765	No
Pennsylvania	Yes	23 Pa.C.S. § 3901	No
Rhode Island	Yes	R.I. Gen. Laws § 15-5-29(a)	No
South Carolina	No		
South Dakota	Yes	S.D. Codified Laws § 25-4-56	Yes (child custody disputes)
Tennessee	Yes	Tenn. Code Ann. § 36-4-130	No
Texas	No		
Utah	Yes	Utah Code Ann. § 30-3-39	Yes
Vermont	No		
Virginia	Yes	Va. Code Ann. § 20-124.4	No
Washington	Yes	Wash. Rev. Code § 26-09-015	No
West Virginia	Yes	W. Va. Code § 48-9-202	Yes (child custody disputes)
Wisconsin	Yes	Wis. Stat. § 767.11(5)	Yes
Wyoming	No		

Note: *Statute does not only apply to family relations; **state rule, not a statute.

HOW EFFECTIVE IS MEDIATION?

Like much research that evaluates the effectiveness of social policy and practice, there have been primarily three types of research conducted on the outcomes of mediation services. First is the research that is driven by consumer satisfaction, and second is research that has used comparison groups. Research from these two categories has produced strong accolades for mediation. Third is research that is more rigorous, using longitudinal data or random assignment of participants to either mediation or litigation groups, which has produced mixed results about this social policy solution. The literature on mediation has been reviewed by several noted scholars, and this survey will draw on some of these reviews [41, 45, 46].

Satisfaction-oriented Research and Descriptive Outcomes

Settlement Rates

There are varying estimates of what percent of couples settle, or come to an agreement, during mediation. Moreover, while some couples resolve all of their conflict in mediation, other couples only come to a partial resolution and then look to the court to bring full resolution. In her review of the literature, Kelly [45] determined that couples were able to settle on an agreement 55 to 77 percent of the time. Sometimes these figures included partial agreements (i.e., the bottom 55 percent) while other times they did not. Thus, a conservative estimate is that parents are able to come to at least a partial agreement somewhere between half and three-quarters of the time. Emery [46] reports that cases randomly assigned to the adversarial system (as opposed to mediation services) were seven times more likely to appear before a judge than those randomly assigned to mediation.

Savings in Time and Money

One of the earliest and often-cited findings about the benefits of mediation was savings in the form of time and money. The use of mediation services reduced the amount of time that cases remained open and that couples remained in limbo without resolution. In one study, successfully mediated cases reduced the length of divorce proceedings by 21 percent [47]. Other research has found that mediation not only allows families to move through the legal system more quickly, it also costs families less money. Parents together took care of issues that would regularly be handled by their attorneys, and in less time. Reports from the late 1970s indicated that couples that used mediation services paid only 70 percent of what couples who litigated paid for their divorce [5]. More recent estimates include cutting the cost of divorce in half [48]. A 1983 *Washington Post* article discussed that rewards in the form of time and finances were among the many benefits of using mediation [49]; these remarks continue to be made today [33].

Despite these reported benefits, savings in the form of time and money vary case by case. As discussed by Beck and Sales [41], the significant savings noted above depend on the characteristics of each case. Families that are able to come to an agreement quickly in mediation will likely spend less time in the legal system and pay fewer legal fees. However, couples who are unable to resolve their differences through mediation must pay for the fees associated with a contested custody case in addition to the cost of mediation. Couples who choose to represent themselves, or *pro se* litigants, must endure much higher fees than if their case had simply moved through the traditional adversarial system. Finally, couples who do not successfully resolve their disputes through mediation have essentially set their cases back approximately four to eight weeks. Beck and Sales ultimately conclude that the findings about savings to divorcing couples have been overstated. They argue that there is not enough evidence to determine if there is, in fact, a savings in using mediation service versus litigation.

Opinions of Attorneys

Early research indicated that attorneys were somewhat hesitant to refer clients for mediation services. In fact, attorneys' preference for mediation was found to be related to the personal experiences of their own lives; attorneys who had experienced a divorce or who had used mediation services themselves were more likely to refer clients for mediation services [50]. An overall failure to refer clients to mediation services can probably be explained by attorneys' lack of faith in these services. One small study found that almost two-thirds of attorneys reported that mediation rarely saved time or money, and 40 percent reported that it was unlikely to expedite conflict resolution. Another 40 percent, however, reported that it was highly likely to result in workable solutions. A number of the attorneys also expressed concern that mediation results in contracts that are not enforceable [51].

Attorney attitudes about mediation may have shifted over time. An Indiana-based study from the mid-1990s found more positive attitudes about mediation, especially among younger attorneys [52]. Study participants cite many benefits including the opportunity for clients to thoroughly express their concerns, to better understand the strengths and weaknesses of their cases, and to take more responsibility than when cases proceed through the adversarial system. Study participants did express caution about mandating mediation for everyone. Results of a more recent study, however, find that some attorneys remain cautious in their enthusiasm about mediation services. An Ohio-based study, with high response rates (between 79 and 85 percent) found that when compared to family mediators and judges, attorneys have more negative attitudes about the usefulness of mediation services [53]. On a Likert scale of 1–5, the mean attitude of attorneys was 2.5. Attorneys were also less likely than mediators or judges to think that mediation resulted in improved parental understanding, better parental coping, fewer arguments, quicker resolutions, less relitigation and better adjusted children. On a Likert scale of 1–4, where 4 is no improvement, the mean responses of attorneys always hovered around 3. In some respects these findings make sense, because attorneys are more likely to hear from clients who are dissatisfied with their divorce agreement and want to relitigate. At the same time, one could make a similar argument about judges.

Early Reports of Endorsement and Approval

The first study to evaluate California's mandated mediation policy reported promising results. In a study of ninety-one clients, Saposnek and colleagues [54] found that 60 percent of the parents who were mandated to use mediation in the first year of the law's implementation reported that they were satisfied with their experiences in mediation. Just over half of the sample, which had no comparison group, reported that their agreements from mediation were still intact and being honored by both parties one year after mediation was completed. Using pre- and postmediation measures, the study determined that parents reported that communication with their former spouses was improving, as were attitudes about one another. Parents reported that child-contact schedules were working better and that their children were pleased to have contact with both of their parents.

Despite these results, just under half of the sample reported that their mediated agreement was not in effect and that of the problems with the former spouses, the majority of them began within the months immediately following the completion of mediation. A quarter of those experiencing problems reported that their disagreements had never ceased since their decision to divorce. Nonetheless, the entire sample provided an 82 percent approval rating of the "concept" of mediation as a tool for divorcing parents to construct their postdivorce lives together.

This latter finding has been repeated elsewhere. Even couples who were unable to come to an agreement in mediation support the use of this type of service and would usually recommend it to other couples. One three-state (California, Minnesota, and Connecticut) study with differing legal mandates and with a sample size of 530, found that 89 percent of those who successfully mediated would recommend it to others. Such high endorsement exists even among those who fail to come to resolution. Almost 70 percent of those who unsuccessfully mediated would also endorse it for others [55]. Kelly [56] found that 74 percent of the forty-five women in her study who voluntarily and successfully mediated reported that they would definitely recommend mediation to a friend.

What Parents Like about Mediation

Satisfaction-oriented research continues to be conducted today and, in general, couples continue to be pleased with mediation. It has been especially well rated by couples who voluntarily, without court order or state mandate, participate in mediation. In one particular study, over 90 percent of participants who voluntarily mediated reported that the mediator was aware of their needs and concerns, as well as the needs and concerns of their spouse. They also reported that the mediator was unbiased and that the divorce decree to which they agreed was fair [57].

Similar findings have been replicated elsewhere, for both voluntary and mandated participants of mediation. Parents report that mediators allow their concerns to be heard, that the mediators do not impose their views on the parents [39], that the process is fair, and that they are treated with dignity and respect by mediators [33]. There is also some evidence to suggest that when parents use mediation, the majority of them (82 percent) do not return to court, even if they had a lengthy history of litigation before using mediation services [58]. This study, however, only assessed relitigation rates nine months after resolution at mediation and did not report the rates of relitigation for parents who did not choose to mediate. The large three-state study previously mentioned found that parents reported that mediation did not change the nature of the relationship with their ex-spouse; however, they also reported that their mediation sessions were not confusing or rushed and that the mediator kept parties on track. Only about half of parents reported that mediation sessions involved tension, were unpleasant, or that they became defensive during mediation sessions [55].

What Fathers Like about Mediation

Very early in the trend toward mediation, fathers reported a preference for using mediation services. Despite the presence of gender-neutral laws (see chapter 5, many fathers felt that the courts were biased against men and that they protected the concerns of women more than men or children. Fathers felt that the courts were blind to the desires of men, who often felt financially drained from the divorce and emotionally devastated from their separation from their children, and that judges were uninformed about the importance of the father-child relationship [59]. Fathers' rights activists argued that alternative dispute-resolution services gave them a medium through which they could express their concerns and desires about their postdivorce life with (and without) their children, which time did not often permit in a traditional courtroom setting [60, 61]. The work of Emery and his colleagues [46] has found that fathers who use the adversarial system are usually more displeased than men who mediate.

Studies Using Comparison Groups

Finding Differences between Those Who Mediate and Those Who Do Not

A second group of studies has focused on using comparison groups between parents who used mediation (either voluntarily or through a court order) and parents who used traditional, adversarial litigation to settle their disagreements. In a study of 200 parents, 141 of whom mediated, Jones and Bodtker [58] found that couples who used mediation services were statistically more likely to feel that the outcome of their legal case was fair, that the legal system heard and respected their concerns, and that, overall, they were satisfied with the outcome of their divorce. This study had response rates ranging from 20 to 47 percent, with the lowest responses from parents who were not referred to mediation; thus response bias could be a factor in the results. In a comprehensive study that examined many different levels of satisfaction with parents who voluntarily mediated, Kelly [56] found that parents who mediated were more likely to report that their case was well handled, that the mediator (as opposed to attorney) helped them to control their feelings of anger, that the process of mediation instilled a sense of responsibility for the continuing family obligations, and that they came away with a better sense of their spouse's concerns. These ratings were all statistically higher than those reported by parents who participated in traditional adversarial services. Kelly has also found that six months after a mediated resolution, spouses who mediated were more cooperative with one another. These results may be skewed by the fact that the couples in this study voluntarily sought out mediation services, as opposed to responding to a state or court mandate [62]. Thus, it is likely that parents who have a more cooperative relationship are those who are more likely to initially enter into mediation services.

Mediation has also been linked to psychological well-being. One such study, with small sample sizes, ranging from eighteen to twenty members per comparison group, found that fathers who voluntarily participated in mediation services reported less "strain" in their lives. The fathers in this pilot project, with a high study response rate of 80 percent, were less likely to report feeling overwhelmed by their responsibilities or that people made too many demands on them, and they reported feeling less nervous and tense than fathers who did not participate in mediation [51].

Some researchers have found meaningful links between mediation services for parents and positive outcomes for children. Fathers who participated in mediation, whether they came to a resolution or not, were more likely to report feeling closer to their children than fathers who did not participate in mediation [51]. Another study found that parents who participated in mediation (both voluntarily and mandated) talked to their children more frequently about the events in their children's lives than parents who did not participate in mediation. Moreover, parents who used adversarial services were more likely to report school behavior problems with their children, problems with the law, drug use, and poor academic performance [63]. These findings should be interpreted with caution, however, as the sample size is small ($n = 58$), the response rate is low (although the exact rate is undeterminable from the study methods), and the authors did not use any statistical significance testing.

The use of mediation services has also been linked to compliance with child support orders. In a study that examined public court and child support records, the authors determined that when couples had used mediation services, fathers were much more compliant with child support orders

[64]. The findings of this study should be interpreted with some caution, as 40 percent of the sample had not yet divorced.

*Studies Finding No Difference between
Those Who Mediate and Those Who Do Not*

While there are some group differences between those who mediate and those who do not, many studies do not find differences between these two groups of parents. Kelly and colleagues found that couples who sought mediation were not any better psychologically adjusted than families who used litigation to resolve their divorce and, surprisingly, mediated couples experienced a significant decline in the level of satisfaction with their divorce when compared with litigation couples [62]. The authors speculate that this negative finding may be linked to a positive finding. The authors had also concluded that parents who voluntarily mediated were more cooperative with one another. This cooperation likely leads to increased contact, which may lead to an increased opportunity for conflict and less overall satisfaction with the divorce. Another study, which again did not use significance testing, found no difference in reports of happiness, parental perception of children, and parent-child relationships [63]. Furthermore, little difference has been found between parents who mediate and those who do not with regard to fostering feelings of empowerment, focusing on the most important issues of the divorce, satisfaction with property agreements, and whether or not the spousal support agreement reached was fair [56].

Finally, it should be noted that the findings of some studies are inconsistent with others. For example, Toews and McKenry [65] found that participation in mediation services was linked to parental conflict. Parents who voluntarily participated in mediation were statistically more likely to have higher levels of conflict than parents who did not participate in mediation. And another study found that while children whose parents did not mediate had academic problems, they reported that their children were more affectionate with them than children whose parents participated in mediation [63]. This finding is based on raw scores without significance testing.

Using Random Assignment or Longitudinal Data

One of the most often cited studies of mediation is that conducted by Emery and colleagues. In this longitudinal examination, families who divorced between 1983 and 1986 were followed and studied periodically, with the last published follow-up taking place twelve years after the initiation of the study. Emery randomly assigned a total of seventy couples who could not resolve their divorce disagreement to either mediation or the traditional adversarial process.

The first data were collected shortly after the resolution of the divorce cases and revealed that fathers who mediated were much more satisfied with legal experiences than fathers who litigated, while there were no differences for mothers. There were also no differences in the psychological adjustment of the parents based on the assignment to their dispute resolution group [32]. Nine years later, noncustodial fathers in the mediation group reported more contact with their children, and there was an overall higher level of communication between mothers and fathers in the mediated group than families in the adversarial/litigation group. Other factors that were considered, but for which there were no significant differences between the two groups, included custody, child-contact or child-support changes, children's behavior, parent-child relationship, and interparental anger [66]. Finally, twelve years later, fathers in the mediated group were still more involved with their children than fathers in the adversarial group.

Among fathers who litigated, 39 percent had seen their children only once or not at all in the past year, compared with only 12 percent of fathers who used mediation services. Frequent contact between fathers and children was striking as well. Only 9 percent of litigation fathers reported seeing their children once a week or more, compared to 30 percent of mediation fathers [46]. Moreover, fathers who litigated were the most dissatisfied with the outcomes of their divorce, even twelve years after dissolution. There were significantly more changes in the child-contact schedule with couples who mediated, but this was in order to achieve more cooperation and flexibility. There was no difference between the two groups with regard to other measures of satisfaction or the effect that the divorce process had on the parents or the children [67].

Problems with Mediation Research

As noted throughout this discussion, there are multiple problems with the research that has been conducted on mediation. Beck and Sales [41, 68] provide a thorough review of these shortcomings and the limited conclusions that can be drawn from the research, as do other scholars as well [46]. The research on mediation suffers from small sample sizes, low response rates, nonrandom samples and assignment to dispute-resolution groups, unequal comparison groups, and sometimes no comparison group and little to no recorded sessions of mediation. In addition, very little research has addressed concepts such as which issues are mediated, the physical setting in which the mediated sessions take place, and models of mediation. Many times parents who voluntarily mediate are compared with parents who do not. This is problematic because parents who willingly seek out mediation services are less likely to report that their spouses took advantage of them during their marriage; are more likely to report that their spouses are honest, fair, and flexible; and more likely to report that they expect that they will be able to cooperate with their spouses about the children than parents who do not seek mediation services [62]. Other times, parents who voluntarily mediated will be combined with those who are court-ordered to mediate. This, too, is problematic because, as Beck and Sales [41] note, couples who voluntarily mediate are generally white, young, middle-class, and college educated, while those who do not mediate come from a low socioeconomic status and are either underemployed or unemployed.

The lack of rigorous research in this field can primarily be attributed to institutional barriers. Courts are reluctant to open their doors to scholars, especially when an element of social experimentation is involved. Families engaged in the emotional turmoil of divorce are hesitant to have mediation sessions recorded and to have their personal catastrophes made the centerpiece of social science research. Finally, well-controlled research is expensive. These factors have provided legitimate obstacles to conducting sound research on this family-policy solution for divorcing families [68].

CONCLUSION

Mediation, as a form of social policy for families of divorce, has received more attention and praise than almost any other social-policy solution. Statutes have been adopted by most states in the nation to regulate the use of mediation, and it has been researched and written about in thousands of publications. As noted, the unique feature of mediation is that it strives to find solutions for families on a case-by-case basis, encouraging parents to settle their disagreements without the use of an adversarial process. It is intended to lay the foundation for the future relationship that a divorced couple will need in order to co-parent their children.

Beck and Sales [41] express serious concerns about the state of mediation research, and they conclude that "it is very difficult to assess the success of mediation given the limitations in both methodology and research designs" (p. 1044). This is true of many social programs and policies [69]. In general, it appears that mediation is highly regarded by many people. Even in the face of their own failed experiences, parents reportedly value the opportunities that mediation provides, and it is usually well regarded by the courts and researchers, even if attorneys are somewhat skeptical of this service.

Many of the shortcomings of the research on the outcomes of mediation make it difficult to draw broad conclusions about the effectiveness of this policy solution and its success in improving the well-being of children of families of divorce. For each study that demonstrates an encouraging outcome, there is one that demonstrates a lack of findings. One is at a loss to draw definitive conclusions of these findings, and even in their thorough review of the literature, Beck and Sales [41] do not. Suffice it to say, the research on mediation suffers from small sample sizes, nonrandom assignment to dispute-resolution groups, and unequal comparison of mediation. Research on mediation has also failed to consider characteristics of the mediation, such as the physical setting of the services and the different types of mediation services used. Professionals within the research and legal communities will need to address these concerns together in order to facilitate more comprehensive research and review of mediation services.

That said, it would be reckless to conclude that all is lost in the field of divorce mediation. Research on mediation has consistently found that those who participate in mediation are more satisfied with the process [56] and there is some indication that it promotes better communication between divorcing parents [66]. The results of research conducted by Emery and colleagues [32, 46, 67] is promising and suggests that there may be a reason to continue to support this social policy intervention. The most important and striking conclusion of this research to date, as demonstrated through a randomly assigned and longitudinal study, is that mediation may increase the contact that children have with their divorced fathers.

Millions of dollars, both on the state and national level, have been devoted to the problem of a "fatherless America," in which children are raised in poverty and suffer from a multitude of risk factors, including low levels of education, criminal activity, substance abuse problems, teenage pregnancy, child maltreatment, and many other problems [70–76]. For all the studies on mediation that are either poorly designed or lack significant findings, Emory's research stands as a possible reason for endorsement of mediation services. Politicians, practitioners, and researchers have tried for several decades to promote father involvement. These efforts have included a variety of mediums, including paternity testing, "deadbeat dad" campaigns, community-outreach interventions, and the federally funded U.S. Department of Health and Human Services *Fatherhood Initiative*. Emery's research on mediation may offer clues on how to reach fathers. The findings suggest that bringing fathers and mothers to the table, together, to discuss and plan for their children's lives may be key in promoting and keeping divorced fathers engaged and active with their children—and ultimately improving outcomes for the children's future.

REFERENCES

1. Haynes, J. M. *Divorce mediation: A practical guide for therapists and counselors.* 1981, New York: Springer Publishing Company.
2. Blades, J. *Family mediation: Cooperative divorce settlement.* 1985, Englewood Cliffs, NJ: Prentice-Hall, Inc.
3. Amato, P. R., and B. Keith. Parental divorce and the well-being of children: A meta-analysis. *Psychological Bulletin*, 1991, 110(1): pp. 26–46.
4. Gentry, D. B. Including children in divorce mediation and education. *Families in Society*, 1997, 78(3) pp. 307–15.
5. Pearson, J., and N. Thoennes. Divorce mediation: An American picture. In *Divorce mediation and the legal process*, ed. R. Dingwall and J. Eekelaar, pp. 71–91. 1985, Oxford, UK: Clarendon Press.
6. Emery, R. E. *Renegotiating family relationships: Divorce, child custody and mediation.* 1994, New York: The Guilford Press.
7. Johnston, J. R., and L. E. Campbell. *Impasses of divorce: The dynamics and resolution of family conflict.* 1988, New York: The Free Press.
8. Irvin, K. K. Including children in mediation: Considerations for the mediator. In *Divorce and family mediation*, ed. J. C. Hansen, pp. 94–107. 1985, Rockville, MD: Aspen Systems Corporation.
9. Beck, P., and N. Biank. Broadening the scope of divorce mediation to meet the needs of children. *Mediation Quarterly*, 1997, 14(3): pp. 179–99.
10. Cornfield, L. A. Are two heads better than one? An examination of the effectiveness of co-mediation: Calling for a new mediation technique. *Conciliation Courts Review*, 1985, 23(2): pp. 55–60.
11. Emery, R. E., and M. M. Wyer. Divorce mediation. *American Psychologist*, 1987, 42(2): pp. 472–80.
12. Glick, P. C. A demographer looks at American families. *Journal of Marriage and Family*, 1975, 37(1): pp. 15–26.
13. Nakonezny, P. A., R. D. Shull, and J. L. D. Rodgers. The effect of no-fault divorce law on the divorce rate across the 50 states and its relation to income, education, and religiosity. *Journal of Marriage and Family*, 1995, 57: pp. 477–88.
14. Kay, H. H. An appraisal of California's no-fault divorce law. *California Law Review*, 1987, 75(29): pp. 291–319.
15. Peterson, R. R. A re-evaluation of the economic consequences of divorce. *American Sociological Review*, 1996, 61(June): pp. 528–36.
16. Peterson, R. R. Statistical errors, faulty conclusions, misguided policies: Reply to Weitzman. *American Sociological Review*, 1996, 61(3): pp. 539–40.
17. Goldstein, J., et al. *Beyond the best interests of the child.* 1980, New York: Free Press.
18. Haynes, J. M. Divorce mediator: A new role. *Social Work*, 1978, (January): pp. 5–9.
19. Folberg, J. The changing family—implications for the law. *Conciliation Courts Review*, 1981, 19(2): pp. 1–6.
20. McIsaac, H. Mandatory conciliation custody/visitation matters: California's bold stroke. *Conciliation Courts Review*, 1981, 19(2): pp. 73–81.
21. Tondo, C.-A., R. Coronel, and B. Drucker. Mediation trends: A survey of the states. *Family Court Review*, 2001, 39(4): pp. 431–53.

22. Blossfeld, H.-P., and R. Muller. Union disruption in comparative perspective: The role of assortative partner choice and careers of couples. *International Journal of Sociology*, 2002, 32(4): pp. 3–35.

23. Walton, L., C. Oliver, and C. Griffin. Divorce mediation: The impact of mediation on the psychological well-being of children and parents. *Journal of Community and Applied Psychology*, 1999, 9: pp. 35–46.

24. Hyden, M. For the child's sake: Parents and social workers discuss conflict-filled parental relations after divorce. *Child and Family Social Work*, 2001, 6: pp. 115–28.

25. Cohen, O., et al. Suitability of divorcing couples for mediation: A suggested typology. *The American Journal of Family Therapy*, 1999, 27: pp. 329–44.

26. Cheung, S.-k. and Kwok, S. Y. C. Predictors of divorcing women's use of divorce mediation. *Journal of Divorce and Remarriage*, 1999, 31(3/4): pp. 37–52.

27. Foy, K. Family and divorce mediation: A comparative analysis of international programs. *Mediation Quarterly*, 1987, 17(Fall): pp. 83–98.

28. National Center for Health Statistics. *Cohabitation, marriage, divorce and remarriage in the United States: Data from the national survey of family growth.* 2002, Hyattsville, MD: U.S. Department of Health and Human Services.

29. Johnson, K. D. Factors predicting outcome of divorce mediation. *Conciliation Courts Review*, 1984, 22(2): pp. 31–38.

30. Association for Conflict Resolution. *Frequently asked questions about conflict resolution.* n.d., http://www.acrnet.org/about/CR-FAQ.htm

31. Brown, E. M. Emotional dynamics of couples in mediation. In *Divorce and family mediation*, ed. J. C. Hansen, pp. 80–93. 1985, Rockville, MD: Aspen Systems Corporation.

32. Emery, R. E., S. G. Matthews, and M. M. Wyer. Child custody mediation and litigation: Further evidence on the differing views of mothers and fathers. *Journal of Consulting and Clinical Psychology*, 1991, 59(3): pp. 410–18.

33. Zuberbuhler, J. Early intervention mediation: The use of court-ordered mediation in the initial stages of divorce litigation to resolve parenting issues. *Family Court Review*, 2001, 39(2): pp. 203–6.

34. Fischer, K., N. Vidmar, and R. Ellis. The culture of battering and the role of mediation in domestic violence cases. *Southern Methodist University Law Review*, 1993, 46: pp. 2117–74.

35. H. A. Magana and N. Taylor. Child custody mediation and spouse abuse: A descriptive study of a protocol. *Family and Conciliation Courts Review*, 1993, 31(3): pp. 50–64.

36. Hahn, R. A., and D. M. Kleist. Divorce mediation: Research and implications for family and couples counseling. *The Family Journal: Counseling and Therapy for Couples and Families*, 2000, 8(2): pp. 165–71.

37. Straus, M. A., and R. J. Gelles. How violent are American families?: Estimates from the National Family Violence Resurvey and other studies. In *Family abuse and its consequences: New directions in research*, ed. G. T. Hotaling and D. Finkelhor, pp. 14–36. 1988, Thousand Oaks, CA: Sage Publications.

38. Ricci, I. Mediator's notebook: Reflections on promoting equal empowerment and entitlements for women. *Journal of Divorce*, 1985, 8(3-4): pp. 19–61.

39. Kelly, J. B., and M. A. Duryee. Women's and men's views of mediation in voluntary and mandatory mediation settings. *Family and Conciliation Courts Review*, 1992, 30(1): pp. 34–49.

40. Slaikeu, K. A., et al. Process and outcome in divorce mediation. *Mediation Quarterly*, 1985, 10(December): pp. 55–74.

41. Beck, C. J. A., and B. D. Sales. A critical reappraisal of divorce mediation research and policy. *Psychology, Public Policy and the Law*, 2000, 6(4): pp. 989–1056.

42. Vestal, A. Mediation and parental alienation syndrome: Consideration for an intervention model. *Family and Conciliation Courts Review*, 1999, 37(4): pp. 487–503.

43. Vanderkooi, L., and J. Pearson. Mediating divorce disputes: Mediator behaviors, styles and roles. *Family Relations*, 1983, 32(4): pp. 557–66.

44. Kelly, J. B. Parents with enduring child disputes: Focused interventions with parents in enduring disputes. *Journal of Family Studies*, 2003, 9(1): pp. 51–62.

45. Kelly, J. B. Family mediation research: Is there empirical support for the field? *Conflict Resolution Quarterly*, 2004, 22(1-2): pp. 3–35.

46. Emery, R. E., D. A. Sbarra, and T. Grover. Divorce mediation: Research and reflections. *Family Court Review*, 2005, 43(1): pp. 22–37.

47. Pearson, J. Family mediation. In *A report on current research findings—implications for courts and future research needs*, ed. S. Keilitz. 1994, National Symposium on Court-Connected Dispute Resolution Research, State Justice Institute, October 15–16, 1993.

48. Kelly, J. B. Is mediation less expensive? Comparison of mediated and adversarial divorce costs. *Mediation Quarterly*, 1990, 8: pp. 15–25.

49. Krucoff, C. Families: Monitoring the mediators. *Washington Post*, June, 1, 1983: p. D5.

50. Smart, L. S., and C. J. Salts. Attorney attitudes toward divorce mediation. *Mediation Quarterly*, 1984, 6: pp. 65–72.

51. Bahr, S. J., B. Chappell, and A. Marcos. An evaluation of a trial mediation program. *Mediation Quarterly*, 1987, 18(Winter): pp. 37–52.

52. Medley, M. L., and J. A. Schellenberg. Attitudes of attorneys toward mediation. *Mediation Quarterly*, 1994, 12(2): pp. 185–98.

53. Hughes, R. J., and J. J. Kirby. Strengthening evaluation strategies for divorcing family support services: Perspectives of parent educators, mediators, attorneys, and judges. *Family Relations: Interdisciplinary Journal of Applied Family Studies*, 2000, 49(1): pp. 53–61.

54. Saposnek, D. T., et al. How has mandatory mediation fared? Research of the first year's follow-up. *Conciliation Courts Review*, 1984, 22(2): pp. 7–19.

55. Pearson, J., and N. Thoennes. A preliminary portrait of client reactions to three court mediation programs. *Mediation Quarterly*, 1984, 2(March): pp. 21–40.

56. Kelly, J. B. Mediated and adversarial divorce: Respondents' perceptions of their processes and outcomes. *Mediation Quarterly*, 1989, 24(Summer): pp. 71–88.

57. Meierding, N. R. Does mediation work? A survey of long-term satisfaction and durability for privately mediated agreements. *Mediation Quarterly*, 1993, 11(2): pp. 157–70.

58. Jones, T. S., and A. Bodtker. Agreement, maintenance, satisfaction and relitigation in mediated and non-mediated custody cases: A research note. *Journal of Divorce and Remarriage*, 1999, 32(1/2): pp. 17–30.

59. Roman, M., and W. Haddad. *The disposable parent: The case for joint custody*, ed. N. York. 1978, New York: Holt, Rinehart and Winston.

60. Thompson, R. A. Fathers and the child's "best interests": Judicial decision making in custody disputes. In *The father's role: Applied perspectives*, ed. M. E. Lamb, pp. 61–101. 1986, New York: Wiley.

61. Bertoia, C. E. An interpretative analysis of the mediation rhetoric of fathers' rightists: Privatization versus personalization. *Mediation Quarterly*, 1998, 16(1): pp. 15–32.

62. Kelly, J. B., L. Gigy, and S. Hausman. Mediated and adversarial divorce: Initial findings from a longitudinal study. In *Divorce mediation: Theory and practice*, ed. J. Folberg and A. Milne, pp. 453–73. 1988, New York: The Guilford Press.

63. Stull, D. E., and N. M. Kaplan. The positive impact of divorce mediation on children's behavior. *Mediation Quarterly*, 1987, 18(Winter): pp. 53–59.

64. Tishler, C. L., L. Landry-Meyer, and S. Bartholomae. Mediation and child support: An effective partnership. *Journal of Divorce and Remarriage*, 2003, 38(3/4): pp. 129–45.

65. Toews, M. L., and P. C. McKenry. Court-related predictors of parental cooperation and conflict after divorce. *Journal of Divorce and Remarriage*, 2001, pp. 57–73.

66. Dillon, P. A., and R. E. Emery, Divorce mediation and resolution of child custody disputes: Long-term effects. *American Journal of Orthopsychiatry*, 1996, 66(1): pp. 131–40.

67. Emery, R. E., et al. Child custody mediation and litigation: Custody, contact, and coparenting 12 years after initial dispute resolution. *Journal of Consulting and Clinical Psychology*, 2001, 69(2): pp. 323–32.

68. Beck, C. J. A., and B. D. Sales. *Family mediation: Facts, myths and future prospects*. 2001, Washington, DC: American Psychological Association.

69. Gelles, R. J. How evaluation research can help reform and improve the child welfare system. In *Program evaluation and family violence research*, ed. S. K. Ward and D. Finkelhor, pp. 7–28. 2000, Binghamton, NY: The Haworth Maltreatment and Trauma Press.

70. Gibson, C. L., and S. G. Tibbetts. A biosocial interaction in predicting early onset of offending. *Psychological Reports*, 2000, 86(2): pp. 509–18.

71. Davis-Maye, D. Daddy's little girl. *Journal of Children and Poverty*, 2004, 10(1): pp. 53–69.

72. Friedman, A. S., A. Ali, and S. McMurphy. Father absence as a risk factor for substance use and illegal behavior by the adolescent sons. *Journal of Child and Adolescent Substance Abuse*, 1998, 8(2): pp. 79–95.

73. Stern, M., J. E. Northman, and M. R. Van Slyck. Father absence and adolescent "problem behaviors": Alcohol consumption, drug use and sexual activity. *Adolescence*, 1984, 19(74): pp. 301–12.

74. Harper, C. C., and S. S. McLanahan, Father Absence and Youth Incarceration. *Journal of Research on Adolescence*, 2004, 14(3): pp. 369–98.

75. Paschall, M. J., C. L. Ringwalt, and R. L. Flewelling. Effects of Parenting, Father Absence, and Affiliation with Delinquent Peers on Delinquent Behavior among African-American Male Adolescents. *Adolescence*, 2003, 38(149): pp. 15–34.

76. Ballantine, J. H. Figuring in the father factor. *Childhood Education*, 2000, 76(2): pp. 104–5.

3

Divorce Education Programs

Each decade brings a new social policy "solution" to families of divorce. The 1970s brought no-fault divorce legislation and gender-neutral custody laws, the 1980s brought policies concerning mandated or recommended mediation, and the 1990s brought divorce education programming to a majority of states in the union. These programs are the focus of the current chapter, where I will describe the types of programs that are available; trace the history of their popularity in the United States; and explore their effectiveness in promoting positive, low-conflict, child-centered co-parenting behavior among divorced parents.

WHAT ARE DIVORCE EDUCATION PROGRAMS?

There are many different types of parenting education programs: general programs for new parents [1, 2], programs for parents of adolescents [3], parents who are at risk for maltreating their children [4, 5], teenage parents [6, 7], incarcerated parents [8], and many others [9–11]. The goal of divorce education programs, which are sometimes mandated and other times voluntary, is to generally educate parents about the stress that divorce inflicts on children and how certain parental behaviors can minimize or maximize that stress.

Program Characteristics

Often called "prevention" or "intervention" programs [12, 13], divorce education classes range in duration from one-time interventions that last a few hours, to sessions that meet over the course of a number of weeks. Because the vast majority of programs, especially those that are mandated by the courts, are one-time interventions and last between ninety minutes and two and a half hours [14, 15], this chapter will focus on this specific type of intervention. More comprehensive interventions will be covered in chapter 7 of this book.

The most thorough research on divorce education program characteristics has been conducted by Blaisure and Geasler [15–18]. Their research has shown that class sizes of divorce education programs range from one to two hundred participants, with a mean of twenty. Most programs permit divorcing parents to attend sessions either together or individually. Between one-half to two-thirds of programs charge parents to participate. The median cost, as of the late 1990s, was thirty dollars; the range was from five dollars to over one hundred dollars [14, 15].

Program Content

Although many program providers have developed their own divorce education curriculum to meet the needs of their local community [17], about half of providers purchase commercially available packaged programs. These are programs that can be purchased from private companies that charge a minimal fee, oftentimes just to cover the cost of development and reproduction. Some organizations that sell packaged programs require program leaders to undergo training before programs are delivered to parents [15].

The topics most often covered in divorce education programs include children's reactions and adjustment to divorce and how parents can respond to their children's adjustment in ways that are appropriately supportive of children. There is instruction about how divorce changes the parent-child relationship, and how certain parental behaviors can have a negative impact on children's adjustment. For example, parents are taught how harmful it is to speak negatively about the "other" parent in front of the children and how triangulating behavior (placing children in the middle of the parents) is especially hard on children. Finally, divorce education programs provide information to parents about the postdivorce roles of parents, the importance of parental cooperation, low levels of conflict, and the significance of keeping both parents involved in children's lives [14, 15, 17].

Program Providers

In their 1998 study of court-connected divorce education programs, Geasler and Blaisure found that providers, or instructors, of divorce education programs vary considerably between programs and states. The most common type of program provider is a mental-health practitioner or social worker. Other providers include mediators, court workers, family-life educators, lawyers, Cooperative Extension personnel, and college faculty [15]. About half of divorce education programs are operated by private, nonprofit human-service agencies [14, 17].

Types of Programs

There are generally three types of programmatic instruction that are used during divorce education programs: (1) passive involvement, (2) limited involvement, and (3) active involvement. In programs that emphasize *passive involvement*, parents watch videos, receive written material, and listen to lectures by professionals who have expertise in child development, family processes, diverse family formations, and the legal system. In programs that have *limited involvement*, parents engage in discussion with one another and the workshop leaders, and they complete some type of worksheet activities that are intended to yield insightful information about themselves, their children, their ex-spouses, and the current relations between members of their divorcing family. In the third type of parenting program, *active involvement*, parents engage in role playing and practice new skills that are intended to promote positive co-parenting behaviors that will minimize triangulating behaviors [14, 16, 18, 19].

Who Attends Divorce Education Programs?

Attendance at divorce education programs varies considerably by state. Today many programs are mandated by the state for all families that are divorcing. In other instances, they are at the discretion of court personnel. Thus, it is difficult to capture a profile of typical parents who attend divorce education programs.

Divorce Education Programs and Intimate-partner Violence

There is some concern about mandating or ordering parents who are in violent relationships to attend parent education programs because these programs emphasize the importance of a cooperative co-parental relationship. In actuality, asking victims to co-parent with their abusers may place them at risk for further victimization. Although Kramer et al. [20] found that attendance at a divorce education program is not, three months later, associated with levels of violent conflict, Fuhrmann, McGill, and O'Connell [21] provide a balanced approach to working with families of violence. Their work explores the perils and possibilities of alternative strategies. Examples include, but are not limited to, granting exemptions for victims of abuse, targeting programming just for victims and offenders, and screening for violence. Of course, it may be difficult to identify victims and offenders of partner violence and, once identified, to adequately provide safety to victims. Even if these challenges can be overcome, Fuhrmann et al. recognize that these are time-consuming and expensive screening procedures. In the end their recommendations to divorce education facilitators include that: (1) the safety of all participants be ensured, (2) attendance lists be held confidentially, and (3) providers be trained in the dynamics and issues of partner violence. These recommendations were, in part, recently supported by the New York State Parent Education Advisory Board [22].

Programs for Children

Programs for children have been slower to develop than programs for divorcing parents. However, using data that were collected by Geasler and Blaisure in 1998–1999, a recent study provided descriptive information about programs for children of divorcing parents [23]. This study, which gathered data from sixty-seven court personnel and eighty-one program providers indicated that children's programs provide information for participants in six general areas:

1. Facilitation of feelings—this includes helping children to identify feelings associated with the divorce;
2. Development of coping skills, such as learning to communicate their feelings;
3. Adjustment to life changes, which includes encouraging children to adjust to new family structures, homes, schools, and communities;
4. Provision of information, such as learning about children's and parents' reactions to divorce and the process of grief that accompanies divorce;
5. Normalization of the divorce experience, which means helping children to realize that their experiences are common and that they are not alone; and finally,
6. Provision of support, which includes trying to bolster children's self-concept and self-esteem and reassuring children that they are not responsible for their parents' divorce.

Depending on the age of the group of children, group facilitation techniques involve a number of different methods including games, making collages, participating in role-plays, play therapy, writing letters to parents, and taking a tour of a court building. Finally, divorce education programs for children tend to last about four hours but have a range of one to fifteen hours; groups usually comprise fifteen children, with a range of two to sixty participants.

HISTORY OF DIVORCE EDUCATION PROGRAMS

Generic parent education programs in the United States date back to at least the 1930s [24–27], with more specific types of parent education, such as education programs for parents of mentally retarded children, and research on the effectiveness of parent education emerging in the 1950s and 1960s [28–32]. The availability of such programming reflected a growing understanding that parental behavior and the nature of children's environments have important implications for overall child well-being.

The First Call for Programming

The Association for Family and Conciliation Courts (AFCC) documents the foreshadowing of the divorce education movement in two papers by Bradford [33] and Brindley [34] who, in 1970, wrote about outreach programs in Michigan for families of divorce. AFCC also reports that divorce education programs were first initiated in some family court systems in the mid-1970s [35]. Indeed, the first known court-connected divorce education program was started as a collaborative relationship between Johnson County Mental Health Center and the Tenth Judicial District of Kansas in 1976 [36].

When dramatic changes in family law made it easier for couples to divorce, professionals noted that divorcing parents needed more adequate supports and education about the divorce process and the effects that it has on family systems and children [37, 38]. This call for education-based interventions was repeated over the next two decades [39–42]. By the early 1990s there were a number of divorce education programs available for families, and several professional meetings, such as the "First International Congress on Parent Education Programs," were organized and attended by legal and mental-health professionals [17]. Programs continued to develop throughout the country [19, 43–45] and by 1996 legal professionals were writing about divorce education providers as a distinct field of practice [46].

The Explosion of Programs for Divorcing Parents

Blaisure and Geasler first systematically studied the availability and characteristics of divorce education programs in 1994 [17]. They surveyed over 3,000 counties regarding court-connected programs for divorcing parents and, with a 74 percent response rate, identified programs in 541 of those counties. The majority of the programs (about 85 percent) were newly started, having been initiated within the then previous five years (after 1989). At the time that this research was conducted (1994), only three states (Connecticut, Utah, and Vermont) mandated that all divorcing parents attend an educational program. Also, there were a handful of states where it was mandated for parents who could not decide on the terms of their divorce. Otherwise, attendance was either voluntary or ordered by judges on a case-by-case basis. Biondi [47] found similar results in her 1995 analysis of divorce education legislation.

In 1998 the initial Blaisure and Geasler study was replicated by the same researchers [15]. For this second study, they again surveyed over 3,000 counties to inquire about the existence of divorce education programs. This study also had a high response rate (72 percent). The authors determined that 1,516 counties and independent cities in the United States had educational programs for divorcing parents. This represented a 180 percent increase between 1994 and 1998—a virtual explosion in the educational services offered for families of divorce. Attendance policies had also greatly changed during this four-year period. They found that approximately two-thirds of county-level divorce education programs were mandated at either the state or county level or by particular judges. When considered at the state level, forty-four states had some type of mandate for participation. Sometimes this was accomplished by state statute, other times it was mandated by local court or administrative statutes [48].

Barriers and Potential Legal Problems

Barriers

Although Geasler and Blaisure [15] found that over 1,500 counties had divorce education programs in 1998, they also found that 726 did not. Using a subsample of the counties without programs, as identified by Geasler and Blaisure, Arbuthnot [49] surveyed 500 counties to determine the possible barriers to implementing divorce education programs. With a response rate of 33 percent, Arbuthnot found that 35 percent (n = 57) of the survey respondents had implemented new programs since the 1998 survey, while 65 percent (n = 105) were still without programs. These nonadopting counties, it was determined, had smaller populations but, significantly, served cases with more children than those counties that had adopted programs.

The most common reason for not having adopted a divorce education program was lack of funding. This was cited by two-thirds of counties without programs. The second most cited reason for nonadoption was the belief that the county lacked professionals who were trained to provide such services to divorcing families. Finally, one-third of nonadopting counties were unaware that divorce education programs existed. In sum, counties that do not adopt divorce education programs lack adequate funding; moreover, court personnel lack pertinent expertise and basic knowledge about divorce education programs that prevent program adoption.

Legal Problems

Clement [48] documents the fact that a number of legal suits have been brought against counties that mandate attendance by local court rule. In some instances these suits have been successful, such as in Campbell County, Kentucky, where parents were mandated to pay for and attend a divorce education program held by the local Catholic Social Services agency. The local court ruled that this constituted an endorsement of the Catholic religion, and the plaintiff was not obligated to attend. In Illinois, parents have successfully objected to the local mandate because it was inconsistent with the criteria established by the state for obtaining a divorce. In such instances mandatory legislation by the state would eliminate the legitimacy of future lawsuits [47].

RESPONSE OF LEGAL PROFESSIONALS TO DIVORCE EDUCATION PROGRAMS

In general, legal professionals have responded favorably to divorce education programs. One study examined judges' views of a nationwide divorce education program that was active in thirty-five U.S. states. With a response rate of approximately 40 percent, Fischer [50] found that judges had very high opinions of educational programming. Between 80 and 98 percent of respondents agreed or strongly agreed that the seminar encouraged parents to more quickly agree on custodial arrangements, that it decreased relitigation between divorcing parties, that it helped to reduce the suffering of children, and that in general it was beneficial for the families who attended. A study from a community-based sample of providers in western Colorado that was primarily comprised of legal professionals found that respondents believed that divorce education was making a positive contribution to their community [51].

Finally, a third study examined the responses of mediators concerning the possible beneficial effects of divorce education on the mediation process [52]. Mediators reported that it had a positive impact on parents who were mediating divorce arrangements. They indicated that divorce education programs helped parents to remain focused on their children and that they increased parental cooperation. They believed that parents who did not receive divorce education programming were less likely to have shared-parenting agreements.

DIVORCE EDUCATION PROGRAMS TODAY

As previously noted, divorce education programs exist throughout the United States. Table 3.1 shows that thirty-two states and the District of Columbia have state-level statutes pertaining to education programming for families who are divorcing. Such regulations usually also apply to families who are returning to court to address a dispute over child custody, parent-child access, or child support. In only eleven states is the completion of a divorce education program mandated before parents can appear in court to have their divorce granted. Utah is one such state.

> *Utah Example*: As a prerequisite to receiving a divorce decree, both parties are required to attend a mandatory course on their children's needs after filing a complaint for divorce and receiving a docket number, unless waived under Section 30-3-4. If that requirement is waived, the court may permit the divorce action to proceed. . . . The mandatory course shall instruct both parties about divorce and its impacts on: (a) their child or children; (b) their family relationship; and (c) their financial responsibilities for their child or children. (Utah Code Ann. § 30-3-11.3)

Research from a Canadian study involving interviews with over 125 professionals who work with families of divorce found that there is considerable disagreement over whether programs should be mandatory, citing reasons such as "freedom of choice" and concerns over whether all parents have the capacity to benefit from educational programs [53]. Research in the United States finds that only 12 percent of participants in divorce education programs believe that classes should not be mandatory [54].

Other times attendance at a divorce education program is mandated under certain conditions, such as in instances of family violence or in contested child-custody cases. In only two instances do states make such stipulations, such as in the state of Alaska.

> *Alaska Example*: The court shall determine custody in accordance with the best interests of the child . . . [and] shall consider . . . (j) If the court finds that a parent has a history of perpetrating domestic violence . . . the court shall allow only supervised visitation by that parent with the child, conditioned on that parent's participating in and successfully completing an intervention program for batterers, and a parenting education program, where reasonably available. (Alaska Stat. § 25.24.150)

Otherwise, attendance at a divorce education program is voluntary or, more significantly, at the discretion of the court, such as in the state of Kansas.

Table 3.1. States with Policies Concerning Divorce Education, and Whether Attendance Is Compulsory

State	Statute	Code	Compulsory
Alabama	No		
Alaska	Yes	AlaskFa Stat. § 25.24.150	Yes—family violence cases
Arizona	Yes	A.R.S. § 25-351	No
Arkansas	No		
California	Yes	Cal. Fam. Code § 3200-3204	No
Colorado	Yes	C.R.S. § 14-10-123.7	No
Connecticut	Yes	Conn. Gen. Stat § 466-69b	Yes
Delaware	Yes	13 Del. C. § 1507	Yes
District of Columbia	Yes	D.C. Code § 16-914	No
Florida	Yes	Fla. Stat. § 61.21	Yes
Georgia	No		
Hawaii	Yes	H.R.S.§ 571-46.2	No
Idaho	No		
Illinois	Yes	750 I.L.C.S.§ 5/404	No
Indiana	No		
Iowa	Yes	Iowa Code § 598.19A	Yes
Kansas	Yes	K.S.A. § 60-1626	No
Kentucky	No		
Louisiana	Yes	La. R.S. § 9:306	No
Maine	Yes	4 M.R.S.A. § 183	
Maryland	Yes	MD Code § 7-103.2	No
Massachusetts	Yes	A.L.M. Probate Ct. Fam. Ct. S.O. 1-03*	Yes
Michigan	No		
Minnesota	Yes	Minn. Stat § 518.157	Yes
Mississippi	No		
Missouri	Yes	§ 452.372 R.S. Mo.	Yes
Montana	Yes	M.C.A. § 40-4-226	No
Nebraska	Yes	R.R.S. Neb. § 42-394.01	No
Nevada	No		
New Hampshire	Yes	N.H.R.S. § 458-D	Yes
New Jersey	Yes	N.J. Stat. § 2A:34-12.3	Yes
New Mexico	No		
New York	No		
North Carolina	No		
North Dakota	No		
Ohio	Yes	O.R.C. Ann. 3109.053	No
Oklahoma	Yes	43 Okl. St. § 107.2	No
Oregon	Yes	O.R.S. § 3.425	No
Pennsylvania	No		
Rhode Island	No		
South Carolina	No		
South Dakota	No		

(*continues*)

Table 3.1. (*continued*)

State	Statute	Code	Compulsory
Tennessee	Yes	Tenn. Code Ann. § 36-6-101	No
Texas	Yes	Tex. Fam. Code § 105.009	No
Utah	Yes	Utah Code Ann. § 30-3-11.3	Yes
Vermont	Yes	V.R.F.P. 14**	No
Virginia	Yes	Va. Code Ann. § 20-103	Yes—contested cases
Washington	Yes	Rev. Code Wash. § 26.12.172	No
West Virginia	Yes	W. Va. Code § 48-9-104	Yes
Wisconsin	Yes	Wis. Stat. § 767.115	No
Wyoming	No		

*Family Court Standing Order
** Rules for Family Proceedings

> *Kansas Example*: The court shall inform the parents, or require them to be informed, about: (1) How to prepare a parenting plan; (2) the impact of family dissolution on children and how the needs of children facing family dissolution can best be addressed; (3) the impact of domestic abuse on children, and resources for addressing domestic abuse; and (4) mediation or other nonjudicial procedures designed to help them achieve an agreement. . . . The court may require the parents to attend parent education classes. (K.S.A. § 60-1626)

Thus, if not mandatory, divorce education services can only reach higher risk families, and only then if their level of risk comes to the attention of the court.

Programs for Children

This book focuses on state-level policy making, and there are few programs that, at the state level, require children to participate in divorce education programs. However, on the county level Geelhoed, Blaisure, and Geasler [23] report that in their 1998–1999 survey of sixty-seven county-level, court-connected programs, 37 percent (n = 25) of divorce education programs for children were mandated.

EFFECTIVENESS OF DIVORCE EDUCATION PROGRAMS

There are a number of features of the research conducted on divorce education programs that make it difficult to evaluate: (1) poor research designs, (2) multiple and varying outcome measures, (3) posttests conducted at varying times, and (4) vast differences between divorce education programs. These problems are not unique to the study of divorce education programs but exist in much of the social science research. Nonetheless, I will outline each of these issues before presenting my examination of the research literature on this social policy intervention.

Challenges within the Research Literature

The research on divorce education programs is characterized by small sample sizes, low response rates, and cross-sectional designs. Research published in peer-reviewed sources has reported on sample sizes as low as 20 (experimental group = 11, comparison group = 9) [55] and response rates ranging from lows of 12–14 percent [56] to 24 percent [57]. Over time, however, the quality of the research has improved, although it continues to suffer from a lack of controls in longitudinal study design. For example, usually the research design includes a group of parents who are mandated to attend the educational intervention compared with a second group of parents who live in a neighboring county or state that does not have a mandate for attendance [58]. Sometimes it compares parents who volunteered for educational services with a group that did not [59]. Or other researchers examine outcomes over time without a comparison group [60]. Thus, rarely have researchers implemented study designs where parents are randomly assigned to groups. Moveover, the growing mandates for this type of intervention will likely make it still more difficult to randomly assign parents to different intervention groups.

Second, in reviewing the literature for this chapter, I discovered many different outcomes that were used to measure or assess the effectiveness of divorce education programs. In order to make the evaluation of the literature more manageable, I created categories of general assessment that seemed to be consistent across most studies. For example, studies that asked parents how often they had spoken negatively about the "other" parent in front of their children, asked the children to carry messages to the other parent, or pressed their children for information about the other parent seemed to be asking about "parenting behaviors." Studies that asked parents how often they discussed the children with the other parent or how often they made decisions about their children jointly were asking about the "co-parental relationship." And studies that asked parents to describe their children's behavior or mood seemed to be asking about "child adjustment to divorce." These are examples of some of the categories that I created in my review of eighteen research papers and reports.

Third, there are important differences within the literature concerning the administration time for posttest measures. Most of the research on divorce education programs uses some type of pretest-posttest study design. Some studies administer posttest measures immediately after program completion, when retention of program material is likely to be quite high. Other studies, in addition to using immediate posttest measures, implement posttest measures several months or even years after program completion.

Finally, the literature on divorce education tends to treat all programs for divorced families the same, when in fact they are not. Some parent education programs use passive teaching techniques [60–62], while others use active teaching techniques [63, 64]. These differences in program characteristics are not usually accounted for in the literature and even less frequently are compared as the focus of research projects—a frequent criticism of the research on divorce mediation and mediation styles as well [65]. The summary of the research reviewed is displayed in table 3.2.

Differences also exist between programs. The majority of divorce education programs are one session long and last a few hours. Such programs and what they have to offer parents are quite different than programs that last for multiple weeks or programs that offer various types of interventions [13, 66–69]. In fact, programs that are comprehensive should rightfully be called something else, and, to remain consistent with the literature, I call these more comprehensive services "prevention" or "intervention" programs for families of divorce. In truth, these programs are not what are mandated by state legislatures or recommended by the courts but are efforts on the part of thoughtful researchers to bring innovative services and programs to divorced families. As noted, these programs will be handled separately in chapter 7 of this book.

Consumer Satisfaction Research

The least sophisticated level of research on divorce education programs reports on parents' level of satisfaction with the content of the program and what they think they have learned. As with many other family interventions, parents report being highly satisfied with divorce education programs, as well as the professionals who lead the seminars. They also indicate that they learned new information and skills that they hope to implement into their changing lives. More specifically, studies have found that parents report learning about the impact of divorce on children [70], their own reactions to divorce [71], how divorce affects parenting [72], and modifications that parents can make in parenting behaviors [73]. One study found that 70 percent of parents reported that attending the seminar may make a difference in how they interact with their children about the divorce [71], while another study found that six months after program completion between 60 and 72 percent of parents reported having used the information that they learned, specifically with regard to making con-

Table 3.2. Summary of Studies Examining the Effectiveness of Divorce Education Programs

	Outcome Measured and Whether Effective in Desired Direction (Yes/No)							
Study	Co-Parenting Relationship	Parental Conflict	Parenting Behaviors	Child Adjustment	Parent Adjustment	Relitigation	Contact w/ Nonresident Parent	Knowledge re Children & Divorce
Posttest Assessment: Immediate								
[64]	—	—	—	—	—	—	—	Yes
[56]	—	Yes	—	—	No	—	—	—
Group Total (# Effective/# Examined)	0/0	1/1	0/0	0/0	0/1	0/0	0/0	1/1
Posttest Assessment: 1-6 Month Follow-Ups								
[58]	No	—	Yes	Yes	Yes	—	—	Yes
[94]	—	—	—	Yes	—	Yes	—	—
[60]	No	Yes	Yes	Yes	—	—	—	Yes
[20]	Yes	Yes	—	No	—	No	—	—
[77]	No	—	Yes*	No	No	—	—	—
[78]	—	—	Yes	—	—	—	—	—
[73]	Yes	Yes	Yes	—	Yes	No	—	Yes
[79]	—	No	Yes	—	—	No	—	Yes
[54]	—	Yes	—	—	—	No	Yes	—

(*continues*)

Table 3.2. (continued)

Study	Co-Parenting Relationship	Parental Conflict	Parenting Behaviors	Child Adjustment	Parent Adjustment	Relitigation	Contact w/ Nonresident Parent	Knowledge re Children & Divorce
Group Total (# Effective/# Examined)	2/5	4/5	6/6	2/4	2/3	1/4	1/1	4/4
Posttest Assessment: One Year and Beyond Follow-Ups								
[61]	—	Yes	—	—	—	Yes	—	—
[80]	—	—	—	—	—	No	Yes	—
[81]	No	No	—	—	No	—	No	—
[59]	—	—	—	—	—	Yes*	—	—
[62]	—	—	—	—	—	No	—	—
[63]	No	—	—	No	No	—	—	No
[57]	No	Yes	—	—	—	—	—	—
Group Total (# Effective/# Examined)	0/3	2/3	0/0	0/1	0/2	2/4	1/2	0/1
Cumulative Total (# Effective/# Examined)	2/8	7/9	6/6	2/5	2/6	3/8	2/3	5/6

*For high-conflict families only

tact with the nonresident parent more successful [54]. Parents have also reported an increase in the responsibility that they feel to protect their children from some of the harmful effects of divorce and to engage in a cooperative communication style with their former spouse [70, 74].

There are some differences among parents in how they rate their experiences with the education seminar. For example, parents who have been married longer or who have had multiple marriages tend to think that divorce education seminars are less useful [74]. Also, parents who engage in higher and more explosive levels of conflict are less likely to report that the program will make a difference in the interactions that they have with their divorcing spouse. [54] Overall, however, most parents report that attending a divorce education seminar is informative and that they would recommend that other parents attend [33, 71, 73]. Similar findings have been reported in qualitative studies as well [75, 76].

Posttest Measurement: Immediate

Two studies were reviewed that used posttest procedures immediately after the completion of the divorce education program. Samples sizes for studies were fifty-eight [56] and over four hundred fifty [64] participants. The Zimmerman study used small, convenience comparison groups; the larger, Yankeelov study used no comparison group. There was little uniformity among the outcomes measured. Zimmerman found a decrease in parental conflict among program participants, but did not find any changes in parental adjustment. The Yankeelov study, which, again, did not have a comparison group [64], found that after participation in the educational seminar, parents were more informed about the unique needs of children whose parents are divorcing than they were before the educational seminar. They also found a positive change in a number of attitudes about children, and parenting and divorce. They did not assess any behavioral changes.

Posttest Measurement: One- to Six-month Follow-ups

There are many more studies that assess the impact of divorce education programs several months after program completion, which is a better measure of program effectiveness. The studies in this category implemented assessments one to six months after program completion. Sample sizes are diverse but overall reasonably large, ranging from 39 to 747, with seven of the nine studies reviewed having sample sizes of more than 100 participants. Two studies [60, 73], both with good sample sizes, did not use a comparison group; all others did. There is more uniformity among the outcomes measured, and thus, one is able to draw conclusions across several studies.

The strongest evidence of success is that even several months after program completion, parents report having maintained parenting behavioral changes that resulted from the divorce education seminar [58, 60, 73, 77–79]. (Parents were usually asked about specific behaviors, as opposed to asking them to subjectively rate their level of change.) In a number of studies, parents had also retained knowledge about the unique needs of children who are part of divorced families [20, 58, 73, 79].

There is some evidence that parents have successfully lowered their conflict several months after attending an educational seminar [20, 60, 73], although only two of the four studies indicating this used a comparison group [54]; another study did not find such a reduction [79]. Two out of three times, parents reported that they, themselves, were better adjusted [58, 73]; this was true for their children only two out of four times [58, 60].

There is less evidence that divorce education programs have a positive impact on the co-parental relationship and on rates of relitigation. In both instances, only once were positive results for the co-parenting relationship [73] and relitigation obtained [58], while others found no difference over time or when compared with nontreatment groups [54, 58, 60, 73, 77].

There is some indication that parents are able to maintain the skills that they learned in class. One study, which assessed parents immediately after program completion, and then six months later, found that parents scored the same when presented with vignettes and asked what they would *say* and what they would *do* in response to a similar situation [58]. However, there was no pretest measure of these parenting skills, thus it is possible that parents possessed these skills before participating in the course.

Finally, one study found that program success was dependent on parental conflict. Kramer and Washo [77] found that, among program participants, parents who at pretest had reported high levels of conflict saw a significant decline in parental triangulating behaviors three months later, when compared to nonparticipants. This reduction in triangulating behaviors was not found among parents who had initially reported moderate and low levels of conflict in either intervention or comparison groups.

Posttest Assessment: Follow-ups after One Year and Beyond

The best well-designed studies to assess brief parent educational seminars are usually those that conduct follow-up assessments several years after program completion. Of the seven studies reviewed, all have sample sizes of at least two hundred participants and all use a comparison group of parents who did not complete a divorce education program. At the same time, the outcome measures are not uniform, making it more difficult to draw conclusions about the effectiveness of divorce education programs.

The most promising finding among these studies is a possible reduction in parental conflict. Two of three studies found that parents who had completed a parenting program, when compared with parents who did not, experienced a reduction in parental conflict [57, 61]. Both of these studies used only posttest procedures with no pretest measures, and there were limited demographic controls. However, the analyses were conducted several years after program completion and both used mandated, as opposed to voluntary, program participants.

There is considerably less support for other positive findings. One study found that there was an overall decrease in relitigation among program participants [61], while another study found that this was true only for participants with high levels of conflict [59]. Meanwhile, two studies found that there was an *increase* in relitigation among those who participated in a divorce education program [62, 80]. There was mixed evidence about the impact of participating in a divorce education program on contact between children and their nonresidential parents. One study found an increase among program participants [80], while another found no difference when compared with nonparticipants [81]. Finally, there was no evidence that there were changes in the co-parenting relationship, adjustments among parents or their children, and no change in the knowledge that parents have about the special needs of children from divorced familes [57, 63, 81]. Although it should be noted that in some instances these outcomes were only measured by one study, the overall lack of findings is supported by a small qualitative study that found that children whose parents attended an educational seminar continue to report family problems such as being put in the middle of their parents and being exposed to parental conflict [82].

Effectiveness of Different Types of Programs

Earlier in this chapter I cited Geasler and Blaisure when outlining the different types of learning and teaching techniques that are used in divorce education programs: passive involvement, limited involvement, and active involvement [18]. Despite the popularity of this topic and the attention paid to it [14], there is little research that compares the efficacy of one type of program with another. Over half of the studies described above used techniques that were consistent with either passive- or limited-involvement teaching styles. Kramer et al. [20] systematically compared a more narrowly focused skills-based program, which involved limited and active involvement, with a broader information-based program, that used passive involvement learning tools. They found that the skills-based program was able to improve parental communication, while the information-based program was not. Such findings support assertions that programs that allow parents to practice new parenting and co-parenting skills, such as in limited- or active-involvement programs, are more likely to be fruitful in bringing about desired behaviors [18].

Programs for Children

Research that evaluates programming for children of divorce is still in its infancy, and most of the current evaluations cover programs that are quite extensive, lasting for many weeks [83–85]. Programs that are shorter in duration and often mandated by the court appear to be well received by families [86]. A qualitative study of children who attended a brief divorce education program found that the program helped children to realize that the breakup of a family is painful for most children. The researchers found that the program support was well received, that children learned about the divorce process, and that the children reported improved relationships within their families [87].

Conclusion

The research on parent education seminars for divorcing parents has methodological problems that make it difficult to truly assess the effectiveness of these brief interventions. The most conclusive evidence comes from studies that assess families several months after program completion, where we see reduction in parental conflict and an increase in positive parenting behaviors and in the knowledge that parents have about divorce and children. There is also some evidence that children and parents have a better adjustment when parents have attended a divorce education program. However, several of these studies did not use control groups, so it is difficult to conclude for certain whether these findings are from the passage of time or because of the intervention. The most promising long-term finding about divorce education programs is a possible reduction in parental conflict. Other measures have not been systematically measured enough to draw strong conclusions.

THE BARNES FAMILY REVISITED

The Barnes family did not live in a state that had any provisions regarding divorce education programs for divorcing parents. However, if they lived, for example, in the state of Delaware, Joanne and Mark would both be required to attend, although not necessarily together, a divorce education seminar before their divorce could be granted. If they lived in a state that does not mandate attendance at programs, such as Montana, a judge might still recommend that they attend an education seminar, since initially Mark and Joanne could not agree on a child custody arrangement.

If Mark and Joanne are similar to most other parents who attend divorce education programs, they are likely to tell friends and family that the seminar was a positive experience and that they would recommend it to other parents who are also divorcing. They are also likely to say that the program covered topics of which they were unaware, especially concerning placing their children in the middle, and that they separately each resolve to speak more kindly of their ex-spouse in front of the children and not to ask the children to carry messages to the other parent. In the short run, Joanne and Mark may experience a decline in their level of conflict, an increase in their knowledge about the unique needs of children and divorce, and an increase in the positive parenting behaviors that they use with their children pertaining to the divorce. In the long run there is a chance that their conflict may remain lower, but any projected changes beyond this would be purely speculation.

SUMMARY

This chapter has documented the rapid growth in popularity of divorce education programs since the mid-1990s. At that time only a handful of states regulated programs, and today over thirty states have legislation pertaining to divorce education programs. What is unique about parenting education programs, unlike mediation or parenting plans, is that they are fairly low cost to parents, both in terms of money and time. Moreover, parents do not have to attend with their divorcing spouse, and therefore, it is an intervention that is likely to be less stressful than other interventions, such as mediation where parents have to face their divorcing spouse and the problems that they share. A low-cost intervention that reaches many parents at one time and that teaches parents about how to be more sensitive to their children: one can easily imagine how this intervention would be well received by policy makers, professionals in the legal professions, and families—which may account for its rise in popularity.

The existing research on divorce education programs makes it difficult to draw conclusions about the effectiveness of these brief interventions in the lives of divorcing families. It is only possible to conclude with some confidence that divorce education programs may result in an increase in positive parenting behaviors concerning living in a divorced family and lead to a reduction in parental conflict. There is also some evidence that participation in divorce education may be associated with an increase in parental knowledge about children and divorce. However, there is little evidence to suggest that there are other positive outcomes from divorce education programs.

From the review presented here, one might be tempted to conclude that divorce education programs are ineffective. I would argue that they are not universally or comprehensively effective. In the words of Thoennes and Pearson, "parent education does not revolutionize relationships between parents" [54, p. 215]; however, there are some encouraging findings. Numerous studies have examined the harmful effects of parental conflict on child adjustment, both in divorced and intact marriages [88–93]. Therefore, the fact that some studies have found a reduction in parental conflict several years after the completion of a divorce education program is a very promising finding. There are also positive findings for families of high conflict, such as a reduction in relitigation and an increase in more positive parenting behaviors. Evidence that a brief intervention might reduce harm to children that is associated with parental conflict is in itself an indication of success, even if there are no other positive program outcomes. It is not my intention to overly and perhaps inappropriately promote the success of parenting education programs. Rather, it is my intention to promote enthusiasm about the prospect of a program that could be useful for children of divorce and that deserves more focused attention from researchers.

REFERENCES

1. Moore, A. A. Utilization of neonatal (birth-age 3) parent education programs by new parents. Dissertation. "Social Work," 1992, New York University, New York.
2. Darmstadt, G. Community-based child abuse prevention. *Social Work*, 1990, 35(6): pp. 487–89.
3. Cohen, M., and C. E. Irwin. Parent-time: Psychoeducational groups for parents of adolescents. *Health and Social Work*, 1983, 8(3): pp. 196–202.
4. Whipple, E. E. Reaching families with preschoolers at risk of physical child abuse: What works? *Families in Society*, 1999, 80(2): pp. 148–60.
5. Peterman, P. J. Parenting and environmental considerations. *American Journal of Orthopsychiatry*, 1981, 51(2): pp. 351–55.
6. Danoff, N. L., K. J. Kemper, and B. Sherry. Risk factors for dropping out of a parenting education program. *Child Abuse and Neglect*, 1994, 18(7): pp. 599–606.
7. Coren, E., J. Barlow, and S. Stewart-Brown. The effectiveness of individual and group-based parenting programmes in improving outcomes for teenage mothers and their children: A systematic review. *Journal of Adolescence*, 2003, 26(1): pp. 79–103.
8. Reilly, J. L. Parenting from prison: What can extension educators do? *Journal of Extension*, 2003, 41(5): http://www.joe.org/joe/2003october/iw4.shtml.
9. Meyers, S. A. Adapting parent education programs to meet the needs of fathers: An ecological perspective. *Family Relations*, 1993, 42(4): pp. 447–52.
10. Owen, M. T., and B. A. Mulvihill. Benefits of a parent education and support program in the first three years. *Family Relations*, 1994, 43(2): pp. 206–12.

11. Ponzetti, J. J., and W. Dulin. Parent education in Washington state Even Start family literacy programs. *Early-Childhood-Education-Journal*, 1997, 25(1): 23–29.

12. Buehler, C., et al. Description and evaluation of the orientation for divorcing parents: Implications for postdivorce prevention programs. *Family Relations*, 1992, 41(2): pp. 154–62.

13. Braver, S. L., and D. A. Gordon. What works and what doesn't? A critical review of the parent education literature. AFCC's 5th International Congress on Parent Education and Access Programs. 2002, Tucson, AZ.

14. Braver, S. L., et al. The content of divorce education programs: Results of a survey. *Family and Conciliation Courts Review*, 1996, 34(1): pp. 41–59.

15. Geasler, M. J., and K. R. Blaisure. 1998 nationwide survey of court-connected divorce education programs. *Family and Conciliation Courts Review*, 1999, 37(1): pp. 36–63.

16. Blaisure, K. R., and M. J. Geasler. The divorce education intervention model. *Family and Conciliation Courts Review*, 2000, 38(4): pp. 501–13.

17. Blaisure, K. R., and M. J. Geasler. Results of a survey of court-connected parent education programs in U.S. counties. *Family and Conciliation Courts Review*, 1996, 34(1): pp. 23–40.

18. Geasler, M. J., and K. R. Blaisure. A review of divorce education program materials. *Family Relations: Interdisciplinary Journal of Applied Family Studies*, 1998, 47(2): pp. 167–75.

19. Arbuthnot, J., et al. Court-sponsored educational programs for divorcing parents: Some guiding thoughts and preliminary data. *Juvenile and Family Court Journal*, 1994, 45: pp. 77–84.

20. Kramer, K. M., et al. Effects of skill-based versus information-based divorce education programs on domestic violence and parental communication. *Family and Conciliation Courts Review*, 1998, 36(1): pp. 9–31.

21. Fuhrmann, G. S., J. McGill, and M. E. O'Connell. Parent education's second generation: Integrating violence sensitivity. *Family and Conciliation Courts Review*, 1999, 37(1): pp. 24–35.

22. Frazee, E. Sensitizing parent education programs to domestic violence concerns: The perspective of the New York State Parent Education Advisory Board. *Family Court Review*, 2005, 43(1): pp. 124–35.

23. Geelhoed, R. J., K. R. Blaisure, and M. J. Geasler. Court affiliated parent education: Status of court-connected programs for children whose parents are separating or divorcing. *Family Court Review*, 2001, 39(October): pp. 393–404.

24. Bigelow, M. A. Sex education in parental education. *Teachers College Record*, 1930, 31: pp. 522–27.

25. Packer, G. M. Ninety-seven hundred parents' questions concerning child development. *Journal of Experimental Education*, 1934, 3: pp. 117–53.

26. Anderson, J. E. Child behavior and parental attitudes. *Mental Health Observer*, 1934, 3: p. 3.

27. Groves, E. R. The family. *American Journal of Sociology*, 1932, 37: pp. 942–48.

28. Albert, G. Learning theory and parent education. *Marriage and Family Living*, 1962, 24(3): pp. 249–53.

29. Neubauer, P. B. Basic considerations in the application of therapy and education to parent groups. *International Journal of Group Psychotherapy*, 1953, 3: pp. 315–19.

30. Pollak, G. K. Family life education for parents of acting-out children: A group discussion approach. *Journal of Marriage and the Family*, 1964, 26(4): pp. 489–94.

31. Terdal, L., and J. Buell. Parent education in managing retarded children with behavior deficits and inappropriate behaviors. *Mental Retardation*, 1969, 7(3): pp. 10–13.

32. Mannino, F. V., and M. M. Conant. Dropouts from parent education groups. *Family Coordinator*, 1969, 18(1): pp. 54–59.

33. Bradford, J. Group orientation. *Conciliation Courts Review*, 1970, 8(1): p. 20.

34. Brindley, J. Group intake. *Conciliation Courts Review*, 1970, 8(1): pp. 21–22.

35. Association of Family and Conciliation Courts. "About AFCC: History." n.d., http://www.afccnet.org/about/history.asp (May 5, 2005).

36. Blaisure, K. R. Personal communication to author. May 26, 2005.

37. Sprenkel, D. H., and C. L. Storm. Divorce therapy outcome research: A substantive and methodological review. *Journal of Marital and Family Therapy*, 1983, 9(3): pp. 239–58.

38. Roeder-Esser, C. Families in transition: A divorce workshop. *Family and Conciliation Courts Review*, 1994, 32(1): pp. 40–49.

39. Di Bias, T. Some programs for children. *Family and Conciliation Courts Review*, 1996, 34(1): pp. 112–29.

40. Zibbell, R. A. A short-term, small-group education and counseling program for separated and divorced parents in conflict. *Journal of Divorce and Remarriage*, 1992, 18(1): pp. 189–203.

41. Warren, N. J., and I. A. Amara. Educational groups for single parents: The Parenting After Divorce programs. *Journal of Divorce*, 1984, 8(2): pp. 79–96.

42. Lyon, E. Stages of divorce: Implications for service delivery. *Social Casework*, 1985, 66(5): pp. 259–67.

43. Lehner, L. Mediation parent education programs in the California family courts. *Family and Conciliation Courts Review*, 1992, 30(2): pp. 207–16.

44. Howe, G. W., et al. Parental decision-making styles during and after divorce. *Conciliation Courts Review*, 1984, 22(2): pp. 63–70.

45. Frieman, B. B., R. Garon, and B. Mandell. Parenting seminars for divorcing parents. *Social Work*, 1994, 39(5): pp. 607–10.

46. Salem, P., A. Shepard, and S. W. Schlissel. Parent education as a distinct field of practice: The agenda for the future. *Family and Conciliation Courts Review*, 1996, 34(1): pp. 9–22.

47. Biondi, E. D. Legal implementation of parent education programs for divorcing and separating parents. *Family and Conciliation Courts Review*, 1996, 34(1): pp. 82–92.

48. Clement, D. A. 1998 Nationwide survey of the legal status of parent education. *Family and Conciliation Courts Review*, 1999, 37(2): pp. 219–39.

49. Arbuthnot, J. A call unheeded: Courts' perceived obstacles to establishing divorce education programs. *Family Court Review*, 2002, 40(3): pp. 371–80.

50. Fischer, R. L. The impact of an educational seminar for divorcing parents: Results from a national survey of family court judges. *Journal of Divorce and Remarriage*, 1997, 28(1): pp. 35–48.

51. Taylor, R. J. Then and now: A follow-up study of professionals' perceptions of parenting after divorce classes. *Journal of Divorce and Remarriage*, 2004, 41(3/4): pp. 135–42.

52. Arbuthnot, J., and K. Kramer. Effects of divorce education on mediation process and outcome. *Mediation Quarterly*, 1998, 15(3): pp. 199–213.

53. Bacon, B. L. Multidisciplinary perspectives on parent education after separation and divorce. *Social Work Forum*, 2004, 37(Spring): pp. 43–62.

54. Thoennes, N., and J. Pearson. Parent education in the domestic relations court: A multisite assessment. *Family and Conciliation Courts Review*, 1999, 37(2): pp. 195–218.

55. Devlin, A. S., et al. Parent education for divorced fathers. *Family Relations: Interdisciplinary Journal of Applied Family Studies*, 1992, 41(3): pp. 290–96.

56. Zimmerman, D. K., J. H. Brown, and P. R. Portes. Assessing custodial mother adjustment to divorce: The role of divorce education and family functioning. *Journal of Divorce and Remarriage*, 2004, 41(1/2): pp. 1–24.

57. Toews, M. L., and P. C. McKenry. Court-related predictors of parental cooperation and conflict after divorce. *Journal of Divorce and Remarriage*, 2001, 35(1): pp. 57–73.

58. Arbuthnot, J., and D. A. Gordon. Does mandatory divorce education for parents work? A six-month outcome evaluation. *Family and Conciliation Courts Review*, 1996, 34(1): pp. 60–81.

59. Kramer, L., and A. Kowal. Long-term follow-up of a court-based intervention for divorcing parents. *Family and Conciliation Courts Review*, 1998, 36(4): pp. 452–65.

60. Bacon, B. L., and B. Mckenzie. Parent education after separation/divorce: Impact of the level of parental conflict on outcomes. *Family Court Review*, 2004, 42(1): pp. 85–98.

61. Criddle, M. N. J., S. M. Allgood, and K. W. Piercy. The relationship between mandatory divorce education and level of postdivorce parental conflict. *Journal of Divorce and Remarriage*, 2003, 39(3): pp. 99–111.

62. McClure, T. E. Postjudgment conflict and cooperation following court-connected parent education. *Journal of Divorce and Remarriage*, 2002, 38(1): pp. 1–16.

63. McKenry, P. C., K. A. Clark, and G. Stone. Evaluation of a parent education program for divorcing parents. *Family Relations: Interdisciplinary Journal of Applied Family Studies*, 1999, 48(2): pp. 129–37.

64. Yankeelov, P. A., et al. Transition or not? A theory-based quantitative evaluation of families in transition. *Family Court Review*, 2003, 41(2): pp. 242–56.

65. Beck, C. J. A., and B. D. Sales. A critical reappraisal of divorce mediation research and policy. *Psychology, Public Policy and the Law*, 2000, 6(4): pp. 989–1056.

66. Wolchik, S. A., et al. Six-year follow-up of preventive interventions for children of divorce. A randomized controlled trial. *Journal of the American Medical Association*, 2002, 288(15): pp. 1874–1881.

67. Wolchik, S.A., et al. The children of divorce parenting intervention: Outcome evaluation of an empirically based program. *American Journal of Community Psychology*, 1993, 21(3): pp. 293–31.

68. Pruett, M. K., B. Nangle, and C. Bailey. Divorcing families with young children in the court's family services unit: Profiles and impact of services. *Family and Conciliation Courts Review*, 2000, 38(4): pp. 478–500.

69. Bloom, B. L., W. F. Hodges, and R. A. Caldwell. A preventive program for the newly separated: Initial evaluation. *American Journal of Community Psychology*, 1982, 10(3): pp. 251–54.

70. Atwood, J. D. The family therapist in the courts: The P.E.A.C.E. program (Parent Education and Custody Effectiveness): A voluntary New York State interdisciplinary program for divorcing parents. *Journal of Prevention and Intervention in the Community*, 2001, 21(1): pp. 113–24.

71. Petersen, V., and S. B. Steinman. Helping children succeed after divorce: A court-mandated educational program for divorcing parents. *Family and Conciliation Courts Review*, 1994, 32(1): pp. 27–39.

72. Mathis, R. D., Z. Tanner, and F. Whinery. Evaluation of participant reactions to premediation group orientation. *Mediation Quarterly*, 1999, 17(2): pp. 153–59.

73. McKenzie, B., and I. Guberman. Evaluation of "For the Sake of the Children": A parent education program for separating and divorcing parents, Phase 2. 2000, Child and Family Services Research Group, University of Manitoba.

74. Feng, P., and M. A. Fine. Evaluation of a research-based parenting education program for divorcing parents: The Focus on Kids program. *Journal of Divorce and Remarriage*, 2000, 34(1): pp. 1–23.

75. Stone, G., K. A. Clark, and P. C. McKenry. Qualitative evaluation of a parent education program for divorcing parents. *Journal of Divorce and Remarriage*, 2000, 34(1-2): pp. 25–40.

76. Bussey, M. Impact of kids' first seminar for divorcing parents: A three-year follow-up. *Journal of Divorce and Remarriage*, 1996, 26(1): pp. 129–49.

77. Kramer, L., and C. A. Washo. Evaluation of a court-mandated prevention program for divorcing parents: The Children First program. *Family Relations*, 1993, 42: pp. 179–86.

78. Kurkowski, K. P., D. A. Gordon, and J. Arbuthnot. Children caught in the middle: A brief educational intervention for divorced parents. *Journal of Divorce and Remarriage*, 1993, 20(3-4): pp. 139–51.

79. Shifflett, K., and E. M. Cummings. A program for educating parents about the effects of divorce and conflict on children: An initial evaluation. *Family Relations: Interdisciplinary Journal of Applied Family Studies*, 1999, 48(1): pp. 79–89.

80. deLusé, S. R. Mandatory divorce education: A program evaluation using a "quasi-random" regression discontinuity design. In *Dissertation Abstracts International: Section B: The Sciences and Engineering*, p. 1349. 1999, Ann Arbor, MI: University Microfilms International.

81. Douglas, E. M. The effectiveness of a divorce education program on father involvement. *Journal of Divorce and Remarriage*, 2004, 40(3/4): pp. 91–101.

82. Hans, J. D., and M. A. Fine. Children of divorce: Experiences of children whose parents attended a divorce education program. *Journal of Divorce and Remarriage*, 2001, 36(1): pp. 1–26.

83. Pedro-Carroll, J. L., S. E. Sutton, and P. A. Wyman. A two-year follow-up evaluation of a preventive intervention for young children of divorce. *School Psychology Review*, 1999, 28(3): pp. 467–76.

84. Fischer, R. L. Children in changing families: Results of a pilot study of a program for children of separation and divorce. *Family and Conciliation Courts Review*, 1999, 37(2): pp. 240–56.

85. Kids' Turn. "Efficacy." n.d., http://kidsturn.org/others/longterm.htm (April 15, 2005).

86. Families in Transition. "FIT evaluation." n.d., http://www.louisville.edu/kent/community/fit/fiteval.html (April 15, 2005).

87. Oliphant, E., et al. Measuring children's perceptions of the Families in Transition program (FIT): A qualitative evaluation. *Journal of Divorce and Remarriage*, 2002, 37(3): pp. 157–64.

88. Tschann, J. M., et al. Conflict, loss, change and parent-child relationships: Predicting children's adjustment during divorce. *Journal of Divorce*, 1990, 13(4): pp. 1–22.

89. Morrison, D. R., and M. J. Coiro. Parental conflict and marital disruption: Do children benefit when high-conflict marriages are dissolved? *Journal of Marriage and the Family*, 1999, 61(August): pp. 626–37.

90. Kline, M., J. R. Johnston, and J. M. Tschann. The long shadow of marital conflict: A model of children's postdivorce adjustment. *Journal of Marriage and the Family*, 1991, 53(2): pp. 297–309.

91. Jekielek, S. A. Parental conflict, marital disruption and children's emotional well-being. *Social Forces*, 1998, 76(3): pp. 905–35.

92. Amato, P. R., and S. C. Rezac. Contact with nonresidential parents, interparental conflict and children's behavior. *Journal of Family Issues*, 1994, 15(2): pp. 191–207.

93. Johnston, J. R., M. Kline, and J. M. Tschann. Ongoing postdivorce conflict in families contesting custody: Do joint custody and frequent access help? In *Joint custody and shared parenting* (2nd ed.), ed. J. Folberg, pp. 177–84. 1991, New York: Guilford Press.

94. Arbuthnot, J., K. M. Kramer, and D. A. Gordon. Patterns of relitigation following divorce education. *Family and Conciliation Courts Review*, 1997, 35(3): pp. 269–79.

4

Parenting Plans

Unlike other social policies for families of divorce, such as gender-neutral custody laws or mediation, the concept of "parenting plans" is relatively recent. Although different in every state, the overriding theme of parenting plans is that it is a contract, to which parents have agreed, that allocates the roles and responsibilities of divorcing parents with regard to their children. Parenting plans are different from traditional divorce decrees in that they usually require that parents develop a plan or schedule of parent-child contact and other parental responsibilities, where traditional divorce decrees do not. As of 2005, twenty-six different states have legislation that addresses parenting plans.

WHAT ARE PARENTING PLANS?

Like many other social policies for families of divorce, parenting plans come in different forms. Intended to head off common areas of postdivorce conflict and multiple bouts of litigation, parenting plans establish the roles and responsibilities of each parent in regard to their joint children before their divorce is finalized.

The Most Common Aspects of a Parenting Plan

The state of Washington defines a parenting plan as "a plan for parenting the child, including allocation of parenting functions, which plan is incorporated in any final decree or decree of modification in an action for dissolution of marriage . . . [or] legal separation" (Rev. Code Wash § 26.09.004). Parenting plans can be more comprehensive, stipulating a child-contact schedule, guidelines for decision making, and criteria for determining changes in case a parent moves [2]. The state of West Virginia provides the most detail concerning not only what a parenting plan is, but the intended goals of such plans (West Virginia Code § 48-9-102).

> (a) The primary objective of this article is to serve the child's best interests, by facilitating: (1) Stability of the child; (2) Parental planning and agreement about the child's custodial arrangements and upbringing; (3) Continuity of existing parent-child attachments; (4) Meaningful contact between a child and each parent; (5) Caretaking relationships by adults who love the child, know how to provide for the child's needs, and who place a high priority on doing so; (6) Security from exposure to physical or emotional harm; and (7) Expeditious, predictable decision-making and avoidance of prolonged uncertainty respecting arrangements for the child's care and control.
> (b) A secondary objective of article is to achieve fairness between the parents.

The process of proposing and writing a parenting plan is intended to help parents identify and resolve potential problem areas before their divorce is finalized. For example, parenting plans most commonly include a proposal for where the children will live and how often they will see each of their parents. It will also note any aberration from the child-contact schedule such as during the summer months, other school vacations, or holidays. Parenting plans often stipulate how much child support will be paid and who will be responsible for paying it. Although such components were and often are part of traditional divorce decrees, they were not mandatory, and therefore, could easily be excluded from divorce decrees.

Another common aspect of parenting plans concerns decision-making authority. Parenting plans stipulate which parent has decision-making authority over children and about which issues. For example, a parenting plan might state that both parents have equal decision-making authority over the major events in a child's life, such as medical treatment, education, and religious training. However, a parenting plan might also stipulate that parental decision-making authority is specific to particular aspects of a child's life. For example, if a mother is heavily invested in her children participating in athletic activities, she might then be responsible for this aspect of the children's upbringing. Likewise, if a father has a strong investment in his children participating in scouting activities, then the divorcing couple might decide that the father will control all decisions pertaining to this aspect of their children's lives [4]. In such instances, a parenting plan would also likely indicate which parent would be financially responsible for these various extracurricular activities.

HISTORY OF PARENTING PLANS

Despite the fact that parenting plans are relatively new, many states have legislation pertaining to their use. Ellis [5] cites that the concept of parenting plans was born within the California chapter of the Association of Family and Conciliation Courts in the early 1980s. Mental-health and family-law professionals who were concerned about unsuccessful postdivorce co-parenting stated that using a detailed joint-custody plan was helpful for families, both psychologically and legally. This concept of a plan for divorcing parents paved the way for the Washington Parenting Act of 1987. This law mandated that all divorcing parents develop a parenting plan before their divorce could be granted. Parenting plans received further attention on the West Coast when, in 1989, the California chapter of the Association of Family and Conciliation Courts unsuccessfully floated the idea to the state legislature [5]. In the same year, the American Bar Association approved the use of parenting plan-type agreements with the ratification of a "Model Joint Custody Statute" at its annual meeting [6].

In the early stages of parenting plans, there was very little national media space given to this social-policy intervention; this paucity of attention was mirrored in the scholarly literature as well. Moreover, when parenting plans were covered, the scope was narrow, as most stories only addressed Washington State's experiences with parenting plans [5, 7]. In 1991, the *UCLA Law Review* published a piece that discussed the potential failures of Washington-style parenting plans in the context of an article that focused on parental equality within divorced families and the near impossibility of forcing parents to cooperate with their ex-spouses [8]. The first mention of parenting plans in national newspapers came in 1993, when the *Wall Street Journal* reported that lawyers from twenty-six states were participating in state-level work groups to consider the costs and benefits of using parenting plans with families of divorce [9].

It was not until the late 1990s that the media and scholarly publications began to report more regularly about parenting plans. The increase in reporting mirrored activity in state legislatures, as this was the period when debates within legislatures about the concept and utility of parenting plans were initiated. In 1997, the *Cleveland Plain Dealer* reported about a bill proposing the use of parenting plans in the state of Ohio [10]. Similar reports were made by newspapers in the states of Minnesota [11] and Colorado [12]. The *Montana Lawyer* reported on the state's adoption of parenting plans in 1997 [13] and in 1998 the *Journal of Juvenile Law* included a piece that recommended the use of parenting plans in order to keep fathers involved in their children's lives [14]. Finally, in 2001 CBS's *Evening News Eye on America* reported on West

Virginia's use of "parenting agreements" that outline parental roles and responsibilities postdivorce [15].

The literature that exists today about parenting plans is primarily published in scholarly legal or family-court journals. The majority of these publications endorse the use of parenting plans or treat this type of social policy as "status quo" within the family-law system [16–19]. If the coverage on parenting plans follows the same trajectory as that on mediation, joint custody, or divorce education, the literature on parenting plans is likely to explode within the next decade. Laws proclaiming no-fault divorce and those declaring gender neutrality in custody awards were the focus of the 1970s. Policies focusing on mediation and then joint custody were highlighted throughout state legislatures in the 1980s. Divorce education programs became the trend of the 1990s, and parenting plans will likely be addressed or adopted by most states within the next ten to fifteen years, by 2020. This movement has also extended outside of the United States, with parenting plan legislation having passed in Canada [20], England [21], Singapore [22], and Australia [23].

THE UNIQUE ASPECTS OF PARENTING PLANS

Many times a parenting plan does not appear to be different than standard divorce decrees that have been used for years by the courts and that usually specify (1) who will have custody and where the child will live; (2) when the child will see his or her parents; (3) who will pay what amount for the rearing of the child; and (4) who will make decisions about medicine, education, and religion. These are the traditional "nuts and bolts" of divorce decrees that involve minor children and that result from an adversarial system. The components of traditional divorce decrees evolved over time and are not usually directed by statutory provisions. Therefore, it would be possible for parents to divorce without addressing when children will see their noncustodial parent or who will make decisions about the children. If parents don't ask for such provisions, and legal systems don't inquire about them, then they can be overlooked. Parenting plans differ from traditional divorce decrees, because state legislatures have outlined what specific details must be included in a parenting plan. Therefore, it becomes impossible for couples to divorce without addressing important decisions such as a child-contact schedule. In addition to mandating what parents must address, parenting plans have several other features that set them apart from other social-policy interventions including (1) the language that is used in parenting plans, (2) the concept of shared parenting, (3) the detail that is required, and (4) planning for the future.

Language

Parenting plans, like mediation services, are intended to offer divorcing parents an alternative to the traditional adversarial system that produces winners and losers. Statutes that mandate parenting plans also commonly mandate the adoption of new language to be used by the family-court system. Terms such as "sole custody," "noncustodial parent," "noncustodian," and "joint legal custody" are retired in favor of more neutral terms that are intended to change the "winner-loser" mentality that plagues the legal system. Instead of using the term "custody," which often translates into which parent has power and control over the child, the term "parenting time" is used. Some states have retained traditional terms, but have linked them with new meaning. For example, "custodial responsibility" is a term that applies to either parent during his or her allotted parenting time with the child. In the Barnes family, the time when Joanne is with the children would be called her period of "custodial responsibility." The same would be true of Mark when he spends time with the children. The term "legal custody," which refers to the parent who has been granted the authority to make decisions about the child's life, has been dropped in favor of "decision-making responsibility"—a role that is usually held jointly by parents [19]. These changes in language are intended to modify the tone of family-court rulings and documentation, and to reduce the level of contention that is now associated with the more traditional language.

As a side note, this trend to move away from using language that implies control is actually not limited just to states with parenting plans. For example, the state of Maine, which does not have legislation pertaining to parenting plans, uses the term "residential care" instead of "physical custody" and also uses the term "rights and responsibilities" when addressing decision-making power and financial support of children (Maine RSA Title 19-A, chapter 55 § 1653-2). Although this type of language is most often found in states that either encourage or mandate a parenting plan, the trend to use more neutral language has spread to other states as well.

Shared Parenting

Although not necessarily inherent in the use of parenting plans, this type of social-policy intervention tends to encourage parents to work together. Although a couple who has decided on sole physical and legal custody for the mother could certainly devise a parenting plan stipulating these restrictions, at some point in the history of parenting plans, this policy solution became linked with the concept of "shared parenting." For example, Tennessee begins its legislative section on parenting plans by stating the importance of both parents remaining active in their children's lives and declares that it is the public policy of the state of Tennessee to ensure that children have regular access to both of their parents.

> The general assembly recognizes the detrimental effect of divorce on many children.... The general assembly finds the need for stability and consistency in children's lives [and] ... recognizes the fundamental importance of the parent-child relationship to the welfare of the child. (Tenn. Code Ann. § 36-6-401)

Thus, parenting plans, unlike traditional divorce decrees, usually imply or actually state that it is in the best interests of children to have both parents involved in postdivorce parenting [26].

In application, if the Barnes family had divorced in a state that mandates parenting plans, it is possible that Joanne would have been more receptive to a shared-parenting arrangement. In that case, Mark would not have pursued legal action, thus reducing legal fees and minimizing stress across the board for both parents and possibly the children as well. That is the intention of parenting plans—to create an environment that fosters shared parenting and cooperation between parents.

Down to the Very Last Detail

Many parenting plans encourage or mandate parents to think beyond who will be the primary parent or who will, for example, make decisions about the educational needs of the children. In 1997, the state of Oregon (ORS § 107.102) stated that, at a minimum, parenting plans must specify what traditional divorce decrees used to state. However, for parents who want to consider other aspects of parenting, the state provided guidelines on how to do this by considering the following child-centered issues: (1) regular child-contact schedule; (2) special events with the children, such as birthdays and holidays; (3) weekends and nonschool days; (4) decision-making responsibilities; (5) sharing of information about the children; (6) relocation of the parents; (7) telephone access; (8) issues pertaining to transportation; and (9) methods for resolving future disputes.

The state of Missouri mandates that parents describe very specific details of parenting responsibilities in their parenting plans. In addition to the information that is also mandated in Oregon, residents of the state of Missouri must also include who will make decisions about education, health care, and health-care providers, extracurricular activities and the times during which they take place, child-care providers and how those providers will be selected, transportation expenses, and any extraordinary expenses (R. S. Mo. § 452.310).

Requiring parents to provide this kind of detail in parenting plans is certainly outside the norm of what most states require. The language used in this statute indicates that Missouri legislators want parents to anticipate potential impediments to co-parenting and to address them before their divorce is finalized. Although some might criticize this approach for being excessive or demeaning to the couples' parenting skills, the parenting functions listed in the Missouri legislation are those that repeatedly bring divorced parents back to court [30, 31].

Planning for the Future

In fact, asking parents to think about the future is one of the most distinct aspects of parenting plans. Garon [18] advocate for the use of a "needs assessment" by mediators or other professionals to aid parents in the development of a parenting plan. Such an assessment, they argue, should consider four developmental components: (1) self-concept of the child, (2) intellectual function on the child, (3) interpersonal functioning of the child, and (4) safety and security pertaining to the child. Moreover, they argue that this needs assessment can be used many times throughout the course of a child's development and growth, unlike in a traditional divorce decree, which treats the postdivorce life as static. In fact, the state of Indiana recommends regularly reviewing and adjusting parenting plans to meet the developmental needs of children in divorced families [32]. This kind of planning by divorced parents throughout the span of their offspring's childhood necessitates a cooperative relationship. Since approximately one in three to one in six of divorces involve couples with higher levels of conflict [30, 61, 62], this model, although thoughtful and potentially very useful, may be unrealistic for some divorced families. At the same time, such a provision may help parents to reframe their need for ongoing professional services. Kelly discusses the notion that having parents revisit mediators or even initiating relitigation does not necessarily mean a breakdown of the divorce agreement. In fact, seeking services postdivorce is often very appropriate, such as in cases of parent relocation or as children mature and their needs and desires evolve [33].

HOW DO PARENTS DRAFT A PARENTING PLAN?

Depending on the level of contention between the parents and also in what state parents live, parenting plans can be developed in a number of different ways. Most states have "forms" that parents can use when drafting a parenting plan. Textbox 4.1 provides an example of a sample

Textbox 4.1. Sample Basic Parenting Plan Form

A. CHILD INFORMATION

Name	Date of Birth	Gender (circle one)
_____	____/____/____	Male Female
_____	____/____/____	Male Female
_____	____/____/____	Male Female

B. PARENT-CHILD CONTACT SCHEDULE
Each parent should use a four-week calendar to indicate when the child/ren will reside with him/her. Make sure to indicate start and end times. If the schedule cannot be displayed on a four-week calendar, write the schedule below.

MOTHER

Week	Sun	Mon	Tue	Wed	Thur	Fri	Sat
1							
2							
3							
4							

FATHER

Week	Sun	Mon	Tue	Wed	Thur	Fri	Sat
1							
2							
3							
4							

Other schedule: _____
_____
_____

How close together do parents plan to live? _____ miles

Child/ren's primary residence (optional) _____

Parent-child communication:
During "off-parenting" times, parents may communicate with their children at all reasonable times:
- ☐ Via telephone
- ☐ Via written communication
- ☐ Via email or other electronic means

C. DECISION-MAKING RESPONSIBILITIES
How will decision-making be shared between the parents? Will a particular parent be responsible for any one thing (such as sports, music lessons, social activities, religious training, etc.)? If so, explain below.
- ☐ Mother will make all decisions
- ☐ Father will make all decisions
- ☐ Parents will make decisions together

Exceptions: _____
_____

D. TRANSPORTATION
How will transportation be shared between the parents?
- ☐ Mother will provide all
- ☐ Father will provide all
- ☐ Parent who currently has child will provide

E. PARENT COMMUNICATION
How will parents communicate with each other? How often will parents communicate? Indicate this plan below.

Parents will communicate about children by
- ☐ Face-to-face discussion
- ☐ Telephone
- ☐ Written letters that are mailed
- ☐ Email

Will parents meet regularly to discuss children?
- ☐ Yes
  - How often? _____
  - Where? _____
- ☐ No

F. OTHER PARENTING RESPONSIBILITIES AND RIGHTS

Responsibility/Right	Mother	Father	Both Parents
Communicating with teachers/schools	☐	☐	☐
Communicating with child care providers (if used)	☐	☐	☐
Scheduling/Taking children to medical appointments	☐	☐	☐
Contact with parents of child's peers (as is age appropriate)	☐	☐	☐
Access to children's school, medical, and legal records	☐	☐	☐

G. ALTERNATIVE CARE
If a parent plans to be away during his/her regularly scheduled parenting time, that parent will notify the other parent about this change _____ 48 hours in advance of the change.

If a parent is away during his/her "parenting time" the child will:
☐ Automatically stay with the other parent
☐ The parent making the change will arrange for an alternative caregiver

H. CHANGES TO PARENTING PLAN
As children grow older, their needs and desires change. Parenting plans often need to be revised to reflect children's growth. How often will parents meet to discuss the parenting plan?
☐ Every six (6) months
☐ At the end of every summer
☐ At the end of every other summer
☐ Other _____

I. PARENTAL RELOCATION
Do both parents make a commitment to reside near one another?
☐ Yes → if so, how close? _____ miles
☐ No

If a parent plans to move more than _____ miles away, he/she will notify the other parent 60 days before doing so.

Cases of parental relocation often require a modification of a parenting plan. If one of the parents proposes to move more than _____ miles away, both parents agree to modify the parenting plan.

H. DISAGREEMENT
If there is a disagreement about a parenting issue, how will this matter be handled?
☐ Discuss the matter between us
☐ Work with a family mediator
☐ Work with a mental health practitioner
☐ Work with our attorneys
☐ Other _____
If the parties choose to see a mediator or a mental health practitioner, list several local providers that both parents agree to see: _____

---

form that is similar to those being used in many states. This form can be used by parents or professionals assisting parents with their divorce. It instructs them to detail the residential schedule, plans for parental communication, the rights and responsibilities of each parent, plans for relocation, and how to resolve a dispute. Textbox 4.2 displays a sample form that outlines how children and parents will spend their holiday and vacation time together. Finally, some states provide suggestions for different child-contact schedules, which are sometimes based on the age of the child. Figure 4.1 provides six examples of possible parent-child contact schedules. Older children are usually more able to endure schedules that are based on weekly or biweekly rotations. This type of information can be used by *pro se* litigants (parents who are presenting

Textbox 4.2. Sample Basic Parenting Plan Form: Holiday, Vacation, and Nonschool Time Schedule

There are often changes to the child-parent contact schedule on holidays, vacations, and non-school days. Indicate your family schedule for such days below. One simple way to explain your family schedule is to indicate if children will be with (1) the mother or father, (2) if parents will rotate years (one parent taking odd-numbered years, another parent taking even-numbered years), or (3) if there will be no change to the schedule. It is advised that parenting times on holidays begin the night before at a specific time (5pm or 6pm) and last for 24 hours.

Occasion	With Mother Every Year	With Father Every Year	Rotate Odd Year/Even Year	No Change in Regular Schedule
VACATIONS				
Winter vacation	☐	☐	Odd Year Parent: _____ Even Year Parent: _____	☐
Summer vacation	☐	☐	Odd Year Parent: _____ Even Year Parent: _____	☐
Summer vacation	☐	☐	Odd Year Parent: _____ Even Year Parent: _____	☐
December vacation	☐	☐	Odd Year Parent: _____ Even Year Parent: _____	☐
HOLIDAYS				
M.L. King, Jr. Day	☐	☐	Odd Year Parent: _____ Even Year Parent: _____	☐
Presidents' Day	☐	☐	Odd Year Parent: _____ Even Year Parent: _____	☐
Easter	☐	☐	Odd Year Parent: _____ Even Year Parent: _____	☐
Mother's Day	☐	☐	Odd Year Parent: _____ Even Year Parent: _____	☐
Father's Day	☐	☐	Odd Year Parent: _____ Even Year Parent: _____	☐
Fourth of July	☐	☐	Odd Year Parent: _____ Even Year Parent: _____	☐
Labor Day	☐	☐	Odd Year Parent: _____ Even Year Parent: _____	☐
Columbus Day	☐	☐	Odd Year Parent: _____ Even Year Parent: _____	☐
Halloween	☐	☐	Odd Year Parent: _____ Even Year Parent: _____	☐
Veteran's Day	☐	☐	Odd Year Parent: _____ Even Year Parent: _____	☐
Thanksgiving	☐	☐	Odd Year Parent: _____ Even Year Parent: _____	☐
Thanksgiving Friday	☐	☐	Odd Year Parent: _____ Even Year Parent: _____	☐
Christmas Eve	☐	☐	Odd Year Parent: _____ Even Year Parent: _____	☐
Christmas Day	☐	☐	Odd Year Parent: _____ Even Year Parent: _____	☐
Other holiday	☐	☐	Odd Year Parent: _____ Even Year Parent: _____	☐
MISCELLANEOUS				
Child (1) birthday	☐	☐	Odd Year Parent: _____ Even Year Parent: _____	☐
First day of school	☐	☐	Odd Year Parent: _____ Even Year Parent: _____	☐
School cancellations	☐	☐	Odd Year Parent: _____ Even Year Parent: _____	☐
Teacher In-service days	☐	☐	Odd Year Parent: _____ Even Year Parent: _____	☐
Other	☐	☐	Odd Year Parent: _____ Even Year Parent: _____	☐

themselves in court), attorneys with their clients, or mediators and mental-health professionals who are working with disputing parents. Because more than half of divorce cases nationwide involve at least one *pro se* litigant [34], the importance of these guides and instructions cannot be overstated. For parents who have legal representation, their at-

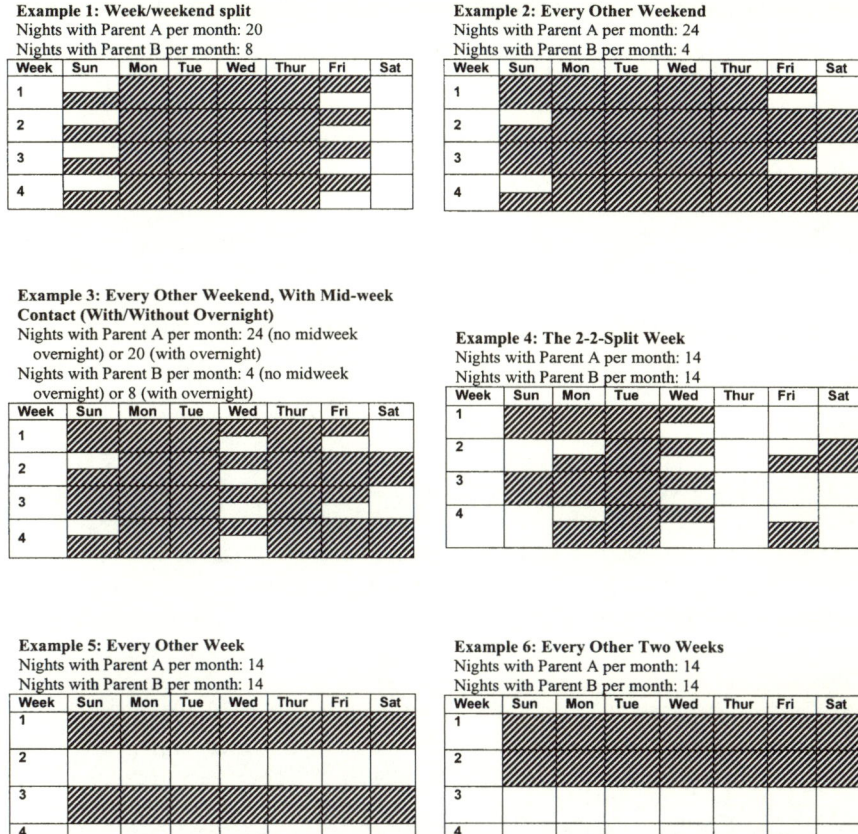

Figure 4.1.   Sample Parenting Plan Child-contract Schedules

torneys help them to draft a suitable parenting plan, using guidelines from their local court. Many parents also develop parenting plans as part of their voluntary or mandated mediation sessions [35]. To date there are no explicit provisions for involving children in the drafting of a parenting plan.

WHAT IF PARENTS DON'T COMPLY?

Just because parents develop and agree to a parenting plan does not mean that they will comply with the agreement. For example, parents may not consult with one another when making decisions about the children, one parent may move the children without consulting the other parent, or parents may fail to follow the child-contact schedule. The legislatures in most states recognize the potential for such problems and ask that parents develop a plan to address postdivorce disputes. States have adopted a variety of procedures for dealing with this phenomenon. Most often, such as in the state of Montana (Mont. Code Anno. § 40-4-234), states simply recommend that parents must designate a method by which they will resolve disputes but do not provide any other details. In the state of West Virginia, parents are fined for a lack of compliance (W. Va. Code § 48-9-501); in Tennessee parents must pay the legal fees of the compliant parent (Tenn. Code Ann. § 36-6-404). Finally, in the state of Washington, parents who violate the residential provisions of the parenting plan can be charged with contempt of court and may be subject to arrest (Rev. Code Wash § 26.09.184).

Nonetheless, it is difficult to say if these "protective" provisions will actually change parental behavior and engender a spirit of cooperation. Noncompliance with court orders and divorce decrees is not especially well documented in the literature, but there is evidence to suggest that both mothers and fathers routinely fail to comply with agreements and that often cases of noncompliance come back to court [39]. The U.S. Census Bureau reported that in 2001 only 74 percent of custodial mothers and 67 percent of custodial fathers reported full or partial compliance with child-support orders [40]. Both mothers and fathers report disruptions in the child-contact schedule. For example, sometimes custodial parents deny noncustodial parents access to their children if those parents are not in compliance with child-support orders [41]. In a review of the literature, Bender and Brannon [42] found that 20–40 percent of custodial mothers reported that they had denied father-child contact out of spite. Another study found that fathers reported that 25–30 percent of mothers tried to interfere with access to their children [43]. This same study found that approximately 85 percent of mothers reported that fathers failed to adhere to the "pick-up" and "drop-off" child-contact schedule. Parental relocation has also become a hotly debated topic among family-law professionals [44]. In a recent study Braver, Ellman, and Fabricius reported that in a study of college-age students from divorced families, 60 percent of study participants had at least one parent move more than an hour away from the original family location [45]. As more parents adopt shared-parenting agreements, the issue of relocation will become even more central to discussion of postdivorce life.

Several states have begun to address the issue of noncompliance with parenting plans through the use of "parenting coordinators." As explained in a recent *Family Court Review* article, "parenting coordination is a process whereby an impartial third person . . . helps . . . parties to implement their parenting plan by facilitating the resolution of disputes" [17, p. 246]. This is a role that is performed by legal or mental-health professionals and combines the tasks of assessment, case management, mediation, and arbitration roles [46]. Parenting coordinators are almost exclusively used in cases involving high conflict and numerous legal battles. Although only three states (Idaho, Oklahoma, and Oregon) legislate the use of parenting coordinators, many other states are beginning to rely on this area of specialization for assistance with their most troubled cases. The use of parenting coordination has not yet been well evaluated, but anecdotal evidence and one unpublished study suggest that parenting coordinators may greatly reduce the rate of relitigation among high-conflict divorced parents [47].

PARENTING PLANS AND FAMILIES OF VIOLENCE

The close link between parenting plans and the concept of shared parenting has led some states to specify that in cases of partner violence victims will not be forced to enter into a parenting plan with an abuser, as in the state of West Virginia (W. Va. Code § 48-9-201), or that parents who have been substantiated for child maltreatment will have their residential time with the child limited, as in the state of Tennessee (Tenn. Code Ann. § 36-6-404). The theory behind this is similar to that which was discussed in chapter 2 on mediation. It is believed to be difficult, if not risky, for victims of partner violence to have to co-parent and to regularly negotiate about the children with their abusers. Moreover, states want to discourage children from being actively raised and influenced by parents who have proved to be abusive or neglectful.

PARENTING PLANS IN PUBLIC POLICY TODAY

Twenty-six states in the nation have some type of statute pertaining to parenting plans. Twelve states mandate the use of parenting plans for all families who are divorcing. Four states mandate parenting plans in cases of disputes or contested custody, and three states mandate it only in the case of joint or shared custody. For those states that do not mandate the use of parenting plans, their legislation may recommend the use of plans, may define what is considered to be a parenting plan in that particular state, or may simply make reference to parenting plans when discussing the roles and responsibilities of parents after divorce. Table 4.1 illustrates which states have laws pertaining to parenting plans.

Table 4.1. Parenting Plans in the United States (n = 25)

State	Statute	Code	Compulsory
Alabama	No		
Alaska	No		
Arizona	Yes	A.R.S. § 25-403	Yes—J.C.† only
Arkansas	No		
California	Yes	Cal. Fam. Code § 3040	Yes
Colorado	Yes	C.R.S. § 14-10-124	Yes
Connecticut	Yes	Conn. Super. Ct. 25-30*	Yes—Disputes only
Delaware	No		
Florida	No		
Georgia	No		
Hawaii	No		
Idaho	Yes	Idaho Code § 32-1402	No
Illinois	Yes	§ 750 ILCD 5/602.1	Yes—J.C. only
Indiana	No		
Iowa	No		
Kansas	Yes	K.S.A. § 60-1623, § 60-1625	No
Kentucky	No		
Louisiana	Yes	La. R.S. § 91332	No
Maine	No		
Maryland	No		
Massachusetts	No		
Michigan	No		
Minnesota	Yes	Minn. Stat. § 518.1705	Yes
Mississippi	No		
Missouri	Yes	§ 452.375 R.S.Mo.	Yes
Montana	Yes	Mont. Code Anno. § 40-234	Yes
Nebraska	Yes	R.R.S.Neb.§ 43-2903-§ 43-2919	No
Nevada	No		
New Hampshire	Yes	N.H. Rev. Stat. Ann. § 461-A:4	
New Jersey	No		
New Mexico	Yes	N.M. Stat. Ann. § 40-4-9.1	Yes—J.C. only
New York	No		
North Carolina	Yes	12.04*	Yes—Disputes only
North Dakota	No		
Ohio	Yes	O.R.C. Ann. § 3109.04	No
Oklahoma	No		
Oregon	Yes	O.R.S. § 107.102	Yes
Pennsylvania	Yes*		Yes
Rhode Island	No		
South Carolina	No		
South Dakota	Yes	S.D. § 25-7-6.14	Yes
Tennessee	Yes	Tenn. Code Ann. § 36-6-404	Yes
Texas	No		
Utah	Yes	Utah Code Ann. § 30-3-10.9	Yes—Disputes only
Vermont	Yes	Vt. A.O. 31**	Yes
Virginia	No		

Washington	Yes	Rev. Code Wash. § 26.09.181	Yes
Washington, DC	Yes	D.C. §16-914	No
West Virginia	Yes	W. Va. §18-9-205	Yes
Wisconsin	Yes	Wis. Stat. §767.24	Yes—Disputes only
Wyoming	No		

†Where J.C. = "joint custody"; *Court Rule; **Administrative Order

EFFECTIVENESS OF PARENTING PLANS

Mediation services and divorce education programs have been evaluated by many different scholars throughout the country. The literature on parenting plans, however, suffers from a lack of empirical evaluations, especially with regard to the well-being of children. Along with laws that declare a presumption for joint custody, parenting plans are one of the least studied interventions for families of divorce. Although there have been some studies that have examined the postdivorce functioning of families who happen to have a parenting plan [50], there have been very few studies that have examined the effectiveness of parenting plans in improving postdivorce life for children and their parents. Moreover, almost all of the research that has evaluated parenting plans has focused on the effectiveness of two particular pieces of legislation: one from the state of Washington and another from the state of Tennessee.

Washington State: Parenting Act

In 1987, the state of Washington enacted the Parenting Act, which was intended to reduce parental conflict by focusing on parenting functions and responsibility, as opposed to custody. In fact, the act outlaws the use of the term "custody" and instead requires parents to write into their parenting plan arrangements for a residential schedule for their children. The law requires that parents provide provisions for how to resolve future disputes, allocation of decision-making authority, and a residential schedule for the children (Rev. Code Wash § 26.09.004).

The Ellis Study

The first review of this law was conducted by Ellis [5] one year after the implementation of the law. The primary purpose of the study was to determine how and if the law was being implemented. Ellis and her students reviewed the records of more than three hundred divorce cases from 1988 (one year after the law was passed) and conducted informal interviews with thirty attorneys. They found that 94 percent of divorce decrees followed the mandates of the parenting plan legislation by specifying a child-contact schedule for both parents, as opposed to using vague language that had been more traditionally used, such as "reasonable visitation" or "visitation with the noncustodial parent will be as the child wishes." This indicates a very high rate of court compliance and implementation for a law that was so new and revolutionary.

One of the most controversial aspects of Washington's Parenting Act was the encouragement of parents to engage in some form of shared parenting. Ellis found significant changes in the allocation of decision-making responsibilities—on paper. Before the act was passed, 27 percent of divorce decrees identified decision making to be jointly held between both parents; after the act this percent rose to 69 percent. Ellis also found a substantial change in the allocation of joint residential custody. Before the law was passed, only 3 percent of divorcing couples chose joint living arrangements for the children; after the law was implemented, shared residential arrangements increased to 20 percent. This study did not investigate how plans on paper translated into reality.

The Dunne et al. Study

Dunne, Hudgins, and Babcock [51] compared parents who divorced in 1987 under the old law with parents who divorced under the new Parenting Act in 1988. They measured level of parental cooperation, parental involvement, and postdivorce adjustment among children and parents. Data were collected via a mail survey at two different time periods—one at the time of divorce (n = 170) and another, two years postdivorce (n = 106). The response rate for the first time period was roughly 25 percent; therefore the results of this study must be interpreted with caution.

The results of this study indicated that the incidence of joint residential custody of children under the new law actually fell, with 87 percent of mothers having sole residential custody under the new law, compared with 71 percent under the old law. These findings are self-reported by the parents, as opposed to examining court records. It is possible that under the old law more fathers thought that they had a shared custodial arrangement and under the new law custodial status rose to a new level of visibility for couples who were divorcing. In other words, since other research has found that divorced fathers are sometimes uncertain of their custodial status [52], fathers who divorced under the old law may have been more uncertain than fathers who divorced under the new law. At the second time period of data collection, Dunne and colleagues found some indication that fathers who divorced under the new law were more likely to have their children living with them, regardless of the official custodial arrangement.

The researchers found that the parenting plan law did not make any difference in terms of how regularly child-support payments were made or in terms of children's postdivorce adjustment. The law did, however, make a difference in terms of parents' level of functioning. Contrary to the researchers hypotheses, parents who divorced under the new parenting-plan law were more likely to have internalizing problems (such as depression, social withdrawal, and anxiety) and externalizing ones (such as irritability, work problems, and parenting problems) than parents who divorced under the old law. These findings were consistent for both time periods of the study. The authors speculate that the results could be due to the fact that the parents divorcing under the new law were subjected to confusion and initial problems with the law, such as lowered child-support awards for families with shared residential living arrangements and initial, temporary parenting plans before divorces were finalized. It is possible that this resulted in more litigation for parents who divorced under the new divorce legislation than for parents who divorced under the old statute.

In truth, the low participant response rate, leaves one to question the validity of this study. It is possible that the conclusions are affected by response bias and that participants with more negative experiences were more likely to respond. At the same time, a previous study, also with a small sample size, found that parents with self-determined agreements reported more conflict than parents who reported minimal participation in the drafting of their divorce decree [53].

The Lye Report

The most recent report on the outcomes of Washington State's parenting-plan legislation was requested by the Washington State Supreme Court Gender and Justice Commission and the Domestic Relations Commission. The report focuses on a review of case records and consumer satisfaction; it does not assess child or family well-being. More specifically, Lye [54] reviewed 403 divorce records that ended in approved parenting plans between 1997 and 1998. She also conducted ten focus groups with parents who had parenting plans that had been approved by the court and who responded to an invitation to participate in the study; the response rate was 11 percent. Finally, Lye interviewed a nonrepresentative purposive and snowball sample of forty-seven Washington State providers who work with divorcing families.

Forty-three percent of the parenting plans that were reviewed were "first-time" plans, another 43 percent represented parenting plans that had undergone their first modification, and 14 percent were on their second or higher modification. Her results of the cases that were reviewed are somewhat different than what Ellis found in 1988. Lye reported that less than 7 percent of the cases that she reviewed had a parenting schedule of

50-50 time with the children. Ellis recorded "joint arrangements," which is substantially different than a schedule that stipulates 50-50 time allotments between the parents. Therefore, it may be unwise to compare these two findings, because it is unclear how many arrangements were considered to be "joint." Notably, Lye found that despite the law, 20 percent of parenting plans did not specify a residential schedule, leaving parents to work out child-contact schedules after their divorce. In accordance with Ellis's prior work, Lye did find that 73 percent of couples arranged for joint decision-making authority. In her focus groups with parents, however, she found that although most parents consented to shared decision making, this agreement was rarely followed in practice. Generally, the primary residential parent makes the decisions about the children's lives.

The providers who work with families of divorce echoed this latter opinion. In the interviews they, too, expressed the opinion that joint decision making is not very successful. The providers stated that joint decision making provides too many opportunities for parents to engage in needless conflict and that it is impractical. Others stated that parents and providers, alike, do not understand the intentions of the law with regard to shared decision-making responsibilities. Although some providers did support the use of joint decision-making responsibilities, these providers were in the minority. Overall, Lye recommends keeping mandates for parenting plans on the books but provides recommendations for improving the Washington law, providing parents with more information and creative residential schedules, encouraging parents to develop more detailed plans, and strengthening provisions for resolving postdivorce conflict such as in cases of parental relocation.

Tennessee: Parenting Plan Law

In 1997, two Tennessee state legislators acting on behalf of divorced, noncustodial fathers, proposed legislation that they hoped would eliminate perceived, gender-based injustices within the family-court system [55]. This legislation, which, among other things, focused on parenting plans, was enacted and permitted the implementation of six pilot programs, initiating the use of parenting plans within the Tennessee family court [56]. This program was evaluated in 1999 with favorable outcomes. The positive reviews of the pilot program resulted in a full implementation of parenting plans statewide (Tenn. Code Ann. § 36-6-401) in the year 2000 [57, 58]. Like the Parenting Act in the state of Washington, Tennessee's Parenting Plan Law does not use the term "custody." Unlike the state of Washington, however, Tennessee legislators provided detailed guidelines for parents who are developing parenting plans, and stated, in a number of different ways, that the welfare of the child in all families of divorce is paramount. More specifically, the law states that parents must provide for the children's changing needs as they mature; establish the responsibilities of each parent that are consistent with the children's needs; minimize children's exposure to parental conflict; include provisions for how to resolve future disputes; allocate decision-making responsibilities with regard to education, health care, extracurricular activities, and religious training; and develop a residential schedule for the children that encourages each parent to maintain a loving, stable, and nurturing relationship with the child.

Evaluation of the Pilot Programs

The evaluation of the parenting-plan pilot program focused on data that were collected from court records and family-law attorneys who had direct experience working with the pilot program [59]. Using a mail survey, the evaluators obtained a response rate of 28 percent, which gave them a sample size of 177 participants. Fifty-eight percent of the attorneys reported being "very" or "somewhat satisfied" with the parenting-plan pilot study, and close to 80 percent reported that the use of parenting plans were either "very" or "somewhat effective." The attorneys also reported a minor savings in cost for the families, with a reduction in billable hours for clients divorcing under the pilot program—moving from an average of eleven hours to ten and one-half hours.

A review of court records demonstrated that the rate of relitigation in the first year after divorce was only 9 percent, down from 18 percent in previous years—a 50 percent decline in the rate of postdecree activity. There was also a similar reduction in the number of orders filed by the court and evidence to support the notion that it led to a decline in the rate of contested cases. Although cases with a parenting plan remained open in the court an average of three weeks longer, the Administrative Office of the Courts interpreted this finding as positive. They found that cases that are open for a longer period of time are less likely to relitigate than cases that are open a shorter period of time.

This report provides favorable reviews of the parenting-plan pilot study; however, the report has a low response rate and focuses on the legal aspects of divorce only. Moreover, it does not assess any outcomes for children or parents. The review of the full law that follows does provide some data collected from parents.

Evaluation of the Full Law

In February 2004 the Administrative Office of the Courts [35] presented an evaluation of the full parenting-plan legislation to several legislative committees. This evaluation was based on survey results and interviews with stakeholders including parents, attorneys, mediators, clerks of the court, and judges, and a review of court records for the years 2001 through 2003. In general, this report offered significant praise for the parenting-plan legislation, stating that "[T]he legislative goal to foster the parent-child relationship when parents divorce is being met by the parenting plan" (p. 2) and the results of the study "do not indicate a need for legislative changes" (p. 3). These are broad and sweeping statements from a study with questionable generalizability.

An overwhelming percentage of parents who responded to the survey believed that the parenting law permitted them to "adequately participate" in their children's lives and that the procedures associated with the plan were adequately clear. A participant response rate of only 15 percent, however, questions the representativeness of these findings.

Response rates among the professionals who were surveyed included 26 percent for mediators, 23 percent for attorneys, 40 percent for court clerks, and 38 percent for judges responding to the questionnaires. Although higher than the response rates for parents, they are still low, and one must question their generalizability. Mediators reported that parents who had attended a parent education seminar (also mandated by the Parenting Plan Law) and learned about the theory and process behind this legislation were more likely to successfully develop a parenting plan together. In general, the vast majority of attorneys were pleased with the procedural steps for completing a parenting plan (i.e., parenting-plan forms) and two-thirds of those responding to the evaluation believed that the parenting-plan law improved divorce procedures within the state of Tennessee.

Although there were no statistics reported about judges' experiences with and opinions of the new parenting law, the evaluators indicated that judges were satisfied with the legislation. The clerks of the court (who are often the first people that divorcing parents encounter in the court system) reported that parents were less confused about the legal process of divorce and more informed about their roles, responsibilities, and options concerning the care of their children. The evaluators also cite the fact that for the study period, only 17 percent of parents initiated legal action to address postdivorce concerns. Although the evaluators do not cite how this statistic is different from the rate of relitigation before the parenting-plan law, other rates of relitigation across the country have been estimated to be between 41 percent [39] and 59 percent [60] for divorced couples with children.

Summary

Research and evaluation regarding parenting plans is in its infancy. The studies that exist about parenting plans have primarily focused on the technical aspects of the law or have been consumer-satisfaction-type reports, with data collected from multiple stakeholders. The research has demonstrated near full implementation and general satisfaction with the use of parenting plans by professionals and parents. The studies reported here, however, have also been plagued with low response rates, and therefore it is difficult to draw any concrete conclusions about their findings. Further problems exist as well. Of the three studies conducted on Washington's Parenting Act, each contradicts each other's findings with regard to the implementation of the law, and there is no attempt to address these contradictions. Moreover, research from the Tennessee Administrative Office of the Courts airs a tone of advocacy as the office seems ready to proclaim the law a success, with research participant response rates ranging from 15–40 percent.

Finally, and most important, parenting plans were intended to improve the lives of children, and yet this measure of "success" is missing from most studies thus far. The Lye report from the state of Washington indicates that parenting plans do not make a difference in families' lives—that parenting plans are treated as traditional divorce decrees, with a new and fancier name. In short, at this point, it is impossible to determine if the good intentions of policy makers are bearing useful fruit for children and families. Examining the implementation of legislation is not without value; however, the research and legal communities must not forget the intended beneficiaries of parenting-plan legislation. How, and if, this legislation affects children should be brought to and kept at the research and policy tables.

CONCLUSION

Parenting plans are the most comprehensive social-policy intervention that has been implemented for families of divorce. Like mediation, parenting plans are intended to be specific to each family and do not, like some other policy solutions (i.e., joint custody or divorce education), make assumptions about what is best for all families that enter the family-court system. For parenting plans that are mandated, parents are required to think through and address the needs and desires of their children now and as they are anticipated to be in the future. Parenting plans without mandates and guidelines are not likely to function any better than traditional divorce decrees, because only those parents with the most cooperative relationships will consider using them. Mandating that all nonviolent divorcing parents develop comprehensive and detailed parenting plans is the only way to ensure that all parents, especially those at highest risk for dysfunction, will develop a plan for working cooperatively with one another.

Decision makers should maintain some caution, however, because even with a mandate, there is no guarantee that parents will follow the plans that they have established. There is little evidence that the public responds to pro-social policies without a "carrot or stick" approach of some type [52], and we have no reason to believe that divorced parents are any different. Asking parents to obey a parenting plan without substantial and enforceable rewards or consequences may result in few behavioral changes, especially with relitigation rates as high as 41 percent in some instances [39]. Many states pledge to implement consequences against parents for noncompliance. Future research will have to determine whether, and how often, such provisions are used.

To date, parenting plans suffer from a lack of empirical assessment. Consumer-satisfaction-type evaluations, with low response rates, indicate that parenting plan laws are fairly well implemented and that most professionals, providers, and parents endorse the concept behind cooperative parenting and thorough planning. There is very little research that targets parents and children. There is also reason to believe that in reality, despite the rise of cooperative parenting plans on paper, parenting plans do not result in increased or better-quality co-parenting.

Clearly, the jury is still out on the effectiveness of parenting plans. With half of the country addressing parenting plans through legislation, this social-policy solution has become a popular way for states to try to remedy the ills associated with divorce; however, to date, there is no evidence that parenting plans result in more cooperative and healthy behaviors between divorced parents. There is also no evidence that parenting plans result in increased child well-being, primarily because this indicator has not been systematically measured by researchers. Only a drastic increase in research and evaluation will inform us about the true usefulness and actual impact on children of this forward-thinking, but possibly unrealistically optimistic, policy option. The greatest contribution of this legislation may be as part of a larger network of policy solutions that serve as a vehicle for creating pro-social attitudes about co-parenting in divorced families.

REFERENCES

1. Kramer, L., and A. Kowal. Long-term follow-up of a court-based intervention for divorcing parents. *Family and Conciliation Courts Review*, 1998, 36(4): pp. 452–65.

2. Minnesota Legislature: *A bill for an act relating to marriage dissolution*, HR1323. 1997.

3. Fuhrmann, G. S., J. McGill, and M. E. O'Connell. Parent education's second generation: Integrating violence sensitivity. *Family and Conciliation Courts Review*, 1999, 37(1): pp. 24–35.

4. Crosby, H. The irretrievable breakdown of the child: Minnesota's move toward parenting plans. *Hamline Journal of Public Law and Policy*, 2000, 21(Spring): p. 489.

5. Ellis, J. W. Plans, protections and professional intervention: Innovations in divorce custody reform and the role of legal professionals. *University of Michigan Journal of Law Reform*, 1990, 24(Fall): p. 65.

6. ABA approves resolutions on joint custody, taxation. *Family Law Reporter*, 1989, 15(August 22): pp. 1494–96.

7. Ellis, J. W. The Washington state parenting act in the courts: Reconciling discretion and justice in parenting plan disputes. *Washington Law Review*, 1994, 69(July): p. 679.

8. Czapanskiy, K. Volunteers and draftees: The struggle for parental equality. *UCLA Law Review*, 1991, 38(August): p. 1415.

9. Woo, J. Divorce lawyers study parenting plans. *Wall Street Journal*, November 15, 1993, p. 5B.

10. Brown, T. C. Bill would let divorced couples set parent rules. *Cleveland Plain Dealer* May 14, 1997, p. 1A.

11. Cummins, H. J. Parenting plans aim to make divorce easier on kids. *Minneapolis Star Tribune*, January 21, 1998, p. 3B.

12. Knight, A. Making custody a bad word. *Denver Post*, March 22, 1998, p. H-03.

13. Scott, P. M. Developments in the law: A successful effort to revamp Montana Domestic Relations Law. *Montana Lawyer*, 1997, 22(July/August): p. 17.

14. Pons-Bunney, J. Non-custodial fathers' rights: State's lack of incentives for the father to remain in the child's life. *Journal of Juvenile Law*, 1998, 19: p. 212.

15. Stewart, J. Easing divorce's impact on kids. *CBS Evening News*, January 22, 2001.

16. Schleuderer, C., and V. Campagna. Substance abuse and child custody evaluations: Assessing substance abuse questions in child custody evaluations. *Family Court Review*, 2004, 42(April): p. 375.

17. Coates, C. A., et al. Parenting coordination for high-conflict families. *Family Court Review*, 2004, 42(April): pp. 246–60.

18. Garon, R. J. From infants to adolescents: A developmental approach to parenting plans. *Family and Conciliation Courts Review*, 2000, 38(April): p. 168.

19. Catania, F. J. Learning from the process of decision: The parenting plan. *Brigham Young University Law Review*, 2001, issue 3 p. 857.

20. Freeman, R. Parenting after divorce: Using research to inform decision-making about children. *Canadian Journal of Family Law*, 1998, 15: p. 79.

21. Freely, M. Children first. *Guardian* (London), 2002, March 27, G2, p. 14.

22. Parenting plan needed before divorce. *Straits Times* (Singapore), May 2, 1997, p. 37.

23. Ferguson, S. Parenting plan for child care. *Herald Sun* (Australia), May 22, 1995.

24. Maine Title 19-A Domestic Relations, 1995.

25. Washington Permanent Parenting Plan, in Title 26: Domestic Relations.

26. Covell, K. Promoting parenting plans: A new role for the psychologist as expert in custody disputes. *Expert Evidence*, 1999, 7: pp. 113–26.

27. Oregon Parent Plans, in Title 11, Domestic Relations.

28. Frazee, E. Sensitizing parent education programs to domestic violence concerns: The perspective of the New York State Parent Education Advisory Board. *Family Court Review*, 2005, 43(1): pp. 124–35.

29. Maine Domestic Relations.

30. Maccoby, E. E., and R. H. Mnookin. *Dividing the child: Social and legal dilemmas of custody*. 1992, Cambridge, MA: Harvard University Press.

31. Ahrons, C. R. The continuing coparental relationship between divorced spouses. *American Journal of Orthopsychiatry*, 1981, 51(3): pp. 415–28.

32. Indiana parenting time guidelines. 2001.

33. Kelly, J. B. Family mediation research: Is there empirical support for the field? *Conflict Resolution Quarterly*, 2004, 22(1-2): pp. 3–35.

34. Wilgoren, J. Divorce court is now in lawyer-free session. *New York Times*, February 9, 2002, p. A12.

35. Tennessee Administrative Office of the Courts. *Parenting plan process evaluation*. Presented to House Children and Family Affairs Committee; Senate General Welfare, Health and Human Resources Committee; House Health and Human Resources Committee; House Judiciary Committee; Senate Judiciary Committee. 2004, Nashville, TN.

36. Missouri Parenting Plans, in Title 30, Domestic Relations.

37. Tennessee Parenting Plans—Findings, in Title 36, Domestic Relations, Chapter 6: Child Custody and Visitation.

38. Montana Final Parenting Plan Criteria, in Title 40, Family Law.

39. Koel, A., et al. Patterns of relitigation in the postdivorce family. *Journal of Marriage and Family*, 1994, 56: pp. 256–77.

40. U.S. Bureau of the Census. *Custodial mothers and fathers and their child support: 2001*. 2003, Washington, DC.

41. Fields, L. F., B. W. Mussetter, and G. T. Powers. Children denied two parents: An analysis of access denial. *Journal of Divorce and Remarriage*, 1997, 28(1/2): pp. 49–62.

42. Bender, W. N., and L. Brannon. Victimization of non-custodial parents, grandparents, and children as a function of sole custody: Views of the advocacy groups and research support. *Journal of Divorce and Remarriage*, 1994, 21(3/4): pp. 81–114.

43. Wolchik, S. A., A. M. Fenaughty, and S. L. Braver. Residential and nonresidential parents' perspectives on visitation problems. *Family Relations: Journal of Applied Family and Child Studies*, 1996, 45(2): pp. 230–37.

44. Hymowitz, P. Relocation: Parents' needs, children's interests. In *A handbook of divorce and custody: Forensic, developmental, and clinical perspectives*, ed. L. Gunsberg and P. Hymowitz, pp. 301–14. 2005, Hillsdale, NJ: Analytic Press, Inc.

45. Braver, S. H., I. M. Ellman, and W. V. Fabricius. Relocation of children after divorce and children's best interests: New evidence and legal considerations. *Journal of Family Psychology*, 2003, 17(2): pp. 206–19.

46. Bailey, D. S. A niche that puts children first. APA Online: Monitor on Psychology. 2005, American Psychological Association. http://www.apa.org/monitor/jan05/niche.html (February 21, 2005).

47. Coates, C. A., et al. Parenting coordination: Implementation issues. *Family Court Review*, 2003, 41(4): p. 533.

48. Washington Court Orders—Required Language, in Title 26: Domestic Relations.

49. Kansas Decree, authorized orders, in Chapter 60, Procedure, Civil, Article 16. Divorce and Maintenance.

50. Pruett, M. K., R. Ebling, and G. Insabella. Parenting plans and visitation: Critical aspects of parenting plans for young children interjecting data into the debate about overnights. *Family Court Review*, 2004, 42(January): p. 39.

51. Dunne, J. E., E. W. Hudgins, and J. Babcock. Can changing the divorce law affect postdivorce adjustment? *Journal of Divorce and Remarriage*, 2000, 33(3/4): pp. 35–54.

52. Douglas, E. M. The influence of public policies on human behavior: Is there an effect of a New Hampshire law stating a presumption for joint legal custody on father involvement in divorced families? Public Policy Program, 2002, Boston: University of Massachusetts, p. 354.

53. D'Errico, M. G., and A. Elwork. Are self-determined divorce and child custody agreements really better? *Family and Conciliation Courts Review*, 1991, 29(2): pp. 104–13.

54. Lye, D. B. Washington State parenting plan study. 1999, Olympia: Washington State Supreme Court.

55. Humphrey, T. Legislators seek rewrite of child custody laws. *Knoxville News-Sentinel*, January 31, 1997, p. A4.

56. de la Cruz, B. M. Parenting plan to ease divorces. *Nashville Tennessean*, May 16, 1999, p. 1B.

57. Humphrey, T. Panel OKs plan to ease child-custody battles. *Knoxville News-Sentinel*, January 26, 2000, p. A4.

58. Keim, D. Change sought in legislation on divorced parenting plan. *Knoxville News-Sentinel*, January 19, 2000, p. A5.

59. Tennessee Administrative Office of the Courts. *Parenting plan pilot project report to the General Assembly.* 1999, Nashville, TN: Alternative Dispute Resolution Department.

60. Arbuthnot, J., and D. A. Gordon. Divorce education for parents and children: Programs for mediators, courts and schools. Presented at the annual conference of the Academy of Family Mediators. 1995, Cincinnati, OH.

61. Ahrons, C. R. The continuing coparental relationship between divorced spouses. *American Journal of Orthopsychiatry*, 1981, 51(3): p. 415–28.

62. Silitsky, D. Correlates of psychosocial adjustment in adolescents from divorced families. *Journal of Divorce and Remarriage*, 1996, 26(1/2): p. 151–64.

5

✣

Joint Custody

The concept of child custody is a remarkable phenomenon because it is a "right" that is never officially granted to parents but that can be taken away by a change in marital status (or because of substantiations of maltreatment). When two people conceive a child, they naturally obtain "parental rights" that grant them the privilege to parent their offspring [1]. However, the occasion of a divorce can terminate those rights, even though it is expected that an emotional relationship between the child and the noncustodial or nonresidential parent will likely continue.

Within the field of divorced families, no other matter has received more attention than the custody of children. The parent who has physical custody of the children is the parent who makes the day-to-day decisions about child rearing: what the children will eat, how they will dress, how much and what television shows they will watch, how much time they spend on their homework, with whom they may interact socially, and the time of their weekend curfews. The parent who is granted the right to exercise such decision making over the children's daily lives is fundamentally the adult who is chosen to be *the* parent. Unless parents have a highly cooperative, postdivorce relationship, the remaining (noncustodial) parent is, in effect, powerless to exercise such rights with any frequency because parenting opportunities are limited by child-contact schedules and the desire to avoid conflict with the former spouse. This limitation of parenting opportunities is often perceived, by groups concerned about fathers and some groups concerned about children, to be a legal and social injustice. Their solution to this "injustice" has been joint custodial arrangements. The joint custody of children and the legislation that supports such arrangements will be the topic of this chapter. In order to enhance comprehension, readers may want to refer back to tables 1.1 and 1.2 in chapter 1 for a reminder of the different types of custodial arrangements.

HISTORY OF CUSTODIAL LAWS

The "tender-years doctrine" prevailed in family-court child-custody decisions for nearly one hundred years. As discussed in chapter 1, this doctrine, which was established in the late 1800s, declared that children of "tender years" needed special care that could only be provided by a mother. This doctrine was eventually extended to all children, regardless of age, as legal professionals and the public at large came to believe that children required a special quality of care that was distinct from mature members of the population. Moreover, it was believed that only mothers possessed the unique ability to properly nurture children. Therefore, the custody of children was, by default, awarded to mothers through the 1950s and into the 1960s and 1970s. However, as women began to play a more active role in the workplace and fathers began to assume more parenting responsibilities, many men expressed a desire for their parenting role and the father-child relationship to continue after divorce. Rotundo [2] described this new development in American family life as "androgynous fatherhood." In this phase of American family life, much of the public viewed women and men as fundamentally alike—rational, nurturing, and assertive. Current theory suggested that it was pure randomness that gave individuals strengths and weaknesses, as opposed to biologically determined, sex-based characteristics.

Between 1975 and 1981, fathers' level of direct interaction with their children increased by 26 percent, although mothers continued to carry two-thirds of all parenting responsibilities. The growing changes in father involvement and the reconceptualization of family roles and responsibilities with regard to child rearing prompted many divorced fathers to condemn the tender-years doctrine. The criticism of the doctrine resulted in sweeping legislation that declared that custody decisions would be gender-neutral [3–9]. While such statutes were widely accepted, mothers continued to predominantly receive sole custody of their children. Many fathers argued that the effects of the legislation garnered little, if any, change in custody outcomes [10–16].

Struggles Associated with Being a Divorced Parent

In the 1960s and 1970s men began to speak about their experiences as divorced fathers, and particularly of wanting to be more involved in their children's lives. They claimed to be restricted from doing so by rigid child-contact schedules and uncooperative custodial parents. Green describes the following about divorced fathers and their children:

> The children gradually come to absorb mother's hostility to father; or they find the two worlds that their separate parents inhabit so impossibly difficult . . . that in the end they too begin to say that they do not wish to see their father. . . . [F]athers tell stories . . . of children who have been paraded before their father with the instruction from mother: "Now tell your father that you don't want to see him." [17, p. 116]

During this same time period of the 1960s and 1970s, many mothers struggled with their role as a divorced parent. They faced prejudices and discrimination about being single parents and sought to legitimize their position within society. Divorced mothers were criticized for actively, and often eagerly, establishing a life "of their own" that sometimes included higher education and, almost always, employment outside of the home. In fact, some women lost custody of their children to their ex-husbands for doing so. Such court decisions were fueled by the traditional belief that men and women had distinct roles in children's lives and that if mothers did not perform their traditional "duty" of staying home to raise their children, then the children would be better off with fathers who, at least, subscribed to the traditional role of providing income for the family [18].

Another obstacle faced by divorced mothers was the daily struggle for financial survival. While there was an active movement to allow fathers to be more involved with their children, there were just as many divorced fathers who had disappeared, rarely saw their children, and paid little, if any, child support. There were numerous studies between the 1960s and 1980s that documented divorced women's financial struggles and divorced fathers' failure to pay child support [19–26].

> Husbands at all income levels contributed to their ex-wives and children in only one-third of cases. A . . . study showed that within one year after the divorce decree, only 38% of the fathers were in full compliance with their support order. . . . Forty-two percent of the fathers made no payment. . . . By the time four years had passed 67% of fathers had ceased providing any money. [19, p. 501]

> Despite the legal obligation for both parents to support the children born in marriage, mothers take primary financial responsibility for children after divorce. In 1981, 81 percent of divorced and 66 percent of separated women with children had support orders. However . . . only 47 percent of all divorced and separated fathers made any child-support payments in 1981. [22, p. 130]

Advocates for women argued that the problems with child support went beyond failure to comply. States at this time did not have, or had poorly implemented, guidelines for child support awards [107, 108] and many support orders were not substantial enough to provide mothers with the financial security necessary to run a household. In addition to a lack of federal and state guidelines, there is evidence that some fathers shirked their financial responsibilities to their children. In her ethnographic study of divorced fathers, Arendell [23] found that many fathers purposely worked limited hours or voluntarily took a significant reduction in the number of hours that they worked so that judges, upon viewing their pay stubs, would order a lower level of child support.

Emergence of Joint Custody

Many divorced fathers ultimately felt that gender-neutral laws had little effect on child custody outcomes. Arguing that they were permitted to be little more than visitors in their children's lives, divorced fathers began voicing their desire for joint custody [10]. In actuality, the first joint physical custody arrangement was awarded in 1948 when the Supreme Court of Virginia ruled:

> The advisability of dividing or alternating the custody of the child has been seriously considered. While there are certain disadvantages in such division, there are also important advantages and benefits. It gives the child the experience of two separate homes. The child is entitled to the love, advice, and training of both her father and her mother. Frequent associations, contact, and friendly relations with both of her parents will protect her future welfare if one of her parents should die. It gives recognition to the rights of parents who have performed obligations as parents. [27, pp. 272–73]

Despite the similarity between the recommendations of this judge and those who currently advocate for joint physical custody, this custodial arrangement has been controversial and continues to be so today.

By the late 1970s and early 1980s, many divorced fathers placed pressure on legislators to acknowledge their rights as parents through joint-custody legislation. This development caused considerable publicity about the issue, which in turn prompted a flurry of research within the fields of psychology and sociology on custodial arrangements in divorced families. Out of this research came several of the most provocative works in the history of child-custody issues. Goldstein, Freud, and Solnit published a series of books, *Beyond the Best Interest of the Child*, *Before the Best Interest of the Child*, and *In the Best Interest of the Child*, which offered guidelines for making child-custody decisions [109, 110, 111]. Grounded in psychoanalytic theory, these authors wrote that a child can only have one "psychological parent" and that this role can never be fulfilled by a partially absent, inactive adult, no matter what his or her legal or biological relationship to the child. In their view, the psychological parent is the parent who provides the day-to-day care for the child and thus the parent who should receive sole physical and legal custody of the child. Their overriding recommendations were as follows:

> Once it is determined who [is] the custodial parent, it is that parent, not the court, who must decide under what conditions he or she wishes to raise the child. Thus, the custodial parent should have the right to decide whether it is desirable for the child to have . . . visits [with the noncustodial parent]. What we have said is designed to protect the security of an ongoing relationship—that between the child and the custodial parent. [109, p. 38]

These recommendations were more widely criticized than embraced. Stack argued that these recommendations would ultimately lead to further problems between divorced parents [112]. Custody battles would become horrendous, as each parent tried to discredit one another in attempts to become the child's "one" psychological parent. She further suggested that these recommendations were derived from a theory that idealized the nuclear family and that viewed alternative family systems as incomplete and dysfunctional.

Bruch [113] wrote that the recommendations of Goldstein, et al. were in direct contrast to current custody laws, which always permitted, and sometimes encouraged, contact between children and noncustodial parents—except in extreme cases. She stated, "No one endorses these authors' proposal for unilateral control of visitation by the custodial parent" (p. 115). She did note, however, that increasingly more researchers were agreeing that children should not be placed in any joint-custody arrangements over the opposition of one parent. Kuehl (1989) wrote that the recommendations of Goldstein and his colleagues were used selectively by fathers who were pushing to have more time with their children. They "had little trouble convincing male legislators and judges that such a notion would simply give vindictive ex-wives the opportunity to unfairly restrict their access to their children" (35, p. 39). Thus, despite the recommendations of these accomplished child psychologists, fathers continued to pursue their goal of joint custody—this time with the support of many legislators. Nonetheless, one must acknowledge that even today, our society continues to embrace a model of single parenting over joint parenting for families of divorce.

Joint Custody: Responses from Women's Advocacy Groups

In general, the fight for joint custody was not supported by most women's advocacy groups or feminist-oriented scholars. Since the 1970s, there have been four central arguments against joint custody: (1) joint custody erodes the traditional role of women as caretakers of children, (2) mandates for joint custody treat men and women equally in unequal situations, (3) fathers are not as interested in care-taking as they are in lowering their child-support payments, and (4) divorced men want to use joint custody as a means to control their ex-wives.

Traditional Role

In an argument that closely parallels the "tender-years doctrine," Chesler stated [114] that mothers were better able to parent than fathers because of the natural bond that mothers share with their children—one that was distinct and superior to the bond between fathers and children. "I believe that mothers and children have a natural and 'ineffable' right to each other. This right transcends *and* is based on genetic and biological ties as well as on the chores of 'psychological' parenting" (p. 439). She questioned why fathers would want to parent their children in the same way that mothers do. "Why are some fathers' rights activists demanding to be recognized as 'mothers'?" (p. 432). Although these arguments were less popular than other rationales, there was a portion of women's advocates who found it threatening to the status of motherhood to have men take a more active parenting role in divorced families. On a related note, others argued that since women primarily cared for children before the divorce, why wouldn't they continue to do so after the divorce had taken place [28]?

Unequal Circumstances

Mandates for joint custody treat men and women equally in unequal situations. Traditionally, a woman cared for children and therefore did not make investments in human capital that would make her marketable in the job market. A man, on the other hand, invested in his human capital, gaining education and work experience that made him infinitely more job marketable than his wife. Some feminist scholars have argued that mandates in joint custody ignore this inherent imbalance in the division of labor within families and instead treat men and women as equals in terms of their parenting. In other words, upon divorce, men continue with their work, in which they have invested, and they gain the benefits of parenting, in which they have invested very little. Women, because of financial strain, are pushed into the job market with little human capital investments and also lose part of their most cherished investments—their children [28–30].

Child Support

When families have joint physical-custody arrangements, sometimes the amount of child support that fathers pay to their ex-wives is reduced. This is because in addition to supporting the children in their mothers' homes, fathers with joint physical custody also support the children in their own homes. For example, they, too, must feed and cloth the children, have adequate living space for them, and pay for activities while the children are in their care. Thus, some advocates for women have argued that fathers seeking joint physical custody are more interested in reducing child-support obligations than in parenting their children [30–36].

Control over Ex-wives

A final argument concerning joint arrangements is that fathers who pursue joint custody seek to control their ex-wives by being involved in the decision-making concerning the children. The following quote illustrates this concern.

> They [mothers] were basically hostile to this arrangement [joint legal custody], for it left their former husbands with considerable power over their lives and the lives of their children [23, p. 19].

One author expressed concern that while divorce gives women "new found" independence, joint custody may return women to a position of dependence if decisions about the children have to be made jointly between parents [37]. Schulman and Pitt describe this interference with parenting as an "attack on women" and their roles as caregivers [38].

Some women's advocacy groups and feminist scholars have especially been opposed to mandated joint custody[28, 30, 34–36, 39–43]. In such instances, the state declares a "presumption" for joint custody, which means that every divorcing family is subject to this custodial arrangement, even over the opposition of one of the parents. Except in instances of violence or maltreatment, families must adhere to this legal preference [44]. The National Organization for Women has suggested that states would be better suited to adopt a mandate that primary caregivers should be awarded sole physical custody [45]. These laws are highly controversial and thus will be the subject of the following chapter.

Introduction of Joint-Custody Legislation

There is evidence that as early as 1920, the state of North Carolina permitted shared residences of children with divorced parents [46]. It was not until the 1960s and 1970s that other states began to address the issue of joint custody in statute (North Carolina, Kansas, Oregon, Texas, and Wisconsin [38, 47]). The statute that broke new ground for custodial arrangements, however, was passed in 1979 in California and stated the first legislative preference for the joint custody of children [48–54]. Shared-parenting arrangements in California at this time were assumed to involve both the residence of and decision making about the children. The legislation also declared a presumption for joint custody, but only when both parents agreed to such an arrangement [50]. In other words, if both parties of a divorcing couple in California wanted joint custody, then the parents would automatically share in the physical care and in the decision making about the children. After this, joint-custody laws spread quickly across the nation for the remainder of the decade [55].

JOINT-CUSTODY LAWS TODAY

The appendix to this book summarizes the different types of joint-custody statutes that exist today throughout the United States. Only four states (Colorado, Montana, North Dakota, and Rhode Island) do not make specific legislative provisions with regard to joint custody. Generally this means that there is no definition provided for this type of arrangement although families may still engage in shared parenting.

Joint Custody as an Option

The most common type of joint-custody statute is that which simply states that joint custody is permitted or is a legitimately recognized custodial arrangement within that state. Joint legal custody is not always distinguished from joint physical custody, but in most instances when one is permitted the other is as well. Statutes are often coupled with language that encourages "frequent and continuing contact" between the child and noncustodial parent; twenty-six states have such language in statute. Sample language is below.

> *Example from Arizona*: In this article, unless the context otherwise requires: 1. "Joint custody" means joint legal custody or joint physical custody, or both. 2. "Joint legal custody" means the condition under which both parents share legal custody and neither parent's rights are superior, except with respect to specified decisions as set forth by the court or the parents in the final judgment or order. 3. "Joint physical custody" means the condition under which the physical residence of the child is shared by the parents in a manner that assures that the child has substantially equal time and contact with both parents. (§ 25-402)

> *Example from New Jersey*: The Legislature finds and declares that it is in the public policy of this State to assure minor children of frequent and continuing contact with both parents after the parents have separated or dissolved their marriage and that it is in the public interest to encourage parents to share the rights and responsibilities of child rearing in order to effect this policy. (§ 9:2-4)

Preference for Shared Custody

In some rare instances (Florida, Kansas, and Utah) legislation states a preference for shared custody without declaring a presumption for any particular custodial arrangement.

Example from Florida: The court shall order that the parental responsibility for a minor child be shared by both parents unless the court finds that shared parental responsibility would be detrimental to the child. (§ 61.13)

Presumptions for Joint Custody

There are five states (Connecticut, Mississippi, Nevada, Tennessee, and Vermont) that declare a presumption for joint custody *only* if both parents agree to that arrangement. This could be joint legal or physical custody.

Example from Connecticut: There shall be a presumption, affecting the burden of proof, that joint custody is in the best interests of a minor child where the parents have agreed to an award of joint custody or so agree in open court at a hearing for the purpose of determining the custody of the minor child or children of the marriage. (§ 46b-56a)

In six states (Minnesota, New Hampshire, New Mexico, Texas, West Virginia, and Wisconsin) there is a presumption for joint legal custody, stating that for every family that divorces, the legislature has determined that joint legal custody is the most suitable arrangement. Such presumptions can be overturned in cases of family violence.

Example from New Hampshire: [I]n the making of any order relative to such custody there shall be a presumption, affecting the burden of proof, that joint legal custody is in the best interest of minor children. (§ 458:17)

Washington, D.C., has a presumption for joint legal and physical custody (§ 16-914). The state of Idaho does not specify if its presumption for joint custody applies to legal custody, physical custody, or both (§ 32-7170). Therefore, it is the court's responsibility to determine which type of joint custody would best serve children [56]. Presumption laws will be more fully addressed in chapter 6.

Protections for Victims of Family Violence

Most states encourage children to have regular contact with both of their divorced parents. At the same time, state legislators also realize how harmful it can be to encourage contact between a child and a parent who is violent or potentially harmful toward the child. Thus, forty-five states have provisions for special protections for victims of violence. The purpose of such provisions is to ensure that victims are not forced to have regular contact with their abusers and that children are not actively parented by a violent adult.

> *Example from Alaska*: Rebuttable presumption that parent with Domestic violence history may not be awarded sole legal, sole physical, joint legal, or joint physical custody of child. (§ 25.24.150[g])

WHO HAS JOINT CUSTODY?

How Many Families Want Joint Custody?

Fathers

While the joint-custody movement is primarily the result of fathers who felt disenfranchised by the family legal system, it is important to know whether this desire for joint custody is widespread, or reflects the wishes of a group of divorced fathers. What little research exists on this topic indicates that a fairly large proportion of fathers desire joint or sole paternal physical custody, even if they do not actively seek it. In a study that I conducted in 2001 in northern New England [44], I found that 80 percent of divorced fathers stated that they had wanted joint or sole paternal physical custody (the data for this question are unpublished, but available upon request). Other studies have had similar findings. Kruk [57] found that 28 percent of the eighty divorced fathers that he interviewed indicated a desire for sole paternal custody and 46 percent wanted joint custody—resulting in 74 percent of fathers wanting some type of custody. Yet, only 19 percent of the sample contested the proposed custody agreement. There were a variety of reasons the fathers gave for not fighting for custody. Frequently cited was advice from legal professionals. Fifty-five percent of the fathers in this study stated that their attorney actively discouraged them from seeking sole or joint custodial arrangements. A very comprehensive study of over twelve hundred families who were divorced in California in the 1980s found that 33 percent of fathers wanted sole physical custody and 35 percent wanted joint physical custody. Another 1.8 percent of fathers wanted split physical custody. In all, close to 70 percent of fathers reported wanting some form of physical custody [51]. These studies indicate that a large proportion of fathers express a desire for physical custodial responsibilities.

Mothers

Mothers have been less likely to embrace the idea of joint custody. In the large California-based study mentioned above, the majority of mothers, 82 percent, desired sole maternal physical custody. The remaining 18 percent expressed a desire for either sole paternal custody, joint custody, or split physical custody [51]. In a study of two hundred divorced mothers, 69 percent of the sample expressed a desire for sole maternal legal custody and 28 percent wanted joint legal custody. Only one mother in this study wanted sole paternal decision-making responsibilities [58].

How Many Families Have Joint Custody?

It is difficult to provide an accurate picture of how many families have joint arrangements. Government agencies rarely collect or report the custodial arrangements of divorced families in their state. Researchers also rarely report information about the custodial arrangements of participants in their studies [59–61], and when they do, it is often dated by the time of publication because the awarding of custodial arrangements changes rapidly over time [62]. The U.S. Census Bureau officially stopped collecting data on physical custodial arrangements resulting from divorce in 1994 [63]; however, other Census Bureau–sponsored surveys—such as the Current Population Survey, the Survey of Income and Program Participation, and the American Community Survey—regularly collect information on child custody or children's living arrangements. The 2001 Current Population Survey gathered data about custodial arrangements from homes that have minor children and an "absent" parent. The data estimate that 24 percent of families have a joint custodial arrangement—for either legal or physical custody, or both. According to this source, about one-quarter of children who live in homes without both of their natural (or adopted) parents, have parents who jointly hold decision-making power, have shared living arrangements, or both [64]. This source is, however, unclear about which of these families are divorced and which were never married. Kuhn [63] used this same data to focus on shared residential living arrangements (as opposed to joint legal custody or shared decision making) and concludes that between 19 and 26 percent of families with one parent "absent" have shared living arrangements. Again, this estimate includes never-married families as well as divorced families. Using data from the 2001 Survey of Income and Program Participation, I estimate that 11 percent of families with child-support orders have joint legal and physical custodial arrangements. Another 18 percent have a joint legal-custody arrangement along with sole physical custody. Thus, data from this survey estimate that about 29 percent of families have some kind of joint arrangement. This is an increase over the 1996 survey, which indicated that 21 percent of all families have joint arrangements, with 17 percent having joint legal custody and 4 percent having joint legal and physical custody [65]. The National Survey of Families and Households collected between 1987 and 1994 provides an estimate that 48 percent of divorced families had joint legal custody, an increase over the data that were collected in the mid-1980s [62, 66].

In the previously mentioned study that I conducted in 2001 in northern New England, I found that 93 percent of families in New Hampshire and 90 percent of families in Maine had joint legal custody [67]. Data compiled by the Vital Records Administration in New Hampshire indicate that 25 percent of families in 2003 had arrangements of joint physical custody, or shared living arrangements. This was an increase of three points over the previous year [68, 69]. Data compiled from court records in the state of Maine show that 13 percent of families divorced between 1996 and 1998 had joint physical custody [44]. A report from the state of Maryland found that in 1999, 35 percent of divorces resulted in joint legal custody (with sole physical custody to one parent) and 13 percent of divorces resulted in both joint legal and physical custody—both shared decision making and shared living arrangements [42]. These figures place joint arrangements in Maryland near 50 percent.

The different estimates presented here illustrate how difficult it is to provide an accurate portrayal of the proportion of families with joint arrangements. There are indications that current postdivorce arrangements involving joint legal custody are considerable, with close to one-half of families having this arrangement. In fact, some scholars have noted that the award of sole physical custody to the mother coupled with joint legal custody to both parents is the "default" custodial arrangement for most divorcing families today [67, 70]. With regard to residential agreements, it appears that 13–25 percent of families have joint or shared living arrangements. One firm conclusion is that joint arrangements have been, and continue to be, on the rise.

Which Families Have Joint Custody?

There are distinct associations between family characteristics and custodial arrangements. Research has fairly consistently demonstrated that fathers with higher levels of income or education are more likely to have joint custodial arrangements. This is true for fathers with joint legal custody [51, 62, 66, 71] and for fathers with joint physical custody [51, 65, 72–74]. Two national studies found that African Americans and Latinos were less likely to have joint custody, including legal and physical custodial arrangements [65, 75]. Another national study, however, that assessed informal shared-parenting arrangements in addition to formal arrangements, found that minorities and families living in urban areas were more likely to practice joint custodial residential arrangements than families living in rural areas [74].

There is also evidence that parents who delayed having their first child until they were somewhat older, families with older children at the time of the divorce, and couples who had longer marriages were more likely to have joint legal custody of their children [71]. Fathers who reside in states that declare a preference for joint legal custody are more likely to receive joint decision-making arrangements, indicating a high level of implementation for this type of social policy [51, 62], which has been independently confirmed [62, 67]. Finally, there is evidence that maternal preference of joint physical custody is a predictor of actual joint residential living arrangements [51] and that mothers' opinions about fathers' capacity to parent is a predictor of whether a divorced family receives joint legal custody [58].

WHAT ABOUT THE BARNES FAMILY?

The Barnes family's legal battle ultimately ended with Joanne having sole legal and physical custody of the children and with Mark, as the noncustodial but fit parent, having "access rights" to his children—traditionally called "visitation rights." In essence, this means that April and Nathan live with their mother and that her home is considered their primary residence. Where their father lives has no legal bearing on their place of residence. Mark also does not have any legal custody rights to his children. This means that he is restricted from participating in any decision-making about the children. Thus, he is not legally entitled to make decisions about the children's education, medical treatment, religious training, or any other matter. There are a number of states, however, that specifically declare that noncustodial parents can make decisions about emergency medical treatment and that noncustodial parents can enjoy the same access to their children's educational or medical records as can the custodial parent, with or without legal custody (e.g., Massachusetts, Domestic Relations, § 208:31, custody of children; shared custody plans, chapter 208, § 31). If Mark lived in one of those states he would enjoy the rights afforded from such legislation.

The Barnes's custodial arrangement is the "traditional" arrangement for divorced families. However, there are other arrangements that might have worked equally well for the family. For example, Mark and Joanne could have arranged for joint legal and physical custody of the children.

In such an instance the children would have split their time between their parents' homes, and Joanne and Mark would both be legally entitled to make decisions about the children's welfare and future. Such an arrangement would not necessarily mean that the children would split their time 50-50 between the two households. There are a number of different residential schedules that divorced families can use. (See chapter 4 on parenting plans for a sample of possible residential schedules.) Under an arrangement that only permitted joint legal custody, April and Nathan would have continued to primarily live with their mother, but Joanne and Mark would share in the decision making about their children. Undoubtedly, if encouraged by the legal system, Mark and Joanne could have explored several different joint custodial agreements, but would their children have benefited or been harmed by such an arrangement?

HOW DO CHILDREN AND FAMILIES WITH JOINT CUSTODY FARE?

A substantial amount of research has been devoted to studying the adjustment of children and parents who live with joint-custody arrangements. In essence, the research shows that children of joint custody are no worse off and are sometimes better off than children living in sole-custody arrangements, as long as there is minimal parental conflict. This research has been praised by fathers' advocates for advancing an idea "whose time has come" [76] and criticized by women's advocates and members of the research community for methodological imperfections [38]. A discussion of this research, as well as its enthusiasts and critics, follows.

Studies Indicating No Difference

There are a host of studies that have found that the adjustment of children in joint-custody arrangements is no different than the adjustment of children living in sole-custody arrangements. Such conclusions have been drawn in studies that have examined families with joint legal custody, joint physical custody, or both.

The literature on divorced families is comprised of studies with different types of samples, measures, and family arrangements. Regardless of these characteristics, a solid group of studies has found that children who either see their parents an "equal" amount of time or whose parents officially have joint physical custody do not fare any better or worse than children who live in sole-custody arrangements. This was true of a small, community-based sample in California of ninety-three children from families seeking free counseling on divorce [77]. Using longitudinal data from two years, the authors studied children from both joint and sole-maternal physical custodial arrangements with regard to behavioral, emotional, and social adjustment. They determined that children from both groups of children had comparable levels of problem behavior, social skills, and emotional adjustment.

Researchers of a relatively large study of over four hundred divorcing couples gathered data at three different points in time to assess overall child well-being among divorced families [73]. They examined families in a number of differing arrangements, including those with maternal sole custody, paternal sole custody, joint legal custody with sole-maternal physical custody, joint legal custody with sole-paternal physical custody, and families with joint physical and legal custody. They found that none of the custodial arrangements examined were predictive of any of the child measures, including depression, aggression, delinquency, social withdrawal, and somatic complaints.

In theory, having joint physical custody means that children spend more time with both parents than children who are in sole physical custodial arrangements. In reality, however, parents can practice any child-contact schedule, regardless of their physical custodial arrangement. Therefore assessing a relationship between child adjustment and the frequency of parent-child contact is likely a better measure of the outcomes of shared parenting, as opposed to whether a parent has joint custody. Using a subsample of a randomly selected, national study, Donnelly and Finkelhor [78] examined the relationship between parent-child access and the quality of the parent-child relationship among 160 divorced families. They found that having a shared physical-parenting arrangement had no relationship with how much support and affection parents offered their children, nor did it predict the level of disagreement between parents in children. The one statistically significant finding was in the opposite direction of what was hypothesized. Children in sole physical-parenting arrangements offered their parents more support and affection than children in shared-parenting arrangements. It is likely that such children play the role of companion to their sole custodians. The lack of findings between parent-child access and children's adjustment is consistent with other research that found that regular and frequent contact with noncustodial fathers or being in a sole physical custodial arrangement had little, if any, bearing on the behavioral [79] or psychological adjustment of children [80].

There are numerous other studies indicating little to no difference between children in joint and sole custodial arrangements. For example, a small study with a sample size of seventy-eight and a response rate below 30 percent found that there was no difference between adolescents from families with sole legal custody and joint legal custody with regard to a number of measures including anxiety, loyalty conflicts, happiness with new stepparents, or change in well-being at the point of parental remarriage [81]. Silitsky [82] also examined outcomes for adolescents, but used a larger sample size of 210 students of divorced families, 32 of which had some form of joint custody (as described by the youth). He found that custodial arrangement did not predict the adolescents' social competence, nor did it predict internalizing or externalizing problem behaviors. A final study interviewed 522 adolescents four and a half years after their parents' divorce and examined the relationship between custodial arrangement and feeling caught between one's parents [83]. These authors found that as long as conflict between the parents remained low, joint physical custody was not a predictor of whether children felt caught between their parents.

Although regularly cited by scholars, these findings have been routinely ignored by members of the public, policy makers, and advocates for one cause or another, primarily because no one knows what to do with them. Is it good that children in joint arrangements appear to be the same as children in sole arrangements, or is it bad? Does it hurt the movement toward joint custody or support it? Because of the uncertainty of how to handle research with these conclusions, the findings have failed to filter down from the research community to the public in any meaningful way. Thus, research with these findings tends to be bypassed for research with less benign conclusions.

Studies Indicating Better Adjustment

Research concluding that children in joint-custody families are better adjusted than children in sole-custody families is similar in nature to studies that have found no difference between these two populations. That is, they, too, have used a variety of sample sizes and measures to study children's adjustment and they have been conducted at all points over the past thirty years, as has the previously mentioned research.

Studies that fall into this category have cited many advantages to living in a family with a shared-custody arrangement. For example, in their study of 133 children whose parents had separated within the past thirty months, Wolchik, Braver, and Sandler [80] assessed children's self-reports of their daily lives. The children in joint shared residential arrangements reported their life events more positively and were found to have higher levels of self-esteem than children who lived in sole-custody arrangements. They were also more likely to see their nonprimary-residential parent. Similar findings were true for families with joint legal custody. Using data from two waves of the National Survey of Families and Households (1987–1988 and 1992–1994), Seltzer examined the relationship between joint legal custodial arrangements and father-child access among 160 divorced families [62]. She found that children of joint legal custodial arrangements were likely to see their fathers more frequently, for both daytime and overnight contact. A study of 254 recently separated families found that fathers who have joint legal custody are more likely to have contact with their children than fathers with no legal or physical custody [84]. The children in joint legal-custody families were also less likely to have adjustment problems than children without shared-parenting arrangements.

Buchanan, Maccoby, and Dornbush [85] examined the adjustment of over five hundred adolescents whose parents had been divorced for four and a half years. Data were collected over a number of years from both children and their parents. In general, the authors found that custodial arrangement did not predict adjustment. When there were differences between the groups, however, children in shared living arrangements showed a marginally higher level of adjustment on a composite score of depression, deviance, and school effort.

The most comprehensive assessment of the effects of joint custodial arrangements was a meta-analysis conducted in 2002 that reviewed thirty-three studies that focused on the adjustment of children in sole and joint (physical or legal) arrangements [86]. Bauserman examined the relationship between any joint (physical or legal) arrangement and a number of child-outcome measures, including general adjustment, behavioral and emotional adjustments, family relations, academic performance, and adjustment to living in a divorced family. When possible, he also controlled for parental conflict. He found that across the board, children from joint-custody homes had better outcomes than children in sole-custody homes, with an effect size that he described as "slightly greater than what would be considered a small effect size" (p. 95). He also broke down the analyses by custody type and found, regardless of whether the study focused on legal custody or physical custody, that children in joint arrangements fared better than children in sole custodial arrangements. For eight studies he also compared children in joint-custody arrangements with children in intact families and found that there was no difference between children from these two family types.

There are additional trends that are consistent with having joint custodial arrangements that are presumed to be beneficial to children. In a study that used self-reported data from 212 fathers, it was determined that fathers who have joint legal custody are more satisfied with their custodial arrangements and have higher levels of self-esteem—although it appears that the author of this study did not control for demographic factors [66]. Finally, one study that controlled for paternal income levels did not find a relationship between levels of child-support payments made after divorce and joint legal custody [87]. This finding was supported by another that failed to find a relationship between custody and support payments [84]. A study that examined one thousand California-based parents who divorced in the mid-1980s found that parents who had shared residential schedules also had more communication with one another. There was, however, no difference in the amount of conflict that they experienced when compared to parents without shared schedules [88].

Some children's advocates, but especially advocates for fathers, cite the findings of these studies to push for mandated joint legal and physical custody for all families of divorce. They argue that since science finds that children are better off when they live with and are parented by both parents, it is in the best interest of all children to be provided with this opportunity [10, 89].

Problems with the Research

Members of the research community and advocates for women's issues have argued that there are serious methodological problems with studies on families of joint legal or physical custody. The primary problem concerns the sample or the subjects with joint custody [73, 90–94]. Because joint legal custody is only mandated in a handful of states and joint physical custody has only ever been mandated in two jurisdictions (currently Washington, D.C., and previously Louisiana), there is a very high likelihood that families who have joint custodial arrangements have chosen these arrangements. Having a shared custodial arrangement is indicative of a cooperative and somewhat amiable co-parenting relationship. Research has consistently demonstrated that parents who have a cooperative relationship have less conflict and when parents have less conflict, children have a better adjustment. Thus, the chief complaint about studies on families of joint custody is that researchers examine the highest-functioning divorced families and conclude that their children are doing well because of the custodial arrangement rather than the cooperative co-parental relationship [33, 35, 40].

What about Families of High Conflict?

One of the primary concerns regarding laws that make joint custodial provisions is that particular custodial arrangements will be preferred or mandated for all families. While professionals and advocates alike are reluctant to interfere with a divorcing couple that agrees on a particular custodial arrangement, there is considerable concern about parents who engage in a high level of conflict and how they would function under a mandate for a joint arrangement. Such a mandate usually operates under a law that declares a "presumption for joint custody." Presumption laws and studies that are relevant to these types of laws will be discussed in chapter 6. It is sufficient to say here, though, that children rarely do well when there is high conflict between their parents and that children who, in addition to experiencing parental conflict, make frequent transitions between their parents' homes have an even poorer adjustment to life postdivorce [53, 83, 95].

IF NOT CUSTODY, THEN WHAT?

Despite all the attention paid to custodial status and the adjustment of children, there seems to be little evidence that children whose parents have joint custody or children who share a considerable amount of time between their parents' homes have a better adjustment than children who live in one home. This is not to say that contact with the noncustodial parent is irrelevant. Although there is some inconsistency within the literature, there is a considerable amount of research that concludes that children who have regular and consistent contact with nonresident parents do better than children who are without this influence in their lives [82, 96–101]. What does seem to be clear, however, is that if all other factors are held constant, children who live primarily with one parent do not fare any better or any worse than children who live with both parents.

If custody does not matter, what does? The findings about parental conflict and children's well-being are indicative of the importance of overall family functioning. Several studies have shown that children whose parents have mental-health problems or are emotionally unstable have a poorer adjustment than children whose parents are more stable [102–105]. This finding is true for children of divorced families as well [77, 95, 99, 106]. Thus, it is apparently not custody that determines a child's well-being, but family functioning—just as with all families, intact or otherwise.

REFERENCES

1. Guggenheim, M. The best interests of the child: Much ado about nothing? In *Child, parent, and state: Law and policy reader*, ed. S. R. Humm, et al., pp. 27–35. 1994, Philadelphia: Temple University Press.

2. Rotundo, E. A. American fatherhood: A historical perspective. *American Behavioral Scientist*, 1985, 29: pp. 7–25.

3. Fetzner, W. N. Fathers deserve equal justice in the courts. *Christian Science Monitor*, June 22, 1990, p. 19.

4. Kellam, S. Custody, courts and kids: Quick rulings urged for sake of children. *Denver Rocky Mountain News*, March 16, 1995, p. 3D.

5. Moody, J. Children benefit when primary parent has custody. *St. Petersburg Times*, May 14, 1990, p. 2.

6. Rankin, D. The new economics of custody suits. *New York Times*, April 6, 1986, p. 11.

7. Dowd, N. E. *Redefining fatherhood*. 2000, New York: New York University Press.

8. Fineman, M. A. *The illusion of equality: The rhetoric and reality of divorce reform*. 1991, Chicago: University of Chicago Press.

9. Depner, C. E. Parental role reversal: Mothers as nonresidential parents. In *Nonresidential parenting: New vistas in family living*, ed. C. E. Depner and J. H. Bray, pp. 37–57. 1993, Newbury Park, CA: Sage Publications.

10. Roman, M. and W. Haddad. *The disposable parent: The case for joint custody*. 1978, New York: Holt.

11. Stamps, L. E., S. Kunen, and A. Rock-Faucheux. Judges' beliefs dealing with child custody decisions. *Journal of Divorce and Remarriage*, 1997, 28(1/2): pp. 3–16.

12. Stamps, L. E., S. Kunen, and R. Lawyer. Judicial attitudes regarding custody and visitation issues. *Journal of Divorce and Remarriage*, 1996, 25(1/2): pp. 23–37.

13. Foster, C. Plea for fathers' rights: divorced but still a dad. *Christian Science Monitor*, July 6, 1982, p. 2.

14. Yenckel, J. T. Families: Fighting for fathers' rights. *Washington Post*, January 13, 1982, p. B5.

15. Wells, K. Divorced dads: Tell their side of the story. *St. Petersburg Times*, May 15, 1989, p. 1D.

16. Herndon, N. Father: Breadwinner or nurturer? *Christian Science Monitor*, February 29, 1988, p. 23.

17. Green, M. *Fathering*. 1976, New York: McGraw-Hill Company.

18. Kelly, M., and J. Goodman. Feminist arguments for a working mother's custody. *Women's Rights Law Reporter*, 1974. 1: pp. 23–25.

19. Brandwein, R. A., C. A. Brown, and E. M. Fox. Women and children last: The social situation of divorced mothers and their families. *Journal of Marriage and the Family*, 1974. (August): pp. 498–514.

20. McLanahan, S. S., and K. Booth. Mother-only families: Problems, prospects, and politics. *Journal of Marriage and the Family*, 1989, 51(August): pp. 557–80.

21. Borenzweig, H. The punishment of divorced mothers. *Journal of Sociology and Social Welfare*, 1976, 3(3): pp. 291–310.

22. Arendell, T. J. Women and the economics of divorce in the contemporary United States. *Signs*, 1987, 13: pp. 121–35.

23. Arendell, T. J. *Fathers and divorce*. 1995, Thousand Oaks, CA: Sage Publications.

24. Cullen, F. T., K. W. Heiner, and P. Sullo. TI: Child support collection: a stick-and-carrot approach. *Social Work*, 1980, 25(5): pp. 397–402.

25. Corcoran, M. The economic consequences of marital dissolution for women in the middle years. *Sex Roles*, 1979, 5(3): pp. 343–53.

26. Nagel, S. and L. J. Weitzman. Double standard of American justice. *Trans-Action*, 1972, 9(5): pp. 18–25.

27. *Mullen v. Mullen*, S.E.2d. 1948, Supreme Court of Virginia. p. 349.
28. Fineman, M. L. Custody determination at divorce: The limits of social science research and the fallacy of the liberal ideology of equality. *Canadian Journal of Women and the Law*, 1987, 3(1): pp. 88–111.
29. Boyd, S. Child custody, ideology and employment. *Canadian Journal of Women and the Law*, 1989, 3: pp. 111–33.
30. Carbone, J. R. A feminist perspective on divorce. *Future of Children*, 1994, 4(1): pp. 183–209.
31. Zuckerman, J. Men's rights groups grow as the battle over child custody in divorce intensifies. *Wall Street Journal*, August, 21, 1986, p. A1.
32. Roman, M., and S. Dichter. Fathers and feminism: Backlash within the women's movement. *Conciliation Courts Review*, 1985, 23(2): pp. 37–45.
33. Hardcastle, G. W. Joint custody: A family court judge's perspective. *Family Law Quarterly*, 1998, 32(1): pp. 201–19.
34. Woods, G. "Father's rights" groups: Beware their real agenda, *National NOW Times*, 1997, 29(2), National Organization for Women.
35. Kuehl, S. J. Against joint custody: A dissent to the General Bullmoose theory. *Family and Conciliation Courts Review*, 1989, 27(2): pp. 37–45.
36. Washington State National Organization for Women. Washington State chapter National Organization for Women position paper joint custody. 1998, Washington State NOW.
37. Hutchinson, E. B. Improving custody law in Virginia without creating a rebuttable presumption of joint custody. *William and Mary Journal of Women and the Law*, 1998, 4: pp. 523–47.
38. Schulman, J., and V. Pitt. Second thoughts on joint custody: Analysis of legislation and its implications for women and children. *Golden Gate Law Review*, 1982, 12: pp. 539–77.
39. Barry, M. M. A leap backwards: D.C.'s joint custody of children act. *The Washington Lawyer*, 1996, Nov/Dec: pp. 41–47.
40. Barry, M. M. The District of Columbia's joint custody presumption: Misplaced blame and simplistic solutions. *Catholic University Law Review*, 1997, 46(Spring): p. 767.
41. Heim, S., et al. *Family court report*. 2002, California National Organization for Women.
42. Women's Law Center of Maryland. *Custody and financial distribution in Maryland: An empirical study of custody and divorce cases filed in Maryland during fiscal year 1999*. 2004, Towson, MD: Women's Law Center of Maryland.
43. Shapero, L. The case against a joint custody presumption. *The Vermont Bar Journal*, 2001(December): pp. 1–2.
44. Douglas, E. M. The influence of public policies on human behavior: Is there an effect of a New Hampshire law stating a presumption for joint legal custody on father involvement in divorced families? Public Policy Program. 2002, Boston: University of Massachusetts. p. 354.
45. National Organization for Women. *NOW 2001 Conference: Conference resolution—Action on family law*. 2001. http://www.now.org/organization/conference/resolutions/2001.html#action.
46. Reynolds, S. Personal communication to author. March 3, 2005.

47. Folberg, J., ed. *Joint custody and shared parenting*. 1st ed. 1984, Washington, DC: Bureau of National Affairs, Inc., Association of Family and Conciliation Courts.

48. McIsaac, H. Mandatory conciliation custody/visitation matters: California's bold stroke. *Conciliation Courts Review*, 1981, 19(2): pp. 73–81.

49. Goldzband, M. G. Current trends affecting family law and child custody: A psychiatrist's perspective. In *Psychiatric Clinics of North America*, 1983, 6(4): pp. 683–94.

50. Cook, J. A. California's joint custody statute. In *Joint custody and shared parenting*, ed. J. Folberg. 1984, Washington, DC: Bureau of National Affairs, Inc., Association of Family and Conciliation Courts.

51. Maccoby, E. E., and R. H. Mnookin. *Dividing the child: Social and legal dilemmas of custody*. 1992, Cambridge, MA: Harvard University Press.

52. Coller, D. R. Joint custody: Research, Theory and Policy. *Family Process*, 1988. 27: pp. 459–69.

53. Johnston, J. R. Children's adjustment in sole custody compared to joint custody families and principles for custody decision making. *Family and Conciliation Courts Review*, 1995, 33(4): pp. 415–25.

54. Woodhouse, B. B. Child custody in the age of children's rights: The search for a just and workable standard. *Family Law Quarterly*, 1999, 33(3): pp. 815–32.

55. Folberg, J. Custody overview. In *Joint custody and shared parenting*, ed. J. Folberg, pp. 3–10. 1991, New York: The Guilford Press.

56. Brandt, E. Personal communication to author. March 23, 2005.

57. Kruk, E. Child custody determination: An analysis of the litigation model, legal practices, and men's experiences in the process. *Journal of Men's Studies*, 1992, 1(2): pp. 163–85.

58. Wilcox, K. L., S. A. Wolchik, and S. H. Braver, Predictors of maternal preference for joint or sole legal custody. *Family Relations*, 1998, 47: pp. 93–101.

59. McKenry, P., et al. Influences on single, noncustodial, father's physical involvement with their children. *Journal of Genetic Psychology*, 1992, 153: pp. 305–19.

60. Lee, M. Y. Post-divorce interparental conflict, children's contact with both parents, children's emotional responses and children's behavioral adjustments. *Journal of Divorce and Remarriage*, 1997, 28: pp. 61–82.

61. Stone, G., and P. McKenry. Nonresidential father involvement: A test of a mid-range theory. *Journal of Genetic Psychology*, 1998, 159: pp. 313–24.

62. Seltzer, J. A. Father by law: Effects of joint legal custody on nonresident fathers' involvement with children. *Demography*, 1998, 35: pp. 135–46.

63. Kuhn, D. R. Shared parenting ranges from 19 percent to 25.8 percent of divorced families in the U.S. *Speak out for children*, 2003, (Winter): pp. 19–21.

64. U.S. Census Bureau, C.P.S. *Child support: 2001—detailed tables*. 2002, Washington, DC: U.S. Census Bureau.

65. Nord, C. W., and N. Zill. *Noncustodial parents' participation in their children's lives: Evidence from the Survey of Income and Program Participation*. Washington, DC: Office of Human Services Policy, Office of the Assistance Secretary for Planning and Evaluation, U.S. Department of Health and Human Services, Contract No. DHHS-100-90-0012, Delivery Order No. 11, 1996.

66. Arditti, J. A. Differences between fathers with joint custody and noncustodial fathers. *American Journal Orthopsychiatry*, 1992, 62: pp. 186–95.

67. Douglas, E. M. The effect of a presumption for joint legal custody on father involvement in divorced families. *The Journal of Divorce and Remarriage*, 2003, 40(3/4): pp. 1–10.

68. Elderkin, P. *2003 New Hampshire divorces*, ed. D. W. Gladstone. 2004, Concord, NH: NH Division of Vital Records Administration.

69. Elderkin, P. *2002 New Hampshire divorces*, ed. D. W. Gladstone. 2004, Concord, NH: NH Division of Vital Records Administration.

70. Kelly, J. B. The determination of child custody. *Future of Children*, 1994, 4(1): pp. 121–42.

71. Phear, W. P. An empirical study of custody agreements: Joint versus sole legal custody. *Journal of Psychiatry and Law*, 1983, 11(4): pp. 419–41.

72. Cancian, M., and D. R. Meyer. Who gets custody? *Demography*, 1998, 35(2): pp. 147–57.

73. Pearson, J., and N. Thoennes. Custody after divorce: Demographic and attitudinal patterns. *American Journal of Orthopsychiatry*, 1990, 60(2): pp. 233–49.

74. Donnelly, D., and D. Finkelhor. Who has joint custody? Class differences in the determination of custody arrangements. *Family Relations*, 1993, 42: pp. 57–60.

75. Huang, C.-C., W.-J. Han, and I. Garfinkel. Child support enforcement, joint legal custody and parental involvement. *Social Service Review*, 2003, 77(2): pp. 255–78.

76. Robinson, H. L. Joint custody: An idea whose time has come. *Journal of Family Law*, 1982, 21(4): pp. 641–85.

77. Kline, M., et al. Children's adjustment in joint and sole physical custody families. *Developmental Psychology*, 1989, 25(3): pp. 430–38.

78. Donnelly, D., and D. Finkelhor. Does equality in custody arrangement improve the parent-child relationship? *Journal of Marriage and the Family*, 1992, 54(4): pp. 837–45.

79. Furstenberg, F. F., S. P. Morgan, and P. D. Allison. Paternal participation and children's well-being after marital dissolution. *American Sociological Review*, 1987, 52(October): pp. 695–701.

80. Wolchik, S. A., S. L. Braver, and I. N. Sandler. Maternal versus joint custody: Children's postseparation experiences and adjustment. *Journal of Clinical Child Psychology*, 1985, 14(1): pp. 5–10.

81. Crosbie-Brunett, M. Impact of joint versus sole custody and quality of coparental relationship on adjustment of adolescents in remarried families. *Behavioral Sciences and the Law*, 1991, 9: pp. 439–49.

82. Silitsky, D. Correlates of psychosocial adjustment in adolescents from divorced families. *Journal of Divorce and Remarriage*, 1996, 26(1/2): pp. 151–64.

83. Buchanan, C. M., E. E. Maccoby, and S. M. Dornbush. Caught between parents: Adolescents' experience in divorced homes. *Child Development*, 1991, 62(5): pp. 1088–129.

84. Gunnoe, M. L., and S. L. Braver. The effects of joint legal custody on mothers, fathers, and children controlling for factors that predispose a sole maternal versus joint legal award. *Law and Human Behavior*, 2001, 25(1): pp. 25–43.

85. Buchanan, C. M., E. E. Maccoby, and S. M. Dornbush. Adolescents and their families after divorce: Three residential arrangements compared. *Journal of Research on Adolescence*, 1992, 2(3): pp. 261–91.

86. Bauserman, R. Child adjustment in joint-custody versus sole-custody arrangements: A meta-analytic review. *Journal of Family Psychology*, 2002, 16(1): pp. 91–102.

87. Seltzer, J. A. Legal custody arrangements and children's economic welfare. *American Journal of Sociology*, 1991, 96(4): pp. 895–929.

88. Maccoby, E. E., C. E. Depner, and R. H. Mnookin. Coparenting in the second year after divorce. *Journal of Marriage and the Family*, 1990, 52: pp. 141–55.

89. Children's Rights Council. *The best parent is both parents*. April 28, 2002 n.d. http://www.gocrc.com/ (January 5, 2005).

90. Shrier, D. K., et al. "Level of satisfaction of fathers and mothers with joint or sole custody arrangements: Results of a questionnaire." *Journal of Divorce and Remarriage*, 1991, 16(3/4), pp. 163–69.

91. Arditti, J. A., and D. Madden-Derdich. Joint and sole custody mothers: Implications for research and practice. *Families in Society*, 1997, 78(1): pp. 36–45.

92. Rothberg, B. Joint custody: Parental problems and satisfactions. *Family Process*, 1983, 22(1): pp. 43–52.

93. Shiller, V. F. Joint and maternal custody: The outcome for boys aged 6–11 and their parents. In *Dissertation Abstracts International*, p. 971. 1985, Ann Arbor, MI: University Microfilms International.

94. Glover, R. J., and C. Steele. Comparing the effects on the child of postdivorce parenting arrangements. *Journal of Divorce*, 1988, 12(2): pp. 185–201.

95. Johnston, J. R., M. Klein, and J. M. Tschann. Ongoing postdivorce conflict: Effects on children of joint custody and frequent access. *American Journal of Orthopsychiatry*, 1989, 59: pp. 576–92.

96. Amato, P. R., and B. Keith. Parental divorce and the well-being of children: A meta-analysis. *Psychological Bulletin*, 1991, 110(1): pp. 26–46.

97. Amato, P. R., and S. C. Rezac. Contact with nonresidential parents, interparental conflict and children's behavior. *Journal of Family Issues*, 1994, 15(2): pp. 191–207.

98. Brody, G., and R. Forehand. Interparental conflict, relationship with the noncustodial father, and the adolescent post-divorce adjustment. *Journal of Applied Developmental Psychology*, 1990, 11: pp. 139–47.

99. Pruett, M. K., et al. Family and legal indicators of child adjustment to divorce among families with young children. *Journal of Family Psychology*, 2003, 17(2): pp. 169–80.

100. Pagani-Kurtz, L., and J. Derevensky. Access by non-custodial parents: Effects upon children's coping resources. *Journal of Divorce and Remarriage*, 1997, 27: pp. 43–55.

101. Thomas, A. M., and R. Forehand. The role of paternal variables in divorced and married families: Predictability of adolescent adjustment. *American Journal of Orthopsychiatry*, 1993, 63(1): pp. 126–35.

102. Leinonen, J. A., T. S. Solantaus, and R.-L. Punamaki. Parental mental health and children's adjustment: The quality of marital interaction and parenting as mediating factors. *Journal of Child Psychology and Psychiatry*, 2003, 44(2): pp. 227–41.

103. Taylor, R. D., and D. Roberts. Kinship support and maternal and adolescent well-being in economically disadvantaged African-American families. *Child Development*, 1995, 66: pp. 1585–97.

104. Scherer, D. G., et al. Relation between children's perceptions of maternal mental illness and children's psychological adjustment. *Journal of Clinical Child Psychology*, 1996, 25(2): pp. 156–69.

105. Cowen, E. L., et al. Follow-up of young stress-affected and stress-resilient urban children. *Development and Psychopathology*, 1997, 93(3): pp. 565–77.

106. Hipke, K. N., et al. Predictors of children's intervention-induced resilience in a parenting program for divorced mothers. *Family Relations*, 2002, 51(2): pp. 121–29.

107. Espenshade, T. J. The economic consequences of divorce. *Journal of Marriage and Family*, 1979, 41(3): pp. 615–25.

108. Jencks, C., Divorced mothers, unite! *Psychology Today*, 1982, 16: pp. 73–75.

109. Goldstein, J., A. Freud, A. J. Solnit, and D. Burlingham. *Beyond the best interests of the child*. 1973, New York: Free Press.

110. Goldstein, J., A. Freud, and A. J. Solnit. *Before the best interests of the child*. 1979, New York: Free Press.

111. Goldstein, J., A. Freud, A. J. Solnit, and S. Goldstein. *In the best interests of the child*. 1986, New York: Free Press.

112. Stack, C. B. Who owns the child? Divorce and child custody decisions in middle-class families. *Social Problems*, 1976, 23(4): 505–15.

113. Bruch, C. S. And, how are the children? The effects of ideology and mediation on child custody law and children's well-being in the United States. *Family and Conciliation Courts Review*, 1992, 30(1): 112–34.

114. Chesler, Phyllis. *Mothers on trial: The battle for children and custody*. 1986, New York: McGraw-Hill Book Company.

6

Declaring a Rebuttable Presumption in Child-custody Statutes

The most controversial social policy for families of divorce concerns a *rebuttable presumption* for child-custody arrangements. These laws mandate that all families adopt a designated custodial agreement, unless one parent can prove that it would not be in the best interests of the child. Most of the presumptive child-custody legislation that has passed in the United States has concerned joint custody or shared parenting, in one form or another. This chapter primarily addresses presumptions for shared parenting, which exist in eight states, and the potential outcomes of this legislation.

WHAT IS A REBUTTABLE PRESUMPTION?

Americans are generally familiar with the concept of presumption laws. These are statutes that declare "truths" that need not be verified or proven in court. In the United States, the most frequently recognized use of this legal standard is the "presumption of innocence until proven guilty." It is embedded in American culture that one cannot be considered guilty of wrongdoing unless proven so in a court of law—whereupon the presumption of innocence is overturned. Gaynor [1] notes that all presumptions are "rebuttable, and proof of the matter is required if one of the parties presents evidence to dispute the presumption" (p. 116). When a state legislature declares a rebuttable presumption that joint custody or shared parenting between divorcing parents is in the best interests of the child, it is assumed that in the absence of evidence to the contrary, joint custody will be granted to all families who present before the court [2, 3]. Should one parent want to obtain sole custody of his or her children, the burden of proof then rests on that parent to overturn the presumption that shared custody is in the best interests of all children in the state.

A presumption for joint custody or shared parenting is substantially different than a preference for sharing custody. One can imagine how innocence in the United States might be handled if our statutes or the Constitution stated that there was a *preference* rather than a *presumption* that everyone be considered innocent upon arrest. A preference is merely that—a statement of public policy, a gesture toward children and families of divorce. It would not require or mandate that all families adopt, or even consider, any specific custody arrangement. A presumption, on the other hand, mandates this for all families. Moreover, it places the burden of proof on any individual who wants to override that presumption.

THE BARNES FAMILY REVISITED

As readers may recall, the Barnes family had a traditional custody arrangement. Joanne received sole physical and legal custody of the children. Despite the fact that his children did not officially reside with him, Mark had "access rights" to his children, seeing them five days out of every two weeks.

If the Barnes family had resided in a state that declared a rebuttable presumption for a particular custody arrangement, Mark and Joanne would have been legally expected to adopt a shared arrangement, unless there was a compelling reason to do otherwise. That means that if the Barnes family resided in Minnesota, their divorce would have concluded with joint legal custody, which means that Joanne and Mark would be expected to share the decision making about their joint children. If they resided in Washington, D.C., their divorce decree would have stipulated joint physical and legal custody, with the understanding that April and Nathan would spend substantial periods of time with both of their parents and that both Mark and Joanne would be involved in decision making about the children.

What if new information about the Barnes family were revealed? What if it were determined that Joanne maltreated the children or that Mark physically assaulted Joanne? Most states that have a presumption for joint custody have provisions that prevent joint arrangements in instances of family violence. A discussion of these provisions follows.

REBUTTABLE PRESUMPTIONS IN CHILD-CUSTODY STATUTES

Rebuttable presumptions have entered into child-custody statutes, or been proposed as legislative bills, in three general areas: (1) joint (legal or physical) custody and (2) protection from perpetrators of maltreatment or violence. Presumption laws concerning joint custody generally declare that the state legislature has determined it to be in the best interests of children for their parents to have joint custody. Most often this legislation addresses joint *legal* custody. Rebuttable presumption laws that address situations of violent parents state that no shared parenting will be granted to perpetrators of violence.

History of Laws Declaring a Presumption for Joint Custody

As suggested in previous chapters, in the late 1970s and early 1980s, the political climate strongly favored joint-custody legislation. Although some sources cite that California was the first state to pass a presumption for joint custody [4], other sources contradict this finding. California was the first state to pass a *preference* for joint custody [5, 6].

Joint Physical and Legal Custody

The first two states to declare a rebuttable presumption for joint physical and legal custody were Idaho and Louisiana—both in 1982. The Idaho legislation states:

> Absent a preponderance of the evidence to the contrary, there shall be a presumption that joint custody is in the best interests of a minor child or children. (§ 32-717B)

An award of joint custody alone would encompass both joint physical and legal custody. However, the court can award either or both types of joint custody at its discretion as described in *Roehl v. Roehl* (Idaho Court of Appeals, 113 Idaho 557 [1987]). Other than this court case, there is little documentation of Idaho's law and its implications for families.

Rigby [7] describes Louisiana's 1982 legislation as resulting in "nonconsensual" joint custody:

> There shall be a rebuttable presumption that joint custody is in the best interests of a minor child. [J]oint custody shall mean that parents shall share the physical custody of children of the marriage . . . and shall enjoy natural cotutorship of such children. . . . Physical care and custody shall be shared

by the parents in such a way as to assure a child of frequent and continuing contact with both parents. [8, p. 117]

"Cotutorship" was considered to be the same as "joint legal custody" or "shared parental rights and responsibilities." In the ten years that followed the implementation of this law, the political and legislative climate shifted, and the presumption was ultimately overturned in 1994.

Louisiana's current child custody statute states:

> If the parents agree who is to have custody, the court shall award custody in accordance with their agreement unless the best interests of the child requires a different award. In the absence of agreement, or if the agreement is not in the best interests of the child, the court shall award custody to the parents jointly; however, if custody in one parent is shown by clear and convincing evidence to serve the best interest of the child, the court shall award custody to that parent. (Louisiana Civil Code: Article 132)

The statute still declares that children should enjoy frequent and continuing contact with both of their parents and that to the greatest extent possible, physical custody of the children should be shared equally. One of the unique provisions of the law is that in cases of joint custody, a "domiciliary" parent is named. The domiciliary parent is the parent with whom the child most frequently resides; this parent is vested with full decision-making power concerning all matters of the child's life. Finally, it is *presumed* that decisions made by the domiciliary parent are in the best interests of the child (Louisiana Revised Statute, 9:335). In essence, these provisions state that if parents cannot agree on a child-custody arrangement, the court will order joint physical custody and will assign one parent to have sole legal custody—the so-called "domiciliary parent." All of these provisions stand without actually stating a presumption for this arrangement.

Why the legislature moved to overturn the presumption in child-custody statute is not well documented. The revision was part of a larger set of reforms to all divorce laws in Louisiana, which were recommended by the Persons Committee of the Louisiana State Law Institute [9]. It is true that the 1982 presumption statute was not well received in the courthouse. Research on the attitudes of Louisiana family-court judges during the 1980s and 1990s indicated that judges generally favored traditional physical custody arrangements and they showed strong support for the tender-years doctrine. Only one-quarter of family-court judges supported the notion of joint physical custody despite the legislative mandate, and the preferred child-contact schedule was for children to see noncustodial parents every other weekend [10, 11], despite the fact that they believed that joint physical custody could protect children from a sense of loss [12].

In 1996 under a firestorm of political conflict, the District of Columbia passed a law with a presumption for joint physical and legal custody. The law states:

> There shall be a rebuttable presumption that joint custody is in the best interest of the child or children, except in instances where a judicial officer has found by a preponderance of the evidence that an intrafamily offense, . . . instance[s] of child abuse, . . . child neglect, . . . [or] parental kidnapping [have occurred]. (District of Columbia, Official Code § 16-914)

The law does not define what a joint custodial arrangement is; however, it is understood that a joint arrangement means that a child will have considerable amounts of time with both parents. According to Henry [13], a family-law attorney and a strong proponent of this law, joint custody is defined by what it is not; it is not a traditional sole-custody arrangement, with a "visitation" schedule for the other parent.

Presumption for Joint Legal Custody

Many more states have a presumption for joint legal custody than for joint physical custody. These are laws that presume that it is in the best interests of children for parents to share in the decision making about their children's lives. Sometimes these statutes began as bills declaring a presumption for joint physical and legal custody, but were ultimately watered down [14]. Legislation declaring a presumption for joint legal custody tends to be more politically acceptable because it does not address the direct transfer of children between two homes, it retains some of the inherent entitlements that come with producing offspring, and it does not substantially increase risk to victims of violence.

Presumption Laws That Address Protection from Violence

About a decade after the debate over joint custody was initiated, a new type of presumption law emerged in many state legislatures. This type of statute, which exists in twenty-one states, declares that in instances of family violence, perpetrators will not be granted joint custody or shared parenting responsibilities of any kind. This legislation was the result of concerns that mandating joint custody in violent families might put children and caregivers at risk [15]. In fact, many states cite partner violence as a deciding factor in child-custody decisions [16], especially among states that declare a presumption for some type of joint custody. For example, the state of Minnesota, which has a presumption for joint legal custody if it is requested by either parent, has a second presumption that overrides the first. It states that in instances of family violence, joint legal custody will not be granted because it is not in the best interests of the child.

> The court shall use a rebuttable presumption that upon request of either or both parties, joint legal custody is in the best interests of the child. However, the court shall use a rebuttable presumption that joint legal or physical custody is not in the best interests of the child if domestic abuse, . . . has occurred between the parents. (§ 518.17)

Other Presumptions in Child Custody Law

Over the years, some social scientists, women's advocates, and legal scholars have proposed a "primary caregiver presumption" that would declare that it is in the best interests of children to be placed in the sole custody of their primary caregivers [17]. There has been no recent legislative activity concerning such a presumption; however, West Virginia case law in the 1980s ruled that the physical and legal custody of children should be awarded solely to primary caregivers [18–20]. This type of custodial arrangement is frequently promoted by feminist legal scholars [21] and women's advocates, such as the National Organization for Women (NOW). The California chapter of NOW recently made the following recommendation to the California state legislature.

> Abolish the tendency to assume joint custody is always in the best interests of the child. This is a false presumption with no support in reality. Joint custody should be voluntary, with sole custody default to the primary caregiver at separation. [22, p. 63]

To date, however, the discussion of a primary caregiver presumption is just that, a discussion. It rarely finds its way into the statehouse.

THE DEBATE OVER PRESUMPTION LAWS

The debate concerning a presumption for joint custody breaks down into similar areas to those that were discussed in chapter 5 regarding nonmandated joint custody. The stakeholders of this debate are: (1) those who are concerned about the presence and influence of fathers or men in children's lives—sometimes called fathers' rights advocates; (2) those who are concerned about the status of women in our country, with specific concern linked to independence, power, financial stability, and special concern about safety from violent partners—often referred to as women's advocates or feminists of one sort or another; and (3) those who are concerned about children's well-being, who sometimes make unique contributions to this debate but whose arguments are usually lumped together with one of the former two categories. It should be noted that these are generalizations about the debates on presumption for joint custody.

Proponents of a Presumption for Joint Custody

A number of scholars who have learned from social-science research that children appear to have a better adjustment to divorce when fathers are involved in their lives have suggested that one way to maintain higher levels of father involvement is to grant all divorced fathers joint legal custody. The easiest way to accomplish this, they argue, is to state a presumption, or mandate, that all divorced families adopt arrangements of joint legal custody [23–25]. As part of their rationale for this, they cite statistics indicating that fathers with joint legal custody are more involved with their children. Research on divorced families has demonstrated that fathers with joint legal custody are more involved with their children and are sometimes more compliant with or pay higher levels of child support [26–29]. This body of research, however, is not without its problems, as some of these findings are correlated with parental income [30]; fathers who earn a higher income are the fathers who seek shared legal decision making. Moreover, it may also be the case that fathers who are more involved with their children are the same fathers who seek shared-parenting agreements. One scholar in particular suggests that implementing a presumption for joint legal custody will help to shape public opinions about divorced families and the role of fathers. Several scholars [23, 24] argue that mandating all families to adopt joint legal custody will send a message to both mothers and fathers that the public and our government expect fathers both in and out of marriage to play influential roles in their children's lives.

While these scholars argue for a presumption of joint legal custody, there has also been a strong and vocal community that has indicated a preference for adopting a presumption for joint physical custody [31–33]. These arguments, too, are based on the research, which shows that oftentimes children who have regular and frequent contact with their noncustodial fathers have a better adjustment to divorce, and have fewer academic, social, and behavioral problems [34–38]. Thus, many authors contend that since (some) research demonstrates that children have a better adjustment when they are exposed to their fathers, mandating that families adopt agreements of shared residential responsibilities should increase the overall mental and physical health of all children of divorce [32, 39–43].

Some proponents believe that this is the only way to reverse what is perceived to be a social injustice against fathers in the courts [44, 45]. As discussed in chapter 5, the vast majority of children from divorced families reside with their mothers. Declaring a presumption for joint custody, it is argued, is one way to overturn this bias. On the other hand, it is also known that roughly 90 percent of divorced families walk into the courtroom with a custody agreement in hand; in other words, custody in families is only contested about 10 percent of the time [46, 47]. Ninety percent of the time, parents agree, at least on paper, about the custody arrangements of their children. Since research has shown that between 70 and 80 percent of fathers would like to have had joint or sole custody of their children [14, 47, 48], it is curious that they settle for an arrangement that they reportedly do not desire. Few studies have documented why this is the case, but as covered in chapter 5, Kruk [48] found that 55 percent of fathers report that their attorneys advised against it, arguing that children are "better off" when they live with their mothers. Divorcing fathers may not understand—especially if they are *pro se* litigants—that they could request joint physical custody; they may want to avoid an expensive custody battle, they may not want to hurt their wives or place their children in the middle of a legal war, and they may have heard rumors that courts are biased against fathers [39]. For those who want to advance the position of universal joint physical custody or shared residential schedules among divorced families, declaring a presumption for joint physical custody may be one way to do this.

Public perception of custodial arrangements has rarely been examined, but results from a 2004 ballot measure in Massachusetts suggest strong public support for a presumption for both joint legal and physical custody [49]. The ballot, which was presented in a quarter of the state's legislative districts, read:

> Shall the state representative from this district be instructed to vote for legislation to create a strong presumption in child custody cases in favor of joint physical and legal custody, so that the court will order that the children have equal access to both parents as much as possible, except where there is clear and convincing evidence that one parent is unfit, or that joint custody is not possible due to the fault of one of the parents? [50]

The measure was overwhelming approved, with 84.5 percent of voters indicating support for a presumption of joint physical custody [50, 51].

Opponents of a Presumption for Joint Custody

The concerns of opponents to joint custody have previously been given in this text, but are summarized here again. Those who express opposition to a presumption for joint custody have several points of concern regarding the potential effects of mandated joint custody on the well-being, primarily, of women. One of the primary concerns has been the potential risk to victims of partner violence. The National Violence Against Women Survey [52] reports that women separated from their spouses experience more partner violence than married women in intact relationships, and the exchange of children between divorced parents provides opportunities for further ill-treatment toward victims of partner violence [15]. Policy makers responded to this concern by passing legislation that mandates that in instances of family violence joint-custody arrangements will not be granted. According to the American Bar Association, almost all fifty states list partner violence or parental maltreatment as one of the criteria used to decide child-custody cases [53]. One potential problem with presumptive legislation in this arena is that it places victims in the position of providing evidence to overturn a presumption for joint custody [54]. This means that absent legal or health-related documentation, it could be difficult to prove that one is a victim of partner violence.

A second concern about a presumption for joint custody centers on the economic stability of divorced mothers. Some scholars worry that child-support orders will be reduced because of a joint physical parenting agreement [4]. The idea behind such reductions is that fathers will need to provide for their children in their own home, as well as the mother's home. If child-support orders are lowered and fathers do not spend their allotted time with their children, divorced mothers will bear an even higher financial burden of raising children than they do now. With only 75 percent of child-support orders to custodial mothers in full or partial compliance [55], legislation with a presumption for joint physical custody may present as a legitimate problem, especially for high-risk families. One of the central objections to the District of Columbia presumption for joint custody was that the law was based on research that studied white, middle-class, educated families. Barry [56] argues that this research has low generalizability to those who live in the District of Columbia, the preponderance of whom are poor, black families. Of course, there is some evidence to suggest that fathers who see, or are permitted to see, their children more frequently are more compliant with their child-support orders [27, 28]. Thus, one could argue that if fathers are spending increasing periods of time with their children, they will be supporting those children in their own homes, which will lower child-related expenses for mothers, and possibly increase fathers' compliance in child-support orders, albeit in lower amounts. This does not ignore the fact that some fathers will continue to fail to be in compliance with their child-support orders. This fact is true of all noncustodial parents, mothers and fathers alike [55].

A third concern about laws declaring a presumption for joint custody centers on the status and power of women and their roles as nurturers. Kuehl [15] specifically argues that since women are in lower positions of power in our society, they may be forced into agreeing to, or fail to fight, presumptions for shared parenting that in actuality they find unacceptable. Moreover, a presumption for joint custody of any type minimizes the important role that most mothers play in their children's lives as primary caregivers. Thus, argue opponents of presumption laws, in addition to a declining standard of living and loss of their marriage, the legislature and courts also expect divorcing mothers to relinquish half of their duties as caregivers [57]—the equivalent of which is not demanded from men. At the same time, some men argue that at a time when federal and state governments, as well as philanthropic organizations, are spending millions of dollars a year to get fathers involved in their children's lives, why would legislators want to limit contact between willingly engaged fathers and their children [58]?

"Best Interest of the Child" Standard

Finally, there are children's advocates who fall on both sides of the argument with regard to mandates in joint physical and joint legal custody. For example, there are some who believe that joint custody is a way to affirm for children that "families are forever" [43]. There are others, however, who, aside from the often bitter and gender-based battles over joint custody, have serious concerns about mandating shared parenting. Most of these concerns center on mandating joint physical custody; other times it is unclear if joint legal custody is also opposed. The primary concern springs from the argument that a presumption for joint custody may override the current foundation for all child-custody decisions: the "best interests of the child" standard. Schulman and Pitt [59] argue that the best interests of the child necessitates a "case-by-case" approach to making custody decisions. Moreover, they argue, not all families may be capable of co-parenting together and as a result children might suffer. This concern is especially raised by the scholars Maccoby and Mnookin [47], who state that "in those cases where the parents are involved in bitter dispute, we believe a presumption for joint custody would do harm" (p. 285). However, these scholars also write that they cautiously support a presumption for joint legal custody. They argue that this kind of legislative action is symbolically important because it acknowledges the dual rights and responsibilities of both mothers and fathers with respect to their children after divorce.

The "best interests of the child" standard serves as the foundation for all custody decisions for divorcing families. This is the primary consideration for all legal decisions affecting children, and unlike the tender-years doctrine is written into state statute. As noted, a few authors have raised concerns about a contradiction between the "best interests" standard and a presumption for joint custody. There have been presumption laws affecting joint custody for well over twenty years at the writing of this book, and there have been no legal cases that have argued that a presumption for joint custody should override the "best interests" standard. This isn't to say that it couldn't be tried. At the same time, most presumption laws leave a "loophole" for instances in which it might be harmful for children to be placed in shared residential arrangements, such as in the state of Wisconsin, as noted below.

> Except as provided in par. (d), the court shall presume that joint legal custody is in the best interest of the child. . . . (d) [I]f the court finds by a preponderance of the evidence that a party has engaged in a pattern or serious incident of interspousal battery . . . or domestic abuse . . . there is a rebuttable presumption that it is detrimental to the child and contrary to the best interest of the child to award joint or sole legal custody to that party. (Wis. Stat. § 767.24)

Targets of Presumption Laws

Any thorough policy analysis should include not only a discussion of stakeholders, but a discussion of intended targets as well. The "majority of divorced families" is the simple answer to this question. Since at most, one-quarter of divorced families have shared living arrangements [60], mandating joint physical custody could substantially change the lives of most divorced families. The discussion of targets, however, is not as simple as one might think. For example, fathers' advocates would argue that all family members are the targets of presumption laws mandating shared residential schedules because they believe that all members of the family would be better off. This would, in turn, improve the quality of the parent-child relationship, and having a shared residential schedule would, for mothers, lift some of the burdens that come with being a sole residential care provider. Those whose arguments are aligned with fathers would also likely highlight the possible rewards to the public in general. If there is a correlation between father-child access and child-support compliance rates, then fathers would likely pay more support and families would therefore be less dependent on government assistance.

Women's advocates, however, who believe that children, as well as women, would be harmed by a mandate for joint physical custody, would argue that the sole beneficiary of presumption laws would be men, who would benefit from a more flexible child-contact schedule, reap the rewards of having the title of "joint physical custodian" without actually coming forward to do any of the work, and enjoy the financial gains that come with lowered child-support orders. They would likely also argue that a mandate for joint physical custody could harm the American public. Since they believe that child-support orders would likely be reduced and that most fathers would not see their children any more regularly than they do now, more female-headed households with minor children would face financial ruin than do so today, and therefore would need to rely on the general support of the public.

Thus, a discussion of intended targets cannot be free from a discussion of ideology. In actuality, all of the targets are the same: children, divorced mothers, divorced fathers, and the American public. The consequences and outcomes for these targets, however, are the source of much contention.

PRESUMPTION LAWS TODAY

Status of Presumption Laws

Today there are eight states or regions—District of Columbia, Idaho, Minnesota, New Hampshire, New Mexico, Texas, West Virginia, and Wisconsin—that have a presumption for joint custody; their statutes are summarized in table 6.1. In Washington, D.C., the statutory presumption is for both joint legal and physical custody. The Idaho statute does not specifically state whether the presumption pertains to legal or physical custody, and it is understood that it can apply to either type of arrangement. The remaining six laws declare a presumption for joint legal custody. Table 6.2 documents that there are twenty-one states with presumption laws that provide protections for victims of violence, ensuring that joint custody will not be granted in cases of child or partner maltreatment.

Implementation of Presumption Laws

There has been almost no research conducted on presumption laws. Thus, it is difficult to know whether presumption laws are passed as a gesture to appease lobbyists or whether they are truly declarations of public policy and implemented as such. Anecdotal evidence of Louisiana's 1982 law suggests that the law was never fully implemented and that joint-custody arrangements are more popular today than they were when there was a presumption for joint legal and physical custody [61]. In a study that I conducted on the state of New Hampshire's presumption for joint legal custody, I found that the law is fully

Table 6.1. States Declaring a Presumption for Joint-custody Arrangements

State	Type of Statute	Statute No.	Language
District of Columbia	Presumption for joint legal and physical custody	D.C. Code § 16-914	There shall be a rebuttable presumption that joint custody is in the best interest of the child or children, except in instances where a judicial officer has found by a preponderance of the evidence that an intrafamily offense . . . an instance of child abuse . . . an instance of child neglect . . ., or where parental kidnapping has occurred. There shall be a rebuttable presumption that joint custody is not in the best interest of the child or children if a judicial officer finds by a preponderance of the evidence that an intrafamily offense . . . an instance of child abuse . . ., an instance of child neglect . . ., or where parental kidnapping has occurred.
Idaho	Presumption for joint custody	Idaho Code § 32-717B	(4) Except as provided in subsection (5), of this section, absent a preponderance of the evidence to the contrary, there shall be a presumption that joint custody is in the best interests of a minor child or children. (5) There shall be a presumption that joint custody is not in the best interests of a minor child if one (1) of the parents is found by the court to be a habitual perpetrator of domestic violence as defined in section 39-6303, Idaho Code.
Minnesota	Presumption for joint legal custody	Minn. Stat. § 518.17	The court shall use a rebuttable presumption that upon request of either or both parties, joint legal custody is in the best interests of the child. However, the court shall use a rebuttable presumption that joint legal or physical custody is not in the best interests of the child if domestic abuse, as defined in section 518B.01, has occurred between the parents.

(continues)

Table 6.1. (continued)

State	Type of Statute	Statute No.	Language
New Hampshire	Presumption for joint legal custody	R.S.A. § 458:17	Except as provided in subparagraph (c), in the making of any order relative to such custody there shall be a presumption, affecting the burden of proof, that joint legal custody is in the best interest of minor children: (a) Where the parents have agreed to an award of joint legal custody or so agree in open court at a hearing for the purpose of determining the custody of the minor children of the marriage . . . (b) Upon the application of either parent for joint legal custody, in which case it may be awarded in the discretion of the court . . . (c) Where the court finds that abuse . . . has occurred, the court shall consider such abuse as harmful to children and as evidence in determining whether joint legal custody is appropriate. In such cases, the court shall make custody and visitation orders that best protect the children or the abused spouse or both.
New Mexico	Presumption for joint legal custody	N.M. Stat. Ann. § 40-4-9.1	There shall be a presumption that joint custody is in the best interests of a child in an initial custody determination. . . . B(9) If a determination is made that domestic abuse has occurred, the court shall set forth findings that the custody or visitation ordered by the court adequately protects the child, the abused parent or other household member . . . L(4) "joint custody" means an order of the court awarding custody of a child to two parents. Joint custody does not imply an equal division of the child's time between the parents or an equal division of financial responsibility for the child . . .

Texas	Presumption for joint legal custody	Tex. Fam. Code § 153.131	(b) It is a rebuttable presumption that the appointment of the parents of a child as joint managing conservators is in the best interest of the child. A finding of a history of family violence involving the parents of a child removes the presumption under this subsection.
West Virginia	Presumption for joint legal custody	W. Va. Code § 48-9-207	(b) If each of the child's legal parents has been exercising a reasonable share of parenting functions for the child, the court shall presume that an allocation of decision-making responsibility to both parents jointly is in the child's best interests. The presumption is overcome if there is a history of domestic abuse, or by a showing that joint allocation of decision-making responsibility is not in the child's best interest.
Wisconsin	Presumption for joint legal custody	Wis. Stat. § 767.24	Except as provided in par. (d), the court shall presume that joint legal custody is in the best interest of the child . . . (d) . . . if the court finds by a preponderance of the evidence that a party has engaged in a pattern or serious incident of interspousal battery . . . or domestic abuse . . . there is a rebuttable presumption that it is detrimental to the child and contrary to the best interest of the child to award joint or sole legal custody to that party.

Table 6.2. Laws Indicating a Presumption against Joint Custody/Shared Parenting in Instances of Family Violence (Yes = 21)

State	Presumption?	Statute No.
Alabama	Yes	§ 30-3-131
Alaska	Yes	§ 25.24.150(g)
Arizona	Yes	A.R.S. § § 25-403(N) and 25-403(E)
Arkansas	Yes	A.C.A. § 9-15-215(c)
California	Yes	Cal. Fam. Code § 3044
Colorado	No	
Connecticut	No	
Delaware	Yes	13 Del C. § 705A(b)
District of Columbia	No	
Florida	Yes	Fla. Stat. § 61.13(2)(b)(2)
Georgia	No	
Hawaii	Yes	H.R.S. § 571-46(9)
Idaho	Yes	Idaho Code § 32-717B
Illinois	No	
Indiana	Yes	Ind. Code Ann. § 31-17-2-8.3
Iowa	Yes	Iowa Code § 598.41
Kansas	No	
Kentucky	No	
Louisiana	No	
Maine	No	
Maryland	No	
Massachusetts	Yes	A.L.M. Ch. 208 §31A
Michigan	No	
Minnesota	Yes	Minn Sta. § 518.17
Mississippi	Yes	Miss. Ann. Code § 93-5-24
Missouri	No	
Montana	No	
Nebraska	No	
Nevada	Yes	N.R.S. § 125.480(5)
New Hampshire	No	
New Jersey	No	
New Mexico	No	
New York	No	
North Carolina	No	
North Dakota	Yes	N.D. Code § 14-09-06.2
Ohio	No	
Oklahoma	Yes	43 Okl. St. § 112.2(B)(2)
Oregon	Yes	O.R.S. § 107.137(2)
Pennsylvania	No	
Rhode Island	No	
South Carolina	No	
South Dakota	No	
Tennessee	No	
Texas	Yes	Tex. Fam. Code § 153.131(b)
Utah	No	

State	Presumption?	Statute No.
Vermont	No	
Virginia	No	
Washington	Yes	R.C.W. § 26.09.191: If adult is a convicted sex offender
West Virginia	No	§ 48-9-207(a)(c)
Wisconsin	Yes	Wis. Stat. § 767.24(2)(d)(1)
Wyoming	No	

implemented, with 93 percent of families having this joint arrangement [62]. One study that used data from the National Survey of Households and Families found that fathers who live in states with a presumption or preference for joint legal custody are more likely to actually have such an arrangement [29]. The conclusions of all of these sources may be confounded by the fact that there appears to be a strong and consistent nationwide trend toward arrangements of joint legal custody between divorced parents in all states, regardless of a presumption [63].

There has been no formal attempt to evaluate the implementation of laws declaring a presumption for joint physical custody in any of the states (regions) that have had a presumption for joint legal custody. An informal survey was conducted by the Children's Rights Council a couple of years after implementation of the District of Columbia's presumption for joint legal and physical custody [64]. The results indicated that roughly 20 percent of families were receiving joint physical custody at that time. The Children's Rights Council indicated that this was an increase over previous years. It thus appears that a presumption for joint physical custody may actually move families toward more joint arrangements.

OUTCOMES OF LAWS DECLARING A PRESUMPTION

The divorce literature is lacking in both quantity and substance for almost every social policy that is addressed in this book. It is, however, most pronounced with regard to laws declaring a presumption for joint legal custody. The reason for this is twofold. First, decision makers continue to make policy decisions without the aid of social-science research, and thus, there has not been a demand for new research to help guide the policy-making process. Second, presumption laws mandating joint custody are rare enough that it is difficult to study their effects. This is less true with regard to presumptions of joint legal custody, but it is especially true with regard to laws that mandate joint physical custody—a law that has only existed in three different states or jurisdictions in the country.

Studies Investigating Outcomes of Presumption Laws

To date, only one study has investigated the effect of a law mandating a presumption for joint custody. In this study, I evaluated the impact of a presumption for joint legal custody in the state of New Hampshire on the involvement of divorced fathers with their children [62]. New Hampshire's presumption for joint legal custody was implemented in 1982 and remained unexamined for almost two decades. Divorced fathers from the state of New Hampshire were compared with divorced fathers from the neighboring state of Maine, which has no presumption. The sample for this study was selected by taking a census from court records of all families that had divorced between 1996 and 1998 in six matched New Hampshire and Maine counties. With a modest response rate of 39 percent (n = 316 divorced fathers), I found that the law was fully implemented, with 93 percent of New Hampshire families having joint legal custody. The results of the study indicated that divorced New Hampshire fathers were not any more involved with their children than divorced Maine fathers. However, Maine was likely a poor comparison state, as 90 percent of families in this state also had joint legal custody, even though there is no stated presumption in favor of this arrangement. As more families adopt this arrangement, it may be difficult to evaluate the success of laws declaring a presumption for joint legal custody because there will be fewer comparison families.

Studies Estimating Outcomes of Presumption Laws

It is uncertain how many children from divorced families are exposed to high levels of parental conflict. Research using small, nonrepresentative samples estimates that it is between 21 and 34 percent [47, 65, 66]. A large and representative sample from California estimates it to be around 15 percent [47]. There is strong consensus that children who are exposed to high parental conflict have poor outcomes [67]. Interparental hostility and lack of cooperation often lead to impaired parent-child relationships, lower adaptive functioning in children [68], behavior problems [69], and children feeling caught between their parents [70]. Conflict appears to be such an important factor in predicting children's outcomes that children of parents in high-conflict marriages who divorce have better outcomes than children of parents in high-conflict marriages who remain married [67, 71]. Such conclusions are drawn from studies in which families do not have joint custody. There have been no studies that have examined the effects of a presumption for joint legal or physical custody on children's adjustment, primarily because so few jurisdictions mandate joint arrangements. Johnston and colleagues have, however, estimated some of the potential outcomes of children living in mandated joint arrangements with parents who have high levels of conflict.

Johnston, Kline, and Tschann [72] examined one hundred California families who were entrenched in custody and child-contact disputes in the mid-1980s; in thirty-five of these families, children had frequent access to their parents' homes—simulating a joint physical custodial arrangement. The remainder of the sample were in sole physical custodial arrangements with either their mothers or fathers. In many instances families had "agreements" that were recommended by a court mediator or mandated by a judge, since parents could not decide on their own; thus, these cases strongly parallel the circumstances of presumption laws. The results indicated that children who had more frequent access to both parents and who made repeated transitions between homes had more behavioral problems and lower scores on measures of social competence. Specifically, their parents rated them as being more depressed, withdrawn, and uncommunicative; as having more somatic problems; and as being more aggressive.

In a review of studies on children of divorce, Johnston [73] discussed in particular one unpublished study that also focused on families of high conflict that had court-recommended or court-ordered arrangements. The sample for this 1992, California-based study comprised seventy-five children from sixty high-conflict families who had been referred by the family court for counseling services. Thirty-six percent (n = 27) of these children were in joint-custody families. According to Johnston, children who had more frequent access to both of their parents' homes were again more likely to have behavioral and emotional maladjustment and to demonstrate physical symptoms of stress, such as stomachaches and headaches. Children of these high-conflict families with shared-parenting arrangements were also more likely to have problems getting along with their peers, when compared to children in sole-custody access families.

Summary

There isn't enough research to draw any substantial conclusions about the effects of presumption laws on child adjustment or family functioning. It is unknown whether a presumption for joint legal custody actually results in more father involvement. Moreover, although children who live in voluntary joint physical-custody arrangements seem to be neither helped nor harmed by these arrangements, there is evidence that mandated joint physical custody in families of high conflict might be harmful to children.

CONCLUSION

At this point, the research on mandated joint custody is insufficient to guide most policy making on the matter of a presumption of joint custody. As a consequence, arguments made in favor of or against presumptions continue primarily to rely on ideology rather than science. Despite my knowledge as a scholar of divorced families, I, too, am at a loss—far more so than with any other social policies addressed in this book—to make a recommendation free from ideology. Using what research is available and holding the notion that children have an inherent need for and right to regular and unrestricted access to both of the parents with whom they have established relationships, I conclude that a presumption for joint legal and physical custody may be in the best interests of children. Much research has demonstrated that children who have regular and frequent access to both of their parents have a better adjustment to living in a divorced family. Moreover, from the research that was reviewed in chapter 5, one can conclude that children in joint-custody families are not routinely harmed by joint custody.

In the concluding chapter of this book, I will explore some of the ways in which social policy can help to shape attitudes and cultural norms. This is even the case when legislative bills are unsuccessful, as the debate that accompanies controversial legislation allows the public to engage in a discussion that may ultimately further social change, even if it is not directed by statute. My conclusion that a presumption for joint legal and physical custody may be in the best interests of children is based on the belief that social policy about divorced families can influence and shape our culture's attitudes about divorced families and the expectations that we hold for both parents after a divorce has occurred. There are many occasions when social policy has effectively influenced social attitudes and brought about more positive social behaviors, such as legislation that outlaws smoking in public spaces and buildings, laws that declare a special status for children and the rights that are afforded them, legislation that outlaws and punishes racial discrimination, and laws that mandate the use of bicycle helmets for children. Often these laws, when coupled with public education, have shaped social attitudes and behaviors of the majority of our culture. There would seem to be no reason to believe that the same would not work for families of divorce.

This said, I have the same concerns as do others about the safety of children and limiting their exposure to parental conflict and parental violence. However, I also agree with Henry, who argues that public policies are not based on pathology [74]. Legislation is based on the majority population, with protections established for aberrations. The majority of divorces do not involve high levels of parental conflict, violence, or maltreatment, and our laws should accurately reflect that. Many states have legislation that establishes protections for victims of violence through a presumption that states that joint custody will not be granted to violent parents. The same kinds of provisions can be made in instances of high conflict. Joint physical custody (and perhaps legal custody as well) should not be awarded in cases where children would be exposed to continuous conflict. Our laws can reflect the attitudes and concerns that we have about protecting children from conflict.

Moreover, legislation could stipulate that parents who cease to have contact with their children could stand to lose their parenting rights. Parents who maltreat and neglect their children lose their parental rights, and a similar system could be put in place for parents of divorce. In no way am I arguing that children should be placed in the residential care of parents who do not demonstrate the skills or willingness to care for their children. Indeed I argue that the best interests of the child should continue to be the overriding principle in all custody matters. This standard should be maintained, perhaps through a presumption of its own, while also promoting shared parenting.

Professionals, policy makers, and the public at large worry about the psychological effects on children who are regularly "shuffled" between two homes—to meet the so-called "50-50 standard" of joint physical custody. Never has a presumption law stated that joint residential custody means that parenting time is divided equally. The spirit behind a presumption law is that both parents remain primary in their children's lives and that neither parent is a visitor. Parents with shared residential parenting plans can arrange for children to split their time in a number of different ways: 50-50, 60-40, 70-30, all of which can depend on the developmental and psychological needs of children as they mature.

In short, I support a presumption for shared decision making and shared residential schedules. I maintain that it is possible to write social policy that both expects and encourages both parents to be involved in their children's lives, while still providing protections for the most vulnerable members of these broken families.

REFERENCES

1. Gaynor, J. K. *Profile of the law*. 1978, Washington, DC: The Bureau of National Affairs, Inc.
2. Lawyers Cooperative Publishing. *American Jurisprudence*. 2nd ed. Vol. 29. 1994, Rochester, NY: Lawyers Cooperative Publishing.
3. Walker, D. M. *The Oxford companion to law*. 1980, New York: Clarendon Press.
4. Hardcastle, G. W. Joint custody: A family court judge's perspective. *Family Law Quarterly*, 1998, 32(1): pp. 201–19.

5. Folberg, J., ed. *Joint custody and shared parenting*. 1st ed. 1984, Washington, DC: Bureau of National Affairs, Inc., Association of Family and Conciliation Courts.

6. Cook, J. A. California's joint custody statute. In *Joint custody and shared parenting*, ed. J. Folberg. 1984, Washington, DC: Bureau of National Affairs, Inc., Association of Family and Conciliation Courts.

7. Rigby, K. 1993 custody and child support legislation. *Louisiana Law Review*, 1994, 55: pp. 103–38.

8. Hawkins, L. E. Joint custody in Louisiana. *Louisiana Law Review*, 1982, 43: pp. 85–117.

9. Rigby, K., and K. S. Spaht. Louisiana's new divorce legislation: Background and commentary. *Louisiana Law Review*, 1993, 54(September): pp. 19–89.

10. Stamps, L. E., S. Kunen, and R. Lawyer. Judicial attitudes regarding custody and visitation issues. *Journal of Divorce and Remarriage*, 1996, 25(1/2): pp. 23–37.

11. Stamps, L. E., S. Kunen, and A. Rock-Faucheux. Judges' beliefs dealing with child custody decisions. *Journal of Divorce and Remarriage*, 1997, 28(1/2): pp. 3–16.

12. Selleck, L. R., et al. Attitudes of attorneys and judges toward joint custody and its litigation. *Journal of Divorce*, 1989, 12(4): pp. 103–16.

13. Henry, R. K. The District of Columbia's new joint custody of children act. *The Washington Lawyer*, 1996, July/August: pp. 50–55.

14. Douglas, E. M. The influence of public policies on human behavior: Is there an effect of a New Hampshire law stating a presumption for joint legal custody on father involvement in divorced families? *Public Policy Program*. 2002, Boston: University of Massachusetts, p. 354.

15. Kuehl, S. J. Against joint custody: A dissent to the General Bullmoose theory. *Family and Conciliation Courts Review*, 1989, 27(2): pp. 37–45.

16. Reihing, K. M. Protecting victims of domestic violence and their children after divorce: The American Law Institute's model. *Family and Conciliation Courts Review*, 1999, 37(3): pp. 393–410.

17. Thompson, R. A. Children after divorce. *The Future of Children*, 1994, 4(1): pp. 210–35.

18. Carpenter, K. Why are mothers still losing: An analysis of gender bias in child custody determinations. *Detroit College Law Review*, 1996, (Spring): pp. 33–61.

19. Polikoff, N. D. The case for the "primary parent." *New York Times*, March 13. 1982, p. 24.

20. Crippen, G. Stumbling beyond best interests of the child: Reexamining child custody standard-setting in the wake of Minnesota's four year experiment with the primary caretaker preference. *Minnesota Law Review*, 1990, 75: pp. 427–503.

21. Huber, A. B. Children at risk in the politics of child custody suits: Acknowledging their needs for nurture. *University of Louisville Journal of Family Law*, 1993, 32: pp. 33–63.

22. California National Organization for Women. *California NOW family court report*. 2002.

23. Barnes, S. N. Strengthening the father-child relationship through a joint custody presumption. *Willamette Law Review*, 1999, 35(Summer): pp. 601–28.

24. Maldonado, S. Beyond economic fatherhood: Encouraging divorced fathers to parent. *University of Pennsylvania Law Review*, 2005, 153(January): pp. 921–1009.

25. Melton, B. J. Solomon's wisdom or Solomon's wisdom lost: Child custody in North Dakota—a presumption that joint custody is in the best interests of the child in custody disputes. *North Dakota Law Review*, 1997, 73: pp. 263–98.

26. Seltzer, J. A. Relationships between fathers and children who live apart: The father's role after separation. *Journal of Marriage and Family*, 1991, 53: pp. 79–101.

27. Seltzer, J. A., N. C. Schaeffer, and H. Charng. Family ties after divorce: The relationship between visiting and paying child support. *Journal of Marriage and the Family*, 1989, 51: pp. 1013–32.

28. Pearson, J., and N. Thoennes. Supporting children after divorce: The influence of custody on support levels and payments. *Family Law Quarterly*, 1988, 22(3): pp. 319–39.

29. Seltzer, J. A. Father by law: Effects of joint legal custody on nonresident fathers' involvement with children. *Demography*, 1998, 35: pp. 135–46.

30. Seltzer, J. A. Legal custody arrangements and children's economic welfare. *American Journal of Sociology*, 1991, 96(4): pp. 895–929.

31. Roman, M., and S. Dichter, Fathers and feminism: Backlash within the women's movement. *Conciliation Courts Review*, 1985, 23(2): pp. 37–45.

32. Roman, M., and W. Haddad. *The disposable parent: The case for joint custody*. 1978, New York: Holt.

33. Children's Rights Council, *The best parent is both parents*. April 28, 2002 n.d. http://www.gocrc.com/ (January 5, 2005).

34. Brody, G., and R. Forehand. Interparental conflict, relationship with the noncustodial father, and the adolescent post-divorce adjustment. *Journal of Applied Developmental Psychology*, 1990, 11: pp. 139–47.

35. Lee, M. Y. Post-divorce interparental conflict, children's contact with both parents, children's emotional responses and children's behavioral adjustments. *Journal of Divorce and Remarriage*, 1997, 28: pp. 61–82.

36. Pruett, M. K., and K. D. Pruett. "Only God decides": Young children's perception of divorce and the legal system. *Journal of the American Academy of Child & Adolescent Psychiatry* 1999, 38 (12): 1544–550.

37. Pruett, M. K., et al. Family and legal indicators of child adjustment to divorce among families with young children. *Journal of Family Psychology*, 2003, 17(2): pp. 169–80.

38. Stern, M., J. E. Northman, and M. R. Van Slyck. Father absence and adolescent "problem behaviors": Alcohol consumption, drug use and sexual activity. *Adolescence*, 1984, 19(74): pp. 301–12.

39. Fetzner, W. N., Fathers deserve equal justice in the courts, *Christian Science Monitor*, June 22, 1990, p. 19.

40. Foster, C. Plea for fathers' rights: divorced but still a dad, *Christian Science Monitor*, July 6, 1982, p. 2.

41. Kruk, E. *The time for shared parenting is now*. 2005, Ontario. 2005, http://www.canadiancrc.com/articles/Nat_Post_Time_for_shared_parenting_is_now_08FEB05.htm (February 8, 2006).

42. Robinson, H. L. Joint custody: An idea whose time has come. *Journal of Family Law*, 1982, 21(4): pp. 641–85.

43. Elkin, M. Joint custody: Affirming that parents and families are forever. *Social Work*, 1987, 32(1): pp. 18–24.

44. Wells, K. Divorced dads: Tell their side of the story. *St. Petersburg Times*, May 15, 1989, p. 1D.

45. Yenckel, J. T. Families: Fighting for fathers' rights. *Washington Post*. January 13, 1982, p. B5.

46. Hastings, H. *The New Hampshire divorce handbook*. 1999, Amherst, NH: Amoskeag Press.

47. Maccoby, E. E., and R. H. Mnookin. *Dividing the child: Social and legal dilemmas of custody*. 1992, Cambridge, MA: Harvard University Press.

48. Kruk, E., Child custody determination: An analysis of the litigation model, legal practices, and men's experiences in the process. *Journal of Men's Studies*, 1992, 1(2): pp. 163–85.

49. Young, C. Equal access to children after a divorce. *The Boston Globe*. October 16, 2004, p. A19, section: opinion.

50. Fatherhood Coalition. *Shared Parenting ballot initiative election results*. 2004.

51. Fathers and Families. *Ballot initiative*. 2004, Boston, Massachusetts.

52. Tjaden, P., and N. Thoennes. *Extent, nature and consequences of intimate partner violence: Findings from the National Violence Against Women Survey*. 2000, U.S. Department of Justice.

53. American Bar Association. *Tables summarizing the law in the fifty states, Table 2*. 2003, http://www.abanet.org/family/familylaw/tables.html (March 23, 2004).

54. Barry, M. M. A leap backwards: D.C.'s joint custody of children act. *The Washington Lawyer*, 1996, Nov/Dec: pp. 41–47.

55. U.S. Bureau of the Census. *Custodial mothers and fathers and their child support: 2001*. 2003, Washington, DC: U.S. Bureau of the Census.

56. Barry, M. M. The District of Columbia's joint custody presumption: Misplaced blame and simplistic solutions. *Catholic University Law Review*, 1997, 46(Spring): pp. 767.

57. Carbone, J. R. A feminist perspective on divorce. *Future of Children*, 1994, 4(1): pp. 183–209.

58. Holstein, N., *Where's dad? Boston Globe*, June 19, 2005.

59. Schulman, J., and V. Pitt. Second thoughts on joint custody: Analysis of legislation and its implications for women and children. *Golden Gate Law Review*, 1982, 12: pp. 539–77.

60. Kuhn, D. R. Shared parenting ranges from 19 percent to 25.8 percent of divorced families in the U.S. *Speak out for children*, 2003, (Winter): pp. 19–21.

61. Spaht, K. S. *Louisiana family law*. E. M. Douglas, Editor. 2005, March 10. Personal communication.

62. Douglas, E. M. The effect of a presumption for joint legal custody on father involvement in divorced families. *The Journal of Divorce and Remarriage*, 2003, 40(3/4): pp. 1–10.

63. Kelly, J. B. The determination of child custody. *Future of Children*, 1994, 4(1): pp. 121–42.

64. Levy, D. Personal communication to author. April 28, 2004.

65. Ahrons, C. R. The continuing coparental relationship between divorced spouses. *American Journal of Orthopsychiatry*, 1981, 51(3): pp. 415–28.

66. Silitsky, D. Correlates of psychosocial adjustment in adolescents from divorced families. *Journal of Divorce and Remarriage*, 1996, 26(1/2): pp. 151–64.

67. Amato, P. R., and B. Keith. Parental divorce and the well-being of children: A meta-analysis. *Psychological Bulletin*, 1991, 110(1): pp. 26–46.

68. Pruett, M. K., et al. Family and legal indicators of child adjustment to divorce among families with young children. *Journal of Family Psychology*, 2003, 17(2): pp. 169–80.

69. Amato, P. R., and S. C. Rezac. Contact with nonresidential parents, interparental conflict and children's behavior. *Journal of Family Issues*, 1994, 15(2): pp. 191–207.

70. Amato, P. R. The consequences of divorce for adults and children. *Journal of Marriage and the Family*, 2000, 62: pp. 1269–87.

71. Jekielek, S. A. Parental conflict, marital disruption and children's emotional well-being. *Social Forces*, 1998, 76(3): pp. 905–35.

72. Johnston, J. R., M. Klein, and J. M. Tschann. Ongoing postdivorce conflict: Effects on children of joint custody and frequent access. *American Journal of Orthopsychiatry*, 1989, 59: pp. 576–92.

73. Johnston, J. R. Children's adjustment in sole custody compared to joint custody families and principles for custody decision making. *Family and Conciliation Courts Review*, 1995, 33(4): pp. 415–25.

74. *The joint custody of children amendment act of 1995*. Ronald K. Henry, testimony, 1995. http://www.horut-shava.org.il/act/legistlation/custody/case_for_joint.htm (May 3, 2006).

7

Emerging Trends: Difficult Cases and Efforts Toward Prevention

New problems and proposed solutions pertaining to families of divorce are routinely emerging in the media, scholarly literature, statehouses, and the courtroom. Some of the issues that emerged over the past five to ten years include the question of what to do when children refuse to see one of their parents [1], when children are denied access to one of their parents [2], the intersection of intimate-partner violence with custody and other divorce-related concerns [3–11], and addressing perceived gender inequalities in custody decisions [12]. A few issues, however, have reached, or deserve, center stage and will be the focus of this chapter: parental relocation—the circumstance in which one parent wants to move with his or her children and the other parent contests this move, prevention programs for families of divorce—which are intended to limit the harmful effects of divorce on children and parents, and covenant marriage legislation—laws that are intended to lower the divorce rate.

PARENTAL RELOCATION

Described by the media as the "most contentious and fastest-growing kind of custody litigation in America" [13], parental relocation cases have become as contentious as presumptions for joint custody and are currently stealing the limelight from other divorce-related issues. Parental relocation problems have traditionally been handled in the courtroom; the recent media attention to these cases, however, has prompted legislative bills and hearings in many statehouses throughout the country. While the particulars in individual relocation cases vary on many different factors, such as child age, custodial arrangement, quality of the parent-child relationship, and motivation for wanting to move, there are, nevertheless, common themes. Almost all parental relocation cases involve the physical custodian of a child wanting to move with the child to a location that would place the child at considerable distance from the nonphysical custodial parent. Cases concerning parental relocation that have been presented in court have ranged from a parent moving less than an hour away [14] to a parent moving to the other side of the globe [15]. Most instances of relocation, however, involve a physical custodian moving across one or several state lines, or at least far enough to substantially reduce and limit frequency of contact between the nonphysical custodian and the child. These cases are substantial enough in quantity that approximately one-third of child-support payments in the 1990s were made across state lines [16].

History of Relocation Cases

The handling of relocation cases has gone through a number of different phases, with most transitions paralleling major social shifts and court rulings. The earliest contested case of parental relocation that appeared in a major news source was in 1981 when a divorced mother residing in New York fought to relocate to Las Vegas with her child, in order to pursue a singing career [17]. The case worked its way through several levels within the state-court system, and ultimately the New York State Appeals Court denied the mother's request for relocation, arguing that limiting contact between father and child would not benefit the child or the father. This ruling reflected the earliest "official" approach for resolving cases of parental relocation. Although state statutes did not usually address this issue, there was a judicially imposed presumption that moving children away from the nonresidential parent would ultimately harm children. Such rulings were based on social-science research that demonstrated that children who have regular and frequent access to both their parents have better outcomes [18, 19]. There were numerous cases where mothers were restricted from moving or, if the mother continued with her relocation plans, physical custody was shifted from the mother to the father.

The frequency with which parental relocation cases have presented in the court system has rapidly increased since the 1970s. This rise in contested cases of relocation corresponds to the increasing strength of organized fathers' groups. It also matches the nationwide movement to keep fathers involved in their children's lives and the increased economic and social mobility of Americans as a whole. There is little evidence that prior to the 1970s relocation cases were seen in the courtroom. This makes sense because divorce rates remained low at that time. Nevertheless, because the tender-years doctrine was fully implemented at that time, it is a safe assumption that when physical custodial parents moved, the move was not likely contested.

Thus, the first well-documented approach to dealing with cases of parental relocation was to deny physical custodial parents the ability to move with their children [20, 21]. Physical custodians who have been denied the right to move with their children have described themselves as feeling like a prisoner or "captive of the state" [22, p. 7A]. Some have argued that the focus on custodial parents who move away is unfair—nonphysical custodial parents routinely move away and little is ever done to force them to stay involved in their children's lives [23]. Shifts in the ideological approach to addressing cases of parental relocation were not uniform across the country. However, the routine denial of parental relocation cases existed in the 1970s and into the 1980s in some parts of the county [17].

In other parts of the country in the early 1980s, however, some state court systems began imposing "tests" that physical custodial parents must pass in order to relocate with their children. In such instances, the courts established criteria that had to be met before relocation would be authorized. The State of New York imposed the "exceptional circumstances test," in which a physical custodial parent must demonstrate exceptional circumstances, such as educational, health, or financial needs or restrictions of the physical custodial parent. The New Jersey courts imposed a "real advantage test," in which four factors were considered: (1) whether the move would improve the quality of life of the custodial unit, (2) whether the custodial parent's motivation for moving is to primarily disrupt contact between the child and the other parent, (3) whether the nonphysical custodial parent is resisting the move because it would mean a higher burden of financial support, and (4) whether a new child-contact arrangement can be devised that would continue to foster a relationship between the other parent and the child. Illinois also imposed a criterion for determining whether a physical custodial parent should be allowed to relocate with his or her child. It was termed the "superficial showing test" and had three areas of consideration: (1) a desire to move must be stated, (2) the desire must be accompanied by a "sensible reason," (3) and a "superficial showing" must be made that the move is in the best interests of the child. In other words, the test must indicate that the move would not harm the child [24].

Relocation "tests" continued to be imposed over the next decade. *Gruber v. Gruber* in Pennsylvania in 1990 set a national precedent for handling relocation cases with a "three-prong approach." It incorporated many of the characteristics from New Jersey's "real advantage test," stating that courts must assess (1) the real advantages that the move would bring to the physical custodial parent and the child, (2) whether the move is proposed in bad faith to circumvent a relationship between the child and noncustodial parent, and (3) whether a contact schedule between the nonresidential parent and the child can be established in order to facilitate a meaningful relationship between that child and his or her parent [21, 25]. This method of imposing a test or a set of criteria on the physical custodial parent was widespread throughout the nation and placed the burden of proof on the parent wishing to relocate [26, 27]. At the same time, one of the primary conclusions that came from *Gruber* was the assumption that what was in the best interests of the physical custodial parent would also be in the best interests of the child [25, 28].

In the mid-1990s, another ideological shift occurred in the ruling of parental relocation cases. At this time, the courts turned to the "best interests of the child" standard that had been used for the previous one to two decades to decide custody cases. In fact, many legal professionals had been encouraging courts to use this model to decide relocation cases for over a decade [24, 25, 29, 30]. In 1996, the New York Court of Appeals, in the relocation case of *Tropea v. Tropea*, broke new ground in stating that previous relocation cases had been ruled on faulty ground. They maintained that the burden of proof should not be on a list of criteria that the physical custodial parent needed to meet—rather, decisions should be based on the best interests of the child. From this point on, the burden of proof on the part of the physical custodial parent has been eased and the tables have turned to favor residential parents [20]. The operating assumption in such cases is that children are better off with their primary caregivers and that what is in the best interests of primary caregivers may also be in the best interests of children. In this same year, the California Supreme Court, *in re: Burgess*, ruled that a physical custodial parent bears no burden to prove that a move is necessary. A custodial parent has a right to move with a child, as long as the move will not be detrimental to the child and as long as the residential parent's primary motive for the move is not to keep the child from the other parent [20, 27]. This is a position from which the California Supreme Court has recently moved away, once again increasing the burden of proof for residential parents.

The year 1996 proved to be a formative one for relocation cases. In addition to these two cases from influential states, Judith Wallerstein, the noted psychology scholar and one of the first social-science researchers to study children of divorce [19, 31, 32], published a paper on relocation cases [33]. In this paper, Wallerstein and Tanke argued that most children should relocate with their primary caregiver. This position is based on research that they cite in which they state that: (1) the psychological adjustment of the custodial parent is a significant predictor for children's adjustment and (2) that it is the quality, not the quantity, of contact between children and their nonresidential parents that mattered most in children's psychological adjustment. Thus, if children were able to maintain quality relationships with both of their parents after divorce, then the location of the child and nonresidential parent mattered not.

This position ignores that fact that the qualities of relationships are, in part, dependent on quantity. Relationship quality does not exist in a vacuum and is at least partially dependent on the amount of time that parties spend together. (How many times have we heard parents of infants despair about the decline in the quality of their marriage since the birth of their child has reduced the amount of time that they spend together?) Wallerstein and Tanke also revisited a conclusion of the *Gruber* case—that children's well-being is intrinsically related to the happiness and satisfaction of residential parents. Therefore, if a parent is denied the opportunity to move it may cause sadness and depression in that parent, which may lead to impaired parenting. They argue that in essence, what benefits a residential parent will benefit the child. Research has, indeed, found that the most salient predictor of child well-being is the psychological well-being of the physical custodial parent [34, 35], but it is a significant leap to assume that being denied the opportunity to move might lead to impaired parenting. One cannot also ignore studies that have determined that aside from high-conflict families, children who have regular and frequent access to their parents are sometimes better adjusted [35–40].

Since 1996, relocation cases have routinely been decided in favor of the physical custodial parent. Parents who want to relocate with their children are rarely prevented from doing so [41]. In fact, a 2003 Arkansas ruling in *Hollandsworth v. Knyzewski* set a judicially imposed presumption in favor of residential parents; "the presumption is in favor of relocation for custodial parents with primary [physical] custody" [42, p. 632]. These cases have also been covered extensively by the media and professional publications [16, 22, 43–45].

The nation's reliance on the use of technology has shaped a number of relocation cases. The courts have ruled that advances in electronic communication can help to foster a closer feeling between children who are separated from their parents. Methods of communication have become much easier, allowing children and parents to communicate daily via landline telephones, cellular telephones, electronic mail, digital photographs, instant messaging, and webcams. Dubbed "virtual visitation," in some instances judges have ordered parents to purchase and establish computers and other equipment that would enable children to communicate with their parents from afar [20]. Although some parents have complained that virtual visitation is no substitute for holding a child on one's lap [46], judges continue to order this as a possible middle ground in cases of relocation.

Responses of State Legislatures

Until recently, states have provided little guidance in how courts should decide cases of relocation. This resulted in widespread discretion in how judges decided relocation cases [16]. The extensive media attention of this issue has caused many state legislators to propose statutory guidelines for how to decide relocation cases. One such case was in the state of California, *in re: the Marriage of LaMusga*, in which the California Supreme Court overruled a lower court decision, concluding that disrupting contact between a nonresidential father and his child would be detrimental to that child. The court indicated that the judicial presumptive right of custodial parents to relocate with their children was granted in bad faith [45]. The case prompted legislation in California that would overturn that judicial ruling. There was a harsh public response to this proposed law, however, which resulted in withdrawal of the bill [13, 41].

In 1998, legislation was passed in Missouri (Missouri Revised Statute § 452.377) that required divorced parents to serve notice to the nonphysical custodial parent when relocation was planned or desired [47]. The National Organization for Women issued a position paper in response to this legislation, declaring that the real intent of relocation laws was to "keep women in their place."[48]. Arizona has a similar statute that requires relocating parents to provide sixty days notification to the nonrelocating parent (Arizona Revised Statute § 25-408[c]). The statute also provides guidelines for contested cases requiring a judicial ruling. These guidelines are similar to those previously used by the courts: the reason for the move, how it would affect the child, and how it would affect the child's relationship with the nonrelocating parent. The state of Washington also requires relocating parents to provide notification to nonrelocating parents (Revised Code of Washington, § 26.09), and specifies that the method of delivery must be in person or through a mail service requiring a return receipt [49]. Similar legislation has been proposed and debated in other states, but it has not always passed (e.g., Idaho House Bill 272, 1999).

Legislatively enacted presumptions for one condition or another have also entered into statutes addressing parental relocation. In 1997, the state of Florida enacted a law stating, "No presumption shall arise in favor of or against a request to relocate when a primary residential parent seeks to move the child and the move will materially affect the current schedule of contact and access with the secondary residential parent" (Florida Statute Title VI: § 61.13[3][d]). The state of Washington adopted legislation in 2000 that declares a presumption that the intended relocation of the child will be permitted (Revised Code of Washington § 26.09.520). In 2001, the state of Colorado General Assembly removed the judicial presumption that children would move with their residential parent [22]. Today the statute contains no language about presumptions and only addresses how a court can determine what is in the best interest of a child (Colorado Revised Statute § 14-10-129).

Research on Relocation

To date, there has only been one study that has empirically examined the effect of relocation on children of divorce. Sanford Braver, a noted scholar on fathers of divorce, and his colleagues studied instances of parental relocation in a sample of 602 freshman college students from divorced families [50]. They questioned students about whether, during their childhoods, a parent had ever moved an hour or more away from the original family's residence, and they examined a number of possible relocation combinations: (1) neither parents moved; (2) mother moved, child went with mother; (3) mother moved, child stayed with father; (4) father moved, child went with father; and (5) father moved, child stayed with mother. The outcome variables that were examined included a number of general life well-being factors, the quality of the relationship between child and parents, and parental conflict. The authors found that only 39 percent of cases did not involve relocation. In 25 percent of cases, students moved with their mothers; 8 percent of the time, students reported having stayed with their fathers when their mothers moved; 4 percent of the time, students reported moving with their fathers; and 26 percent of the time when their fathers moved, students stayed with their mothers. In other words, according to this study in three out of five divorced families, a parent moves and children are separated from one parent or another by at least an hour's traveling time.

The authors conducted a series of one-way analyses of variance considering the five relocation situations as predictors of student outcomes. They found considerable differences between the relocation situations. In general, students whose parents relocated performed worse than students whose parents did not relocate. The outcomes, however, vary by relocation situation. For example, students who lived with their fathers after their mothers moved performed worse on the personal hostility and general life-satisfaction measures than students who stayed with their mothers when their fathers moved. Students who stayed with their mothers when their fathers moved were also likely to report more inner turmoil related to their parents' divorce. Students were more likely to feel that the parent with whom they lived after relocation was the parent who provided more support for them. Students who worried more about college-related expenses were those students who either moved with their mothers or remained with their fathers. Students were least likely to report that both of their parents were good role models if they moved away with their fathers. Students who reported the least hostility between their parents were those students who stayed with their fathers when their mothers moved away (this was even better than for students who did not experience a relocation).

The findings also varied by gender. Females were more hostile and males were less hostile when their fathers moved away than when both parents remained in the same region. Females who moved away with their mothers reported lower levels of global health than did males, when compared with families that did not move. The findings of this study prompted the authors to conclude that that there is no empirical reason to establish a presumption in favor of a parental relocation.

This study has been the target of criticism. In an interview, Judith Wallerstein argued that the methodology of this study is flawed. She stated that the conclusions were drawn on short self-reports by the students, without any context for whether the relocation was contested. She suggests that the study would have been more effective if Braver and colleagues would have examined the outcomes of children who had been ordered to move with a parent versus children who had been ordered to stay with a parent [51]. I, too, have noted problems with this study. It appears that the authors did not control for any demographic factors, such as socioeconomic status, parental conflict or hostility, gender, why parents had relocated, and so on. It is possible that families with the most contentious relationships are those that moved. Therefore, the researchers may be picking up on the effects of parental conflict rather than the effects of relocation. The authors also failed to control for parental general well-being, physical health problems, substance issues, or mental-health conditions. Since previous research has found a link between parental well-being and child adjustment, and since parental well-being has been the focus on the debate in cases of parental relocation, it is imperative to include these measures in future research. An additional problem with the Braver et al. study is that often the students with poorer outcomes were those who remained or moved with their fathers. Because this is an uncommon postdivorce living situation, one must inquire as to what the conditions were that led mothers to move away without their children, or of children moving away with their fathers. Another area of concern is the fact that the many different relocation situations result in small sample size "cells." For example, there were only twenty-two respondents who moved with their fathers. This may not produce enough statistical power to draw firm conclusions about the results. Finally, this study was conducted on a group of college students, and the findings are probably not generalizable to the larger population, something that is noted by the authors.

In the end, I predict that this study is the first of many in a new area of divorce-related problems. It is a good starting place; overall, the study had a large sample size and measured a number of different outcome variables. Early studies have routinely had problems; this study is no exception. The limitations of the study, however, are not so significant to disregard the importance of the findings: children appear to be worse off when one of their parents moves.

Conclusion

The problem of parental relocation has captured the attention of the media and many legal and legislative professionals. The majority of these cases are settled outside of court, and what percentage make their way to the courtroom is unknown. As noted, however, one-third of child-support payments are made across state lines, and three out of every five divorced families appear to experience a parental relocation. Thus, the issue of a parent's relocation after divorce is substantial and may affect at least half of children from divorced families. The judicial system has tried a number of different approaches to address this problem. The media attention given to cases with multiple appeals prompted state legislatures to take up the issue. They, too, have grappled with the complexity of parental relocation, which has resulted in considerably different legislative provisions betweem states. The common theme in the guidelines for handling these cases today is to base each move on the best interests of the child, and because this is the gold standard used to decide any contested case involving children, the transition to using such guidelines is wise. As yet, there is insufficient research to determine the potential harmful or beneficial effects of relocation on children. The social-science literature could benefit from a longitudinal study that follows a large sample of newly divorced families to examine the outcomes of those families with and without parental relocation. Researchers could also heed the advice of Wallerstein and study families where children have been ordered to stay with a nonrelocating parent or to move with a parent that is relocating. In any study, regardless of its design, researchers must be careful to consider demographic controls and any preexisting conditions (e.g., parental conflict) that might be related to the intent of the move.

PREVENTION PROGRAMS

Prevention programs are educational- and skills-based intervention programs for families that are currently divorcing or recently divorced. Lasting between five and twelve weeks, these programs are not intended to prevent divorce; they are intended to prevent the harmful effects of divorce on children and parents. Prevention programs are intended to be research based [52] and usually focus on a number of different problem areas, including child adjustment and parent adjustment to divorce, parent-child relationships postdivorce, parenting practices, single parenting, the coparental relationships, legal issues, and financial management [52–55].

Prevention programs are not mandated but are experimental programs that are initiated by university-based researchers [56–59]. One of the strengths of the research that is conducted on these prevention programs is that random assignment is used. Participants are recruited using a number of different techniques, including media publicity, public schools, social-service agencies, or direct appeal from researchers who have obtained public records of recent divorces. Participants are comprised of divorced parents, with some programs specifically targeting divorced, residential mothers [55] and others targeting divorced, nonresidential fathers [54, 59]. Some programs also include children in the programming [53]. Participants are sometimes paid for their involvement in the study [58]. Once a sample has been established, parents are then randomly assigned to either a treatment group (of which there may be more than one) or a control group. Sometimes the control group is actually a "delayed treatment" group and will receive services at a later time. The second strength of the research on prevention programs is that most of them are longitudinal, collecting data at multiple points posttreatment, including follow-ups as extensive as four [56] and six years later [53]. The results of the research from a number of different studies conducted over the past two decades is promising, especially among families that present with more problems at baseline.

What Does the Research Say?

Programs for Mothers and Fathers

One of the most comprehensive programs to have been tested is the Collaborative Divorce Project that was implemented in Connecticut by Pruett and colleagues [35, 57, 60–62]. This randomized clinical trial collected data from 161 divorcing couples, their attorneys, children's teachers, and court records. The program included an introduction to the legal system, a four-hour divorce education program that used small groups and discussion, private sessions with parenting counselors, mediation sessions, a settlement conference with legal professionals, and a follow-up meeting eighteen months after the beginning of the intervention. Families were identified through public records, and families with the highest levels of conflict were excluded from the study. One of the primary components of this program was to increase contact between nonresidential fathers and their children, in part by educating mothers about "gatekeeping," or interfering with father-child contact. The mothers in the intervention group were more likely to report that the father-child relationship was a benefit to their children, and the reports from fathers in the intervention group confirmed the maternal reports. Other positive program outcomes included decreased parental conflict and increased father involvement. Children whose parents participated in intervention groups had smoother play sequences and were more likely to express themselves verbally than behaviorally. Consistent with this finding, teacher reports indicated fewer cognitive and attention problems among children whose families were in the intervention group. This program did have some shortcomings. Mothers in the intervention group were more likely to report negative changes in the relationship with their children (perhaps because they are more aware of possible problems); the Collaborative Divorce Project also appears to be ineffective for minority families [57].

Not all programs have demonstrated changes in so many different areas. The five-week program, Orientation for Divorcing Parents, which was implemented with 242 divorcing parents, conducted a pretest and ten-week posttest follow-up. The researchers examined a number of different outcome variables, including parent psychological well-being, stress, social support, child behavior problems, health problems, social competence, parent-child relationship, household organization, and parent-child access patterns. Program participants were found to have more positive outcomes only in their reduced need for social support and a decline in children's hopes for parental reconciliation. Parents who participated in Orientation for Divorcing Parents were not randomly assigned to this group and actually had a higher level of preprogram conflict than the comparison group. Thus, the groups were not comparable to one another, meaning that the interventions might yield different outcomes. Also, the posttest was administered only ten weeks after program completion, making it difficult to know whether the program produced lasting results [63].

Programs for Fathers

The most polished program to date for fathers of divorce is Dads for Life, which is run in Arizona by Braver and colleagues [59, 64]. A recent report describes a randomized clinical trial of this program that was implemented with 214 recently divorced fathers. Dads for Life lasts eight weeks and is a total of fourteen hours long; it is a heavily scripted program, relying on videos, skill building, and role playing. Fathers were recruited from public divorce records; data were collected from fathers, mothers, and teachers before the program, and at four- and twelve-month follow-up assessments. The results indicated that both mothers and fathers reported a decrease in child internalizing problems, especially for children who had more problem behaviors at the start of the study. There were no significant findings for child externalizing behaviors or total behavior problems [59].

Another program, Parenting for Divorced Fathers, is a six-week divorce-education program for divorced fathers [81]. This program underwent a very small, nonrandomized evaluation study using a convenience sample. The results indicated that fathers increased their skills in communicating with their children and that at the end of the program they were more satisfied with their role as a father. There were no differences between participants and the comparison group with regard to the parent-child relationship, weekly contact with children, and likelihood of leaving the state. The small sample size may account for the lack of findings, and the one-time immediate posttest follow-up does not indicate if the successes of this program were lasting.

Programs for Mothers

Two programs show encouraging findings for divorced mothers. An Oregon-based program recruited divorcing mothers of boys through media advertisements to participate in a course that focused on five parenting modules: appropriate discipline, skill encouragement, mother's monitoring of son, problem solving, and positive involvement. The data were collected primarily through observation of mothers and their sons in a laboratory setting where they solved puzzles, played games, and addressed topics over which there was disagreement (e.g., chores). Data collection took place at pretest and twelve- and thirty-month posttests. There were positive findings for the experimental condition in the areas of coercive discipline, child noncompliance, and positive parenting. In each of these areas, the control group declined in their performance and the program participants stayed the same. Thus, the program prevented the onset of some poor parenting practices [65].

Bloom and colleagues conducted a random clinical trial of a prevention program for 134 newly separated divorced mothers in Colorado [55]. The six-month program focused on socialization, childrearing and single parenting, career planning and employment, legal and financial issues, and homemaking concerns; the program was delivered by paraprofessionals in group and individual settings. Data were collected at multiple posttest times, including six, eighteen, thirty, and forty-eight months, on more than one hundred different measures. At the four-year mark, program participants had better adjustment in a number of different areas including anxiety, general life well-being, general psychological adjustment, and work performance (competence, satisfaction, general performance). There were a number of indicators on which participants performed better at the thirty-month mark, but on which performance had diminished by forty-eight months: loneliness, feelings of guilt, relationship problems, health problems, work performance (trouble concentrating and effectiveness), and personal growth. On these final indicators, program participants did not perform any better than the control group at the concluding follow-up test [56].

Mother and Child Programs

Some programs for mothers also include participation for children. In such instances, a number of different program delivery methods and group compositions have been tested against one another. A well-studied example of this is the New Beginnings Program that has been implemented in Arizona for divorcing mothers and their children by Wolchick and colleagues [53, 66, 67]. The New Beginnings Program is ten weeks long, with individual sessions for mothers. The program is highly structured, and places an emphasis on learning new parenting and postdivorce coping skills. This program, which has been tested on two different samples, has used a variety of different group assignments. The first randomly assigned divorcing mothers to an experimental or control condition. The results indicated that ten to twelve weeks after program completion, mothers in the intervention group reported a higher quality of mother-child interaction, had fewer divorce-related negative events, and engaged in more consistent and less authoritarian parenting. Children, however, reported having less positive support.

A more recent trial of the New Beginnings Program randomly assigned families to one of three conditions: (1) mother-only program, (2) mother and child, and (3) mother and child self-study group—which served as a comparison group. Families in the latter group were given books about divorce to read. There were positive findings for mothers and children, both at the six-month and six-year follow-up times, although the mother-child group did not yield greater program benefits than the mother-alone condition. Positive program findings included better child adjustment, fewer behavioral problems, fewer mental-health problems and less drug use, better academic performance, and fewer negative attitudes by the mother about nonresidential fathers. These findings were especially true for families that entered with lower levels of functioning [53, 66].

In another prevention program design, Stolberg and Garrison [68] examined eighty-two mother-child pairs in a study using a volunteer, convenience sample. They compared four groups: (1) children alone, (2) mothers alone, (3) mothers and children together, and (4) a comparison group. The sample size of each group was small, with one group having only eleven participants; data were collected at pretest, posttest immediately following intervention, and at five-month follow-up. The twelve-week program produced some positive effects for program participants. Children who participated in the program by themselves had a significant positive increase in their perception of self-concept, and adults who participated in the group alone avoided a deterioration in their adjustment to postdivorce living. These findings were maintained over five months. The mother-child groups did not yield any changes in adjustment or behavior, and there were no other significant differences between the groups with regard to child behavior or parenting behavior.

Conclusion

Prevention programs for currently divorcing or recently divorced families appear to have promising effects. Even studies that used small sample sizes and nonrandom assignment to treatment conditions found some encouraging results for children and parents. Unlike most of the studies reviewed in this book, the vast majority of prevention programs have been well-designed and have few major methodological flaws. Their ability to show positive improvements on mothers, fathers, and children over a wide array of social indicators is encouraging. The areas that appear to be most receptive to intervention are parenting practices, child behaviors, and parent and child psychological- and social-adjustment indicators. The fact that prevention programs are most effective with families that presented with the highest level of problems may be instructive when considering what social-policy interventions to mandate for families. Families with higher levels of conflict or children with poor adjustment may universally be an excellent target for court or legislatively mandated prevention programs.

COVENANT MARRIAGE LAWS

Covenant marriage laws establish a provision that allows marrying or married couples to opt out of "no-fault" divorce laws. Adopted by only three states, these special provisions make it difficult to obtain divorce; in fact, specific requirements that mirror old divorce legislation must be met in order for a divorce to be granted [69]. Couples who marry under the covenant marriage provision and who seek divorce have to prove that the marriage faces severe hardship, such as criminal behavior, abandonment, family violence, or adultery [70, 71]. In other words, couples are only supposed to divorce under extreme circumstances [72]. In truth, there is a loophole in the law that states that couples who have been legally separated for a specific period of time (i.e., eighteen months) but have not suffered significant hardship are also eligible for divorce [73]. Before couples can enter a covenant marriage they have to engage in premarital counseling and sign a contract indicating that they understand that their marriage will be held to a different level than standard marriages, and that covenant marriages are "for life."

History of Covenant Marriage

Just like laws declaring a presumption for joint legal and physical custody, the history of covenant laws begins in Louisiana, where the first covenant marriage law was adopted in 1997. At that time, Florida, Illinois, Washington, and Indiana had discussed, but failed to pass, legislation that would toughen requirements for divorce. Regardless of the state of origin, however, the covenant marriage movement is largely the result of the Christian Right interest group in the United States. This special interest group has increasingly become involved in social issues, and the political responses to them. They have tackled issues such as abortion, same-sex marriage, and gambling—always as staunch opponents to each of these areas. As a result, their image in the media is often negative—as a pious group in opposition to social issues that are perceived by many to be social advances. Not insensitive to their image problem, the Christian Right wanted to tackle a "positive" social initiative—to be supportive of, rather than against, a new piece of legislation. A small group of religiously motivated leaders in Louisiana, comprised of legislators, a judge, a law professor, and a social activist, drafted legislation to sponsor covenant marriages in Louisiana. It passed with an overwhelming majority in both the House and the Senate [72].

While only Arizona, Arkansas, and Louisiana have passed covenant marriage laws, the issue of toughening divorce laws has been addressed or debated in about half of the states in the nation [70]. These numbers are reflected in attitudes about divorce, with roughly 50 percent of Americans from a national study agreeing that "it should be harder for married couples to get a divorce," and 61 percent of Americans agreeing that "it should be harder for married couples *with children* to get a divorce" (emphasis added) [74]. Similar attitudes were found among residents in the states of Louisiana, Arizona, and Minnesota [75], where two states have covenant marriage laws. While many Americans may be eager to lower the divorce rate, they are reluctant to let the government step into their "private lives" and perceived freedoms. In a national study, only 37 percent of respondents stated that they thought "the government should make it harder for people to get a divorce" [74]. On the other hand, there does appear to be more support for legislation that would mandate premarital counseling [74, 75]. In states that already have covenant marriage laws, four in ten residents are very supportive of new marriage provisions. Those who favor covenant marriage tend to be more religious and hold more traditional attitudes about the respective roles of men and women [75].

Current Covenant Marriage Laws Today

Since Louisiana passed its covenant marriage law in 1997, Arizona and Arkansas have followed suit with their own similar laws. The legislation from each of the three states have almost parallel provisions. There are two components to the legislation: requirements that must be met before marriage can take place and the circumstances under which married persons can divorce. First, couples planning to marry under covenant provisions must provide evidence that they have engaged in premarital counseling, and they must sign a statement indicating their commitment to the special provisions of the law. Second, the law outlines the conditions under which couples can seek divorce. Examples of each of these follow.

> *Arizona premarital counseling requirement*: A declaration of intent to enter into a covenant marriage shall contain . . . the following: An affidavit by the parties that they have received premarital counseling from a member of the clergy or from a marriage counselor. Premarital counseling shall include a discussion of the seriousness of covenant marriage, communication of the fact that a covenant marriage is a commitment for life, a discussion of the obligation to seek marital counseling in times of marital difficulties and a discussion of the exclusive grounds for legally terminating a covenant marriage by dissolution of marriage or legal separation. (Arizona Revised Statute, § 25-901)

> *Louisiana statement of commitment to covenant marriage*: We do solemnly declare that marriage is a covenant between a man and a woman who agree to live together as husband and wife for so long as they both may live. We have chosen each other carefully and disclosed to one another everything which could adversely affect the decision to enter this marriage. We have received premarital counseling on the nature, purposes, and responsibilities of marriage. We have read the Covenant Marriage Act, and we understand that a Covenant Marriage is for life. If we experience marital difficulties, we commit ourselves to take all reasonable efforts to preserve our marriage, including marital counseling. . . . With full knowledge of what this commitment means, we do hereby declare that our marriage will be bound by Louisiana law on Covenant Marriages and we promise to love, honor, and care for one another as husband and wife for the rest of our lives. (Louisiana Revised Statute § 9:273)

Arkansas specifications under which divorce can be granted: The circuit court shall have power to dissolve and set aside a marriage contract, not only from bed and board, but from the bonds of matrimony, for the following causes: (1) Where either party, at the time of the contract, was and still is impotent; (2) Where either party shall be convicted of a felony or other infamous crime; (3) Where either party shall be addicted to habitual drunkenness for one (1) year, shall be guilty of such cruel and barbarous treatment as to endanger the life of the other, or shall offer such indignities to the person of the other as shall render his or her condition intolerable; (4) Where either party shall have committed adultery subsequent to the marriage; (5) Where husband and wife have lived separate and apart from each other for eighteen (18) continuous months without cohabitation, the court shall grant an absolute decree of divorce at the suit of either party, whether the separation was the voluntary act of one party or by the mutual consent of both parties or due to the fault of either party or both parties; (6)[For reasons of mental insanity]; (7) Where either spouse legally obligated to support the other, and having the ability to provide the other with the common necessaries of life, willfully fails to do so. (Arkansas Code § 9-12-301)

In addition to Louisiana, Arkansas, and Arizona, legislation in twenty other states has been proposed, but ultimately defeated [70]. These pieces of legislation can be viewed on the website of Americans for Divorce Reform (http://www.divorcereform.org/cov.html). Even though legislation has not been adopted by these states, the covenant marriage movement appears to be strong, with many websites devoted to this topic (http://www.covenantmarriage.com/, http://www.covenantmarriages.com/, http://www.family.org/married/comm/a0017718.cfm, and http://www.divorcereform.org/cov.html). Moreover, many states have implemented provisions that are intended to make it more difficult to obtain a divorce even if a covenant marriage provision has been unsuccessful. For example, the state of Florida now requires marriage education in high school, alongside driver's education. The state also passed a law mandating a three-day waiting period after applying for a marriage license. Oklahoma passed laws that give incentives to couples who obtain premarital education and, like the state of Arizona, is dedicating unspent welfare funds to initiatives intended to strengthen marriage [76].

Who Uses Covenant Marriage Laws?

Covenant marriage laws are used by a small and distinct group of couples. Only 2.5 to 3 percent of couples marrying in Louisiana choose to have a covenant marriage [70, 77]. Nock, Sanchez, Wright, and colleagues have extensively analyzed Louisiana couples who married since the covenant marriage law went into place. Their research primarily focused on over one thousand people, or five hundred couples, roughly half of whom are in covenant marriages. Couples who were married between 1997 and 1998 were selected for participation (the law was implemented in 1997); the mail survey response rate was 55 percent, and data were collected at multiple intervals over a five-year period. The results of this study reveal a number of different demographic and attitudinal differences between couples who choose covenant versus standard marriages.

Couples who chose to have a covenant marriage were slightly younger and had more education than those who chose standard marriages, although there were no racial differences between the two types of couples. Husbands in covenant marriages were more consistently engaged in the labor force than husbands in standard marriages, although there was no statistical difference in the salaries that they earned. There was also no difference in the amount of time that wives from the two marriage types spent in employment, but wives in standard marriages statistically earned more money than wives in covenant marriages. Couples in covenant marriages were also less likely to have children together prior to their marriage, wives were less likely to have children from a previous relationship, and covenant marriage couples were also less likely to have cohabited together when compared with couples with standard marriages [71, 78].

Couples with covenant marriages were statistically more religious than couples with standard marriages. They were more likely to be Baptist, or, in general, Protestant, than Catholic or any other type of religion. When compared with couples from standard marriages, couples from covenant marriages were more likely to participate in religious activities, to have participated in these activities together, to have come from a "very" religious home, and to have described themselves as a "religious fundamentalist" [71, 78].

Couples with covenant marriages also had different social attitudes than couples with standard marriages. Wives were more likely to see childbearing as a social duty, but they were more likely to be worried about childrearing responsibilities than women in standard marriages. Covenant marriage couples were also more likely to have traditional attitudes about gender [71, 78]. A study of ninety-two married persons from covenant and standard marriages in one Baton Rouge parish found that 72 percent of respondents from covenant marriages believed that men and women should have separate responsibilities during marriage, compared with only 27 percent of respondents from standard marriages. Those from covenant marriages were also more likely to believe that husbands should be "the head of the household for making family decisions." Seventy percent of respondents from covenant marriages felt that this was the case, compared with 18 percent of respondents from standard marriages [79].

When compared with couples in standard marriages, those who entered into covenant marriages reported several differences in the circumstances surrounding their marriage and family. Data from the longitudinal study of Louisiana marriages indicated that couples who chose covenant marriages reported more community support prior to their marriage than couples who chose standard marriages. Covenant couples reported that their weddings were attended by more people and that they received more support from friends and families when their engagement was announced. Couples from covenant and standard marriages did not differ in their level of satisfaction with or the level of affection in their marriage. Covenant couples, however, were more committed to their marriages, reported seeing marriage as essential to the intimate relationship, and (when reported by wives) had a higher degree of consensus in their marriage than couples with standard marriages [77]. Husbands in covenant marriages report that they were more likely to "give in" during an argument than husbands in standard marriages. Furthermore, when compared with those in covenant marriages, partners in standard marriages reported a higher tendency to use sarcasm and violence in marital conflict [78].

Implementation and Outcomes of Covenant Marriage Laws

As noted, few couples choose covenant marriage. There are a number of possible reasons for this. First, since those who choose covenant marriage are so different from those with standard marriages, it is possible that covenant marriage provisions appeal to a small number of couples. Second, there is some indication that the public is not aware of covenant marriage options. Results from a 1998 Gallup poll indicate that 56 percent of the sample of 540 randomly selected Louisiana respondents had not heard of covenant marriage and only 36 percent remembered when the covenant law was passed. Only a small fraction of the respondents, 2 percent, knew someone who had a new covenant marriage [76].

A third possible explanation for why covenant marriages have not taken a stronger hold points to problems with implementation. Two years after the passage of Louisiana's covenant marriage law, a team of researchers sent a confederate couple to seventeen different parishes to apply for a marriage license. They found that the procedures for marriage application and the information that they received about covenant marriage differed greatly between parishes. In only 35 percent of parishes were couples asked if they wanted a covenant marriage. In only 12 percent of parishes did the confederate couple receive accurate information about covenant and standard marriages. And, over half of the time the clerks at the parishes had a negative attitude about covenant marriages. In addition, the majority of clerks failed to mention some of the basic information about covenant marriages, such as premarital counseling, the declaration of intent, and fault-based criteria necessary for divorce [76].

Some question the potential "success" of covenant marriages. The option is not well used or well known, and there is little indication that it will substantially reduce the divorce rate [80]. At best, covenant marriages appear to target couples who have a stronger commitment to marriage than the general population, although some who enter into covenant marriages have been previously married and divorced. Its current popularity is among couples who are a distinct group—those who are religious, are deeply committed to the notion of lifelong marriages, and hold traditional notions of men's and women's respective roles in the home and in society. Although covenant marriage laws make it more difficult for couples to obtain a divorce, those who obtain covenant marriages are far less likely to pursue divorce in the first place. Unless something about these laws changes, covenant marriage laws do not hold much hope of lowering the divorce rate. Their greatest contribution has been to put the discussion about the longevity of marriage back on the policy table—which in many ways is a success in and of itself [71].

SUMMARY

Each of the problems and perceived solutions presented in this chapter is substantial enough to stand alone. However, there has been no national movement on any of these issues. Based on the popularity and media attention of these matters, I expect that relocation will continue to be a problem among families of divorce, that state legislatures will increasingly address this problem, and that the proposed solutions will become more similar than dissimilar between states. I expect that comprehensive prevention programs for families of divorce will primarily be offered in university research laboratories, unless something substantial changes in the way that our nation responds to social problems in general. The popularity of covenant marriages may increase, paralleling the nation's recent rise in religiosity. Nevertheless, I do not expect that the presence of covenant marriage will have an impact on the divorce rate, nor do I see the popularity of these laws growing significantly outside of traditionally conservative, southern states.

REFERENCES

1. Johnston, J. R., M. G. Walters, and N. W. Olesen. Resilience and risk for alienation in children of high conflict divorce. In *Association of Family and Conciliation Courts: Solving the Family Court Puzzle—Integrating Research, Policy, and Practice.* Conference May 17–21, 2005, Seattle, WA.

2. Fields, L. F., B. W. Mussetter, and G. T. Powers. Children denied two parents: An analysis of access denial. *Journal of Divorce and Remarriage*, 1997, 28(1/2): pp. 49–62.

3. Reihing, K. M. Protecting victims of domestic violence and their children after divorce: The American Law Institute's model. *Family and Conciliation Courts Review*, 1999, 37(3): pp. 393–410.

4. Toews, M. T., P. C. McKenry, and B. S. Catlett. Male-initiated partner abuse during marital separation prior to divorce. *Violence and Victims*, 2003, 18(4): pp. 387–402.

5. Logan, T. K., et al. Divorce, custody and spousal violence: A random sample of circuit court docket records. *Journal of Family Violence*, 2003, 18(5): pp. 269–79.

6. Hardesty, J. L. Separation assault in the context of postdivorce parenting. *Violence Against Women*, 2002, 8(5): pp. 597–625.

7. Austin, W. Partner violence and risk assessment in child custody evaluations. *Family Court Review*, 2001, 39(4): pp. 483–96.

8. Ayoub, C. C., R. M. Deutsch, and A. Maraganore. Emotional distress in children of high-conflict divorce: The impact of marital conflict and violence. *Family and Conciliation Courts Review*, 1999, 37(3): pp. 297–314.

9. Fischer, K., N. Vidmar, and R. Ellis. The culture of battering and the role of mediation in domestic violence cases. *Southern Methodist University Law Review*, 1993, 46: pp. 2117–74.

10. Jaffe, P. G., and R. Geffner. Child custody disputes and domestic violence: Critical issues for mental health, social services and legal professions. In *Children exposed to marital violence: Theory, research, and applied issues*, ed. G. W. Holden, R. Geffner, and E. Jouriles, pp. 371–408. 1998, Washington, DC: American Psychological Association.

11. Jaffe, P. G., S. E. Poisson, and A. Cunningham. Domestic violence and high-conflict divorce. In *Domestic violence in the lives of children: The future of research, intervention and social policy*, ed. S. A. Graham-Bermann and J. L. Edleson, pp. 332–42. 2001, Washington, DC: American Psychological Association.

12. Finley, G. E. Divorce inequalities. In *National Council on Family Relations Report*. 49(3): 2004, pp. 9–10.

13. McElroy, W. Child custody laws poised for change. 2004, Foxnews.com. (September 10, 2005).

14. Puente, M., Custody wars: Relocating Courts allow parent with kids to move. *USA Today*, April 22, 1996, p. 1A.

15. Mazzoli, E. A. The court's role facilitating an effective relationship between the noncustodial parent and child when the custodial parent relocates with child. *Brandeis Law Journal*, 1999, 37(Winter): pp. 259–71.

16. Masters, B. A. Child custody's moving problem: Judges intervene as parents relocate. *Washington Post*, September 20, 1998, p. B01.

17. Meislin, R. J. Court limits freedom of a divorced parent in choosing residence. *New York Times*, February 25, 1981, p. 1.

18. Hetherington, E. M. Divorce: A child's perspective. *American Psychologist*, 1979, 34(10): pp. 851–58.

19. Wallerstein, J. S., and J. B. Kelly. The effects of parental divorce: Experiences of the child in later latency. *American Journal of Orthopsychiatry*, 1976, 46(2): pp. 256–69.

20. Gottfried, S. L. Virtual visitation: The new wave of communication between children and non-custodial parents in relocation cases. *Cardozo Women's Law Journal*, 2003, 9: pp. 567–96.

21. Weissman, H. N. Psychotherapeutic and psycholegal considerations: When a custodial parent seeks to move away. *American Journal of Family Therapy*, 1994, 22(2): pp. 176–81.

22. Garner, J. Captives of Colorado: Rights of custodial parents to relocate at heart of legal battle. *Rocky Mountain News*, September 14, 2004, p. 7A.

23. Rotman, A. S., et al. Reconciling parents' and children's interests in relocation: In whose best interest? *Family and Conciliation Courts Review*, 2000, 38(July): pp. 341–67.

24. Surace, P. T. A proposed "best interests" test for removing a child from the jurisdiction of the noncustodial parent. *Fordham Law Review*, 1982, 51(December): pp. 489–514.

25. Adams, F. G. Child custody and parental relocations: Loving your children from a distance. *Duquesne Law Review*, 1994, 33(Fall): pp. 143–58.

26. Kisthardt, M. K., and B. E. Handschu. Custody relocation cases. *The National Law Journal*, 2000(November 13): p. A17.

27. Handschu, B. E., and M. K. Kisthardt. Relocation Battles. *The National Law Journal*, 2004, 26(43): p. 11.

28. Hawkins, A. Family law relocation case takes parent's quality of life into consideration; Superior Court rules child's best interests inextricably linked with mother's happiness. *Pennsylvania Law Weekly*, April 5, 2004, p. 7.

29. Bulow, J., and S. G. Gellman. The judicial role in post-divorce child relocation controversies. *Stanford Law Review*, 1983, 35(May): pp. 949–74.

30. Rankin, B. High court reverses child custody ruling. *Atlanta Journal and Constitution*, July 22, 1994, p. C2.

31. Wallerstein, J. S., and J. B. Kelly. The effects of parental divorce: The adolescent experience. In *Child in his family: Children at psychiatric risk*, ed. E. J. Anthony and C. Koupernik. 1974, Oxford, UK: John Wiley and Sons.

32. Wallerstein, J. S., and J. B. Kelly. Effects of divorce on the visiting father-child relationship. *American Journal of Psychiatry*, 1980, 137(12): pp. 1534–39.

33. Wallerstein, J., and T. J. Tanke. To move or not to move: Psychological and legal considerations in the relocation of children following divorce. *Family Law Quarterly*, 1996, 30(Summer): pp. 305–32.

34. Johnston, J. R., M. Kline, and J. M. Tschann. Ongoing post-divorce conflict in families contesting custody: Do joint custody and frequent access help? In *Joint custody and shared parenting* (2nd ed.), ed. J. Folberg, pp. 177–84. 1991, New York: Guilford Press.

35. Pruett, M. K., et al. Family and legal indicators of child adjustment to divorce among families with young children. *Journal of Family Psychology*, 2003, 17(2): pp. 169–80.

36. Brody, G., and R. Forehand. Interparental conflict, relationship with the noncustodial father, and the adolescent post-divorce adjustment. *Journal of Applied Developmental Psychology*, 1990, 11: pp. 139–47.

37. Amato, P. R., Children of divorce in the 1990s: An update of the Amato and Keith (1991) meta-analysis. *Journal of Family Psychology*, 2001, 15(3): pp. 355–70.

38. Amato, P. R., and B. Keith. Parental divorce and the well-being of children: A meta-analysis. *Psychological Bulletin*, 1991, 110(1): pp. 26–46.

39. Lee, M. Y., Post-divorce interparental conflict, children's contact with both parents, children's emotional responses and children's behavioral adjustments. *Journal of Divorce and Remarriage*, 1997, 28: pp. 61–82.

40. Tschann, J. M., et al. Conflict, loss, change and parent-child relationships: Predicting children's adjustment during divorce. *Journal of Divorce*, 1990, 13(4): pp. 1–22.

41. Mother granted permission to relocate abroad; Father awarded generous visitation rights. *New York Law Journal*, 2005, 234(August 9): p. 19.

42. Carrington, C. From parent to paycheck. *University of Arkansas at Little Rock Law Review*, 2004, 26(Spring): pp. 615–40.

43. Jacobs, M. A. Legal beat: Courts let custodial parents move. *Wall Street Journal*, February 10, 1998, p. B1.

44. McElroy, W. Child custody laws poised for change. 2004, Foxnews.com. (September 19, 2005).

45. McKee, M. Divorced parents must consider ex if moving away. *San Francisco Recorder*, 2004. p. 1.

46. Gallagher, M. P. A state appeals court orders a Family Part judge to reconsider his rejection of a plan, by a parent who wants to relocate, to enhance child visitation by use of a Web cam. *New Jersey Law Journal*, 2001(January 15).

47. Kingsbury, J. S. "Mommy, are we moving? No . . . Maybe . . . Yes. . . ."—The evolution of Missouri's relocation law. *Journal of the Missouri Bar*, 2004, 60(2), 83–91.

48. Gomes, H. Relocation laws keep women in their place. *National NOW Times*, 2000, National Organization for Women. http://www.now.org/nnt/fall-2000/family.html#relocation (September 27, 2005).

49. Law Offices of Raj Baines. Current events: Custody relocation bill becomes law. 2000, Divorcenet. http://www.divorcenet.com/states/washington/wa_art12 (September 10, 2005).

50. Braver, S. H., I. M. Ellman, and W. V. Fabricius. Relocation of children after divorce and children's best interests: New evidence and legal considerations. *Journal of Family Psychology*, 2003, 17(2): pp. 206–19.

51. Carpenter, M. The struggle to quantify children's well-being. *Pittsburgh Post-Gazette*, August 3, 2003 p. A-13.

52. Grych, J. H., and F. D. Fincham. Interventions for children of divorce: Toward greater integration of research and action. *Psychological Bulletin*, 1992, 111(3): pp. 434–54.

53. Wolchik, S. A., et al. Six-year follow-up of preventive interventions for children of divorce. A randomized controlled trial. *Journal of the American Medical Association*, 2002, 288(15): pp. 1874–81.

54. Devlin, A. S., et al., Parent education for divorced fathers. *Family Relations: Interdisciplinary Journal of Applied Family Studies*, 1992, 41(3): pp. 290–96.

55. Bloom, B. L., W. F. Hodges, and R. A. Caldwell. A preventive program for the newly separated: Initial evaluation. *American Journal of Community Psychology*, 1982, 10(3): pp. 251–54.

56. Bloom, B. L., et al. A preventive intervention program for the newly separated: Final evaluations. *American Journal of Orthopsychiatry*, 1985, 55(1): pp. 9–26.

57. Pruett, M. K., G. Insabella, and K. Gustafson. The Collaborative Divorce Project: A court-based intervention for separating parents with young children. *Family Court Review*, 2005, 43(1): pp. 38–51.

58. Wolchik, S. A., et al. The children of divorce parenting intervention: Outcome evaluation of an empirically based program. *American Journal of Community Psychology*, 1993, 21(3): pp. 293–331.

59. Braver, S. H., W. A. Griffin, and J. T. Cookston. Prevention programs for divorced nonresident fathers. *Family Court Review*, 2005, 43(1): pp. 81–96.

60. Pruett, M. K., B. Nangle, and C. Bailey. Divorcing families with young children in the court's family services unit: Profiles and impact of services. *Family and Conciliation Courts Review*, 2000, 38(4): pp. 478–500.

61. Pruett, M. K. and T. D. Jackson. Perspectives on the divorce process: Parental perceptions of the legal system and its impact on family relations. *Journal of the American Academy of Psychiatry and the Law*, 2001, 29(1): pp. 18–28.

62. Pruett, M. K., R. Ebling, and G. Insabella. Critical aspects of parenting plans for young children: Interjecting data into the debate about overnights. *Family Court Review*, 2004, 42(1): pp. 39–59.

63. Buehler, C., et al. Description and evaluation of the orientation for divorcing parents: Implications for postdivorce prevention programs. *Family Relations*, 1992, 41(2): pp. 154–62.

64. Braver, S. H., and D. A. Gordon. What works and what doesn't? A critical review of the parent education literature. AFCC's 5th International Congress on Parent Education and Access Programs, 2002. Tucson, AZ.

65. Martinez, C. R., and M. S. Forgatch. Preventing problems with boys' noncompliance: Effects of a parent training intervention for divorcing mothers. *Journal of Consulting and Clinical Psychology*, 2001, 69(3): pp. 416–28.

66. Wolchik, S. A., et al. Programs for promoting parenting of residential parents: Moving from efficacy to effectiveness. *Family Court Review*, 2005, 43(1): pp. 65–80.

67. Wolchik, S. A., et al. Inner-city, poor children of divorce: Negative divorce-related events, problematic beliefs and adjustment problems. *Journal of Divorce and Remarriage*, 1993, 19(1): pp. 1–20.

68. Stolberg, A. L., and K. M. Garrison. Evaluating a primary prevention program for children of divorce. *American Journal of Community Psychology*, 1985, 13(2): pp. 111–24.

69. Gallagher, M. Marriage-saving. *National Review*, 1999, 51(21): pp. 38–40.

70. Nock, S. L., J. D. Wright, and L. Sanchez. America's divorce problem. *Society*, 1999, 36(4): pp. 43–52.

71. Nock, S. L., et al. Covenant marriage turns five years old. *Michigan Journal of Gender and Law*, 2003, 10: pp. 169–88.

72. Feld, S. L., K. B. Rosier, and A. Manning. Christian right as civil right: Covenant marriage and a kinder, gentler, moral conservatism. *Review of Religious Research*, 2002, 44(2): pp. 173–83.

73. Sanchez, L., et al. Setting the clock forward or back? Covenant marriage and the "divorce revolution." *Journal of Family Issues*, 2002, 23(1): pp. 91–120.

74. Kim, W., and W. King. The ties that bind. *Time*, 1997, 150(7): pp. 148–50.

75. Hawkins, A. J., et al. Attitudes about covenant marriage and divorce: Policy implications from a three-state comparison. *Family Relations*, 2002, 51: pp. 166–75.

76. Sanchez, L., et al. The implementation of covenant marriage in Louisiana. *Virginia Journal of Social Policy and Law*, 2001, 9(Fall): pp. 192–222.

77. Brinig, M. F., and S. L. Nock. What does covenant mean for relationships. *Notre Dame Journal of Law, Ethics and Public Policy*, 2004, 18: pp. 137–88.

78. Sanchez, L., et al. Is covenant marriage a policy that preaches to the choir? A comparison of covenant and standard married newlywed couples in Louisiana. 2002, Center for Family and Demographic Research, Bowling Green State University, Bowling Green, Ohio. Working paper series 02–06.

79. Rosier, K. B., and S. L. Feld. Covenant marriage: A new alternative for traditional families. *Journal of Comparative Family Studies*, 2000, 31(3): pp. 385–94.

80. Zurcher, K. E. "I do" or "I don't?" Covenant marriage after six years. *Notre Dame Journal of Law, Ethics and Public Policy*, 2004, 18: pp. 273–301.

81. Devlin, A. S., E. H. Brown, J. Beebe, and E. Parulis. Parent education for divorced fathers. *Family Relations: Interdisciplinary Journal of Applied Family Studies*. 1992, 41(3): 290–96.

8

Conclusions and Recommendations

In this book we have traveled through five social-policy responses to the problems of divorced families. We have examined each policy and its effectiveness to promote healthier relationships among family members of broken marriages. What remains to be examined is the net value of these various social experiments, the ability of social policy to influence social behavior and attitudes, and recommendations for the divorce-related profession—including policy makers and researchers alike. First, however, I will begin with a brief summary from the preceding chapters.

CONCLUSIONS FROM EACH SOCIAL-POLICY INTERVENTION

For each of the social-policy interventions that have been discussed in this book, what follows is a brief review of the intention of the law, the status of the research, and the conclusions of that research.

Mediation

The rationale for bringing mediation into the family legal system was to reduce the adversarial nature of the divorce process. The theory was that by bringing parents to the table, they could work to resolve their disputes together rather than relying on the court to do that for them. Inherent in this idea was the notion that if parents could establish a method of communication for dispute resolution, they could draw on this to resolve future disputes. Although mandated in a handful of states, the use of mediation services is primarily at the discretion of the court.

There is a vast body of research that has examined the outcomes and effectiveness of mediation. This research has been summarized and critiqued by a number of scholars, and most have concluded that mediation is not the "magical intervention" that it was once thought to be [1]. That does not mean that all is lost, however. Many studies have found positive outcomes for mediation. There is strong evidence from both studies with comparison and studies with control groups that mediation may foster more parental communication and cooperation. Evidence from longitudinal, randomized research indicates that mediation may result in more father involvement with their children. These are important findings and their significance should not be minimized.

Divorce Education Programs

Divorce education programs are intended to sensitize parents to the needs of children who live in divorced families. Most programs provide parents with guidelines about how they can minimize the harmful affects of divorce, primarily by lowering parental conflict, encouraging positive coparenting behaviors, and emphasizing the importance of avoiding triangulating behaviors that place children between their parents. Most programs also cover "normal" adult responses to divorce.

Like the social policies that regulate the use and mandate of mediation, the majority of laws do not mandate the use of divorce education programs. In most instances, the court can recommend that parents attend an educational seminar or parents can voluntarily attend educational programming—something that is usually undertaken by parents who recognize that divorce is stressful on children.

The research on the effectiveness of divorce education programs has varied considerably in its rigor. There are, however, some positive and encouraging findings about the effectiveness of this social policy. There is some evidence that parents who participate in divorce education programs have reduced their triangulating behaviors, such as asking their children for information about the other parent, speaking negatively about the other parent in front of the child, or generally using the child to satisfy a destructive curiosity about the other parent. There is also evidence that divorce education programs may result in less parental conflict, which is no small feat. And parents who participate in divorce education programs generally have more knowledge about children and their responses to divorce than parents who do not receive such education. These particular findings are fairly consistent between studies, and they are important indicators of the potential preventative nature of even short-term educational programs for families of divorce.

Parenting Plans

Parenting plans are a relatively new type of intervention in which parents outline their future roles and responsibilities as parents of a divorced family with minor children. This type of social-policy intervention is intended to encourage parents to be proactive in the planning for their life ahead, rather than reactive to unanticipated problems. Rarely mandated by state legislatures, parenting plans vary considerably in their breadth. Some parenting plans differ little from traditional divorce decrees in which custody of the children, parent-child contact schedules, and child-support orders are outlined. More comprehensive parenting plans discuss parenting responsibilities, including which parent will be responsible for specific aspects of the children's lives; parental decision making, including which and when each parent may participate in decisions about the children; residential or child-contact schedules, including vacation times, holidays, and birthdays; transportation arrangements, including how children will be transported to school, extracurricular activities, and between their parents' homes, and who will pay for those transportation costs; if and how co-parenting may change over the coming years, depending on the developmental needs and desires of the children; if parental and child relocation will be permitted; and, how future disputes will be resolved. Parenting plans have yet to be rigorously examined, and thus, there is no solid empirical evidence that can speak to the effectiveness of this social policy.

Joint Custody/Shared Parenting

Joint-custody or shared parenting agreements, whether residential or joint decision making, are not only permitted but encouraged in the majority of states. State legislatures, as well as social scientists, have declared it beneficial for children to have frequent and continuing contact with their parents. Social policy also encourages parents, to the greatest extent possible, to cooperate with one another and to make decisions jointly. The research on the benefits of joint custody and shared parenting are unclear. There is some evidence that shared parenting results in higher father involvement and higher compliance with child-support orders, but these findings are often confounded with the fact that fathers who have shared parenting arrangements would be more involved regardless of their parenting agreement, and that fathers of higher income and education tend to be more compliant with their child-support orders.

The research about the well-being of children from families of joint-custody arrangements has been criticized for generalizing from nonrepresentative samples to the population at large. Children in joint arrangements generally appear to have a better adjustment to postdivorce life than children who are not in shared arrangements. Often this is because of the cooperative and good-natured relationships between parents, rather than the joint-custody arrangement itself. Nevertheless, most researchers are comfortable concluding that unless parents are engaged in a high level of conflict or violence, joint custody or shared parenting neither helps nor harms children.

Presumption for Joint Custody/Shared Parenting

As noted in chapter 6, laws that declare a presumption for joint custody or shared parenting are more contentious and politically sensitive than any other social-policy response to divorced families—although policy responses to instances of parental relocation are quickly taking a close "second place." The primary problem with the public debate over mandating joint custody or shared parenting is that little to no research has been conducted in this area of divorced families. This is in part because only a handful of states/jurisdictions have a presumption for joint custody; thus it is difficult to study this phenomenon. The only research that has been conducted on presumption laws indicates that where presumption laws are present, they appear to be well-implemented and there is a high rate of shared parenting on paper. The results are inconclusive regarding the effect of a presumption for joint legal custody on father involvement. Thus, essentially little can be concluded about presumption laws. As a result, the debate about a presumption for joint custody continues to rest on ideology.

I argue for a presumption of joint residential custody and shared decision-making responsibilities as an initial starting place for all families. The research about the benefits of father-child contact is inconclusive [2–4], but I err on the side of caution, encouraging substantial involvement by both divorced parents. I also argue that it is possible to create legislation with language that provides appropriate protection for children and caregivers from violent parents and unhealthy relationships and, finally, that the best interests of the child should continue to be the overriding criterion for all child-custody decisions.

LOOKING ACROSS THE STATES AT SOCIAL POLICIES

Table 8.1 summarizes all of the social-policy interventions addressed in this book. The table provides a summary for each state and the social policies

Table 8.1. Social-policy Responses to Divorce across the Nation, by State

	MEDIATION		DIVORCE EDUCATION		PARENTING PLANS		JOINT CUSTODY		TOTAL	
State	Statute?	Mandated?	Statute?	Mandated?	Statute?	Mandated?	Statute?	Presumption?	Any Policy	Mandated Policy‡
AL	Yes	By request	No		No		Yes	No	2	1
AK	Yes	No	Yes	Family viol. only	No		Yes	No	3	1
AZ	Yes	No	Yes	No	Yes	JC** only	Yes	No	4	1
AR	Yes	No	No		No		Yes	No	2	0
CA	Yes	Contested cases	Yes	No	Yes	Yes	Yes	No	4	2
CO	Yes	No	Yes	No	Yes	Yes	No		3	1
CT	Yes	No	Yes	Yes	Yes	Disputes only	Yes	No	4	2
DE	Yes	Yes	Yes	Yes	No		Yes	No	3	2
DC	Yes	No	Yes	No	Yes	No	Yes	Yes	4	1
FL	Yes	Yes	Yes	Yes	No		Yes	No	3	2
GA	No		No		No		Yes	No	1	0
HI	Yes	No	Yes	No	No		Yes	No	3	0
ID	Yes	Yes	No		Yes	No	Yes	No	3	1
IL	Yes	No	Yes	No	Yes	JC only	Yes	No	4	1
IN	Yes	No	No		No		Yes	No	2	0
IA	Yes	No	Yes	Yes	No		Yes	No	3	1
KS	Yes	No	Yes	No	Yes	No	Yes	No	4	0
KY	Yes	No	No		No		Yes	No	2	0
LA	Yes	No	Yes	No	Yes	No	Yes	No	4	0
ME	Yes	Custody disputes	Yes	Yes	No		Yes	No	3	1
MD	Yes	No	Yes	No	No		Yes	No	3	0
MA	No		Yes	Yes	No		Yes	No	2	1
MI	Yes	No	No		No		Yes	No	2	0
MN	Yes	No	Yes	Yes	Yes	Yes	Yes	Yes (JLC)†	4	3
MS	No		No		No		Yes	No	1	0

(continues)

Table 8.1. (Continued)

State	MEDIATION		DIVORCE EDUCATION		PARENTING PLANS		JOINT CUSTODY†		TOTAL	
	Statute?	Mandated?	Statute?	Mandated?	Statute?	Mandated?	Statute?	Presumption?	Any Policy	Mandated Policy‡
MO	Yes	No	Yes	Yes	Yes	Yes	Yes	No	4	2
MT	Yes	No	Yes	No	Yes	Yes	Yes	No	4	1
NE	Yes	No	Yes	No	Yes	No	Yes	No	4	0
NV	Yes*	Yes*	No		No		Yes	No	2	1
NH	Yes	No	Yes	Yes	Yes	Yes	Yes	Yes (JLC)	4	3
NJ	Yes		Yes	Yes	No		Yes	No	3	1
NM	Yes	No	No		Yes	JC only	Yes	Yes (JLC)	3	2
NY	No		No		No		No	No	1	0
NC	Yes	Custody disputes	No		Yes	Disputes only	Yes	No	3	2
ND	Yes	No	No		No		No	No	1	0
OH	Yes	No	Yes	No	Yes	No	Yes	No	4	0
OK	Yes	No	Yes	No	No		Yes	No	3	0
OR	Yes	No	Yes	No	Yes	Yes	Yes	No	4	1
PA	Yes	No	No		Yes	Yes*	No		3	0
RI	Yes	No	No		No		Yes	No	1	0
SC	No		No		No		No	No	1	0
SD	Yes	Custody disputes	No		Yes	Yes	Yes	No	3	2
TN	Yes	No	Yes	No	Yes	Yes	Yes	No	4	1
TX	No		Yes	No	No		Yes	Yes (JLC)	2	1
UT	Yes	Yes	Yes	Yes	Yes	Disputes only	Yes	No	4	3
VT	No		Yes	No	Yes	Yes	Yes	No	3	1
VA	Yes	No	Yes	Contested cases	No		Yes	No	3	1
WA	Yes	No	Yes	No	Yes	Yes	Yes	No	4	1
WV	Yes	Custody disputes	Yes	Yes	Yes	Yes	Yes	Yes (JLC)	4	4
WI	Yes	Yes	Yes	No	Yes	Disputes only	Yes	Yes (JLC)	4	3
WY	No		No		No		Yes	No	1	0

Note: *In certain counties; **JC = joint custody of any type; †JLC = joint legal custody. ‡Any mandates are counted.

that have been implemented for that state: mediation, divorce education, parenting plans, and joint custody. For each of these interventions, the table indicates if the intervention is mandatory. For joint-custody legislation, the column that indicates whether the policy is mandatory is titled "presumption," because a presumption for joint custody is a mandate for this custodial arrangement. The final two right-hand columns indicates how many total social policies have been enacted by each state. For example, the state of Michigan has enacted two social policies to target families of divorce: mediation, parenting plans, and joint-custody legislation; none of these are mandated. One line below Michigan, Minnesota has implemented four different policies: mediation, divorce education, joint custody, and a presumption (or mandate) for joint custody; three of these are mandatory. The most proactive states, as defined by the number of mandates on their books, are Minnesota, New Hampshire, West Virginia, and Wisconsin.

Figure 8.1 illustrates how many total social policies have been enacted by all states, mandatory or otherwise. The figure shows that most states have implemented a number of different social-policy responses to problems associated with families of divorce, but very few states mandate the majority of their policies. Only one state mandates all four different policies. All states have adopted at least one type of policy for divorced families.

There is virtually no research that examines the joint impact of legislation on families. Some studies have included families that have received either mediation or divorce education, but they have failed to consider the

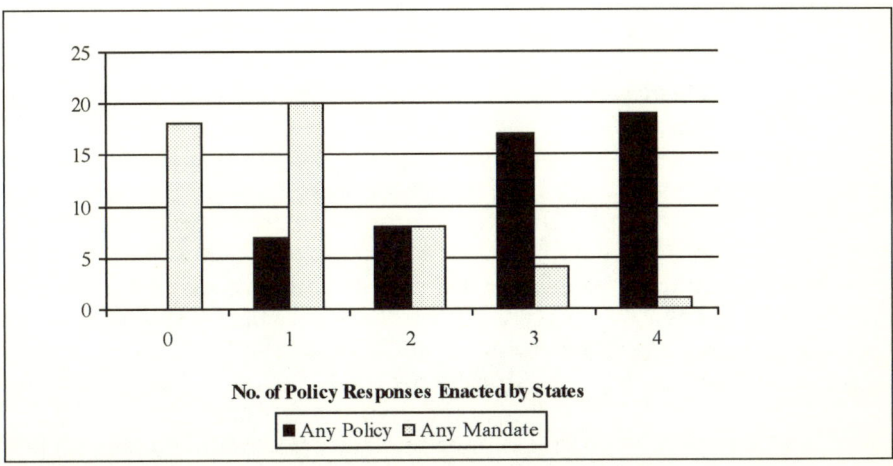

Note: Minimum number of policies enacted = 0, Maximum of policies enacated = 5

Figure 8.1. Number of Different Social Policies Enacted by States

interaction of these two variables [5]. More research is needed on the interaction of receiving multiple types of intervention, since most social-policy interventions do not exist in a vacuum. One could speculate, however, that prevention programs, such as those reviewed in chapter 7, that combine multiple types of programs and services together are a good indication of the potential success of using multiple methods of intervention at the state level [6–8].

USING SOCIAL POLICY TO INFLUENCE BEHAVIOR AND SOCIAL ATTITUDES

Social policies target problem behavior, social ills, and social injustices that would not likely be eliminated or alleviated without legislative action. Policies have been enacted to encourage safer driving practices (e.g., mandatory seat belt laws and drunken driving laws); to promote environmentally friendly behavior (e.g., mandatory recycling laws and antilittering legislation); to deter and punish criminal sexual activity (e.g., rape laws and harsher sentencing for sex offenders); to punish caregivers who kill their children (e.g., child fatality sentencing legislation); and to correct racial and gender discrimination (e.g., civil rights legislation and hate crime laws). The effects of such legislation are often difficult to assess, as it is usually coupled with public awareness campaigns and media attention—factors for which it can be difficult to account in statistical analyses. These issues are also often addressed at the national level and can thus promote behavior change regardless of state legislation.

Some public and social policies, which are primarily local in nature, have been effectively evaluated to determine the success of recently enacted legislation. Most often this body of research evaluates seat belt legislation, laws addressing the use of bicycle helmets, recycling laws, criminal justice legislation, and other similar changes in state-level policies.

Research indicates that a number of different types of legislative actions result in behavioral changes. The effects of mandatory seat belt legislation in Kansas were monitored for one year after implementation. The law was found to be effective in both promoting more positive attitudes about using seat belts and in changing actual use of seat belts, increasing compliance with the law by 78 percent [9]. The state of California passed legislation mandating that 25 percent of all solid waste be streamed out of landfills by increasing recycling; towns effectively met this goal by encouraging "curbside" recycling at the local level [10].

Mandates appear to be more effective than allowing the public to self-regulate undesirable behavior. One study examined the effectiveness of different bicycle helmet laws in three New York City suburbs: one in which all residents were required to wear helmets or face a fine of fifty dollars; another in which children under the age of twelve were required to wear helmets, with no penalty for failure to comply; and, in a third county, in which residents were encouraged, but not mandated, to wear helmets [11]. The authors found that the county with the least restrictive law had the lowest rate of helmet use and the county with the most restrictive law had the highest rate of compliance. Similar success has been found with laws that regulate motorcyclists wearing helmets [12]. Research found that two months after a Taiwanese law took effect, 95.95 percent of cyclists used helmets, compared with only 21 percent before the law was enacted. Moreover, in the year after implementation, motorcycle-related head injuries decreased by 33 percent.

New drunk-driving laws in Canada have been known to result in lowered self-reports of drunk driving [13]. The former law penalized an intoxicated driver by suspending the offender's license for twelve hours at the time the charge was laid. The new law mandated suspending the license for ninety days. Following the implementation of the harsher law, there was a significant change in the number of persons who, in a public-wide survey, said that they drove after consuming two drinks.

Changes in public policy have also effectively increased compliance with child-support orders. In one year, the state of New York lowered child-support arrears from $872 million to $574 million by enacting "get-tough" policies that included suspending driver's licenses of nonpaying parents, placing liens on property, requiring welfare recipients to help locate nonpaying parents, and by using state labor records to locate parents in arrears [14].

Public awareness or public education campaigns have also successfully resulted in behavioral and attitudinal changes. Antitobacco campaigns have been successful in both California and Massachusetts, resulting in steeper decreases in adult smoking when compared to national rates [15]. Many other antitobacco campaigns have successfully prevented or delayed youth from starting to smoke and increased cessation rates among adults who smoke [16, 17]. Some social-welfare scholars attribute the national increase in reporting of child maltreatment to public awareness campaigns and the mandatory reporting laws that accompanied them. In the thirty years between 1963 and 1993, there was a twenty-fold increase in the number of child maltreatment cases that were reported to social-service agencies [18].

The state of Washington launched an educational campaign about the use and availability of emergency contraceptive pills. In a four-month period, calls per month to an emergency contraceptive hotline increased by ten times the pre-campaign level [19]. Finally, one of the most successful public awareness campaigns has been the "back-to-sleep" promotion that targeted parents of infants in an effort to reduce cases of sudden infant death syndrome. Ten years after this campaign was initiated, cases of sudden infant death syndrome decreased by 50 percent [20].

I have provided these examples of behavioral changes to demonstrate that social-policy and public-education campaigns can change social behavior. I believe that the same may be true for policies that target families of divorce. I am not the first author to suggest that there is a link between social policy and social behavior and attitudes. Salazar and colleagues suggest that domestic-violence policies may lead to new social norms that are less tolerant of family violence [21]. Elkin suggests that shared parenting arrangements remind family members and society at large that "families are forever" [22]. Maldonado, more than anyone, however, links together changes in divorce policy with changes in social norms and social behavior [23]. She argues that a presumption for joint legal custody will change expectations among parents and society. Moreover, she maintains that social expectations resulting from such legislation that both parents should be involved in their children's lives will educate many non-residential parents enough to increase their involvement, and others will be "shamed" into changing their behavior since their actions will fall outside of appropriate social norms.

I concur with this approach to social policy and families of divorce. Let us use research-based social policy not only to improve the lives of children from families of divorce, but also to shape social attitudes and ultimately social behavior to have higher expectations of divorced parents and to promote more parental cooperation and parental involvement in children's lives.

RECOMMENDATIONS TO POLICY MAKERS

The conclusions that result from this book concern recommendations to policy makers and recommendations to researchers. I also provide a final recommendation that is made jointly to both of these audiences.

Policy recommendation 1: Mandate interventions for all families rather than relying on the goodwill of divorcing parents. There is evidence that parents who voluntarily seek or use intervention services for divorcing families are different from parents who do not use such services. For example, couples who voluntarily mediate tend to be better educated, have less ethnic diversity, and earn more income than couples who do not mediate. They also tend to experience more depression and guilt about the divorce, and they tend to view their spouses as more fair-minded than couples who chose not to mediate [24, 25]. Families that voluntarily choose joint physical-custody arrangements are significantly different from families that do not. A greater percentage of families with joint residential living arrangements have attended graduate school and have higher combined household and maternal income than families without joint arrangements [26–28]. Similar differences have been found between families that select joint legal custody and families that do not [29]. Most research of divorce education programs has used parents who have been mandated to receive such training; however, Arbuthnot and colleagues note that voluntary divorce education programs are likely to only draw the most motivated parents [30].

Families that are most at risk will be least likely to use interventions. In fact, these families will likely only receive assistance if their family situation reaches a crisis point (e.g., repeated court cases or child psychopathology) and they are referred for services. In such instances, damage to children that could have been prevented may have already been done. Let us not leave children and families at risk for problems when there is ample evidence that some interventions reduce harmful behavior and risk factors in families of divorce.

Moreover, divorce decrees sometimes include penalties (e.g., payment of a hundred dollars) that would be enacted if a parent fails to co-parent or abide by child-contact schedules. There is little research to indicate whether courts follow through on such threats. If not, perhaps courts should. If legislators are uncomfortable "punishing" or "threatening" parents as a means to get them to cooperate with each other, another way to change social behavior is to offer incentives. Perhaps parents who revisit their parenting plans every two years or who seek formal education about parenting in a divorced family could receive a financial "reward" for their participation.

Policy recommendation 2: Expand what is mandated. Parenting education programs, which usually involve a two- to four-hour seminar, produce promising findings. Prevention programs that are more comprehensive and longer in duration produce findings that are even more promising. Mandating that all divorcing parents attend an eight- to twelve-week intervention is not likely to be politically feasible, but it is possible that currently mandated interventions could be made more comprehensive.

Policy recommendation 3: Promote shared parenting. From the moment that state legislatures became involved in drafting legislation for divorcing families they have promoted a paradigm of shared parenting. Moreover, the propensity to do so over the last several decades has only increased. Mediation, divorce education programs, parenting plans, and joint custody are all intended to move parents closer to staying involved with their children, financially supporting their children, and having parents work with one another for the sake of their children. Although there is some research that has found no positive association between parent-child contact and psychosocial measures for children [3, 4], the vast majority of social programs aim to keep, if not encourage, an engaged co-parenting relationship and contact between children and both of their parents [6, 8, 31–33].

Policy recommendation 4: Use social policy to change social behavior and attitudes. One way to change behavior is to change the rules and laws that regulate those behaviors. Public policy, for instance, is a form of regulation, as it reflects societal standards. In every state in the nation it is against the law to abuse a child. Such laws reflect a social attitude that it is not only cruel, but also unacceptable to abuse children. It is against the law to drive while intoxicated. This reflects the social attitude that it is unacceptable to engage in a behavior that would jeopardize human lives. Social policy declares that if one bears a child, one must either directly provide for that child or provide financial support to meet that child's basic needs. Such regulation is a reflection of the social belief that parents, as opposed to others or the government, have primary responsibility to financially support and provide for a child.

In each of these instances we expect that the presence of legislation itself may shape human behavior. Some parents might want to use severe corporal punishment on their children, but refrain from doing so because it is against the law. Others might, and certainly did in past generations, want to drive while under the influence, but now refrain from doing so because of legislation. Furthermore, individuals may be deterred from bearing children, knowing that they will, for the life of the child, be financially responsible for their offspring.

Before child support legislation was enacted, there was little legal or public expectation that a noncustodial parent would support his or her children. While we still lack full compliance with such legislation [34], we have at least changed public [35] and legal expectations, and in many instances, behavior (e.g., increases in child-support compliance) [14, 34]. There is no reason that legislation that promotes shared parenting cannot promote similar changes. Over the past several decades, father involvement in divorced families has increased, which is likely the result of multiple efforts: more awards of joint decision-making responsibilities, multiple calls at all levels of government for father involvement, social-service agencies that promote father involvement, parenting education that targets fathers, and public policy that calls for "frequent and continuing contact" between children and both of their parents. We can use social policy to shape social attitudes and ultimately social behavior. If we expect parents to work together and to cooperate with one another, these positive co-parenting behaviors are more likely to occur than if we do not. For example, our attitudes about race and discrimination in the United States might not have evolved over the last fifty years without legislation. It is unlikely that grassroots efforts alone would have produced the same social advances for people of color, or for women. Likewise, it is difficult to imagine advances in our nation's treatment of gays and lesbians without legal protection and declarations of equality in the eyes of the law. I make this same argument with regard to co-parenting. Let our social policies declare that parents should and must work together for the sake of their children.

Public education campaigns have effectively shaped a multitude of different behaviors and addressed many social problems, ranging from drug use to sudden infant death syndrome, from smoking behavior to child abuse reporting laws. Public awareness campaigns have educated the public about the hazards of driving while intoxicated and the importance of not tolerating family violence. They have encouraged parents to read to their children, stop smoking because of their children, and to stay informed of their children's after-school activities as a way to prevent drug use. I have yet to see general education or awareness campaigns that remind parents about the importance of keeping both (nonviolent) parents involved in children's lives, and the benefits to children when parents put aside their differences to focus on their children. Social change results from multiple different efforts: public policy, grassroots efforts, social programming, and general public education. I strongly recommend that we provide divorced parents with clear messages about the importance of keeping both parents engaged in their children's lives, and what they can do to help achieve this.

RECOMMENDATIONS TO RESEARCHERS

The research on social policies for families of divorce suffers from problems that are common throughout the social sciences but are nonetheless important and worthy of discussion. My recommendations follow the discussion of the following problem areas.

Problems with the Research

Random Assignment

Rarely, if ever, are rigorous research methods applied to the examination of social-policy interventions. This has been true of the research on social-policy interventions for families of divorce. Only one study that examined the efficacy of mediation has used random assignment [33, 36–38]. No other policy intervention that has been addressed in this book has been subjected to such scrutiny (although some prevention programs have been [6–8]). Part of the problem with using randomly assigned groups is the perception that some residents of a state or county will be denied the "better" service. Legislators and advocates on both sides of the aisle may be convinced of the "success" of a social-policy intervention and want it implemented statewide. Since the decision makers believe that this intervention is effective, it may be difficult, if not nearly impossible, to convince them of the importance of testing the intervention for its efficacy. Because that particular intervention has become equated with success, policy makers may perceive that families that do not receive the intervention are being denied the opportunity to have a "successful" postdivorce family [39–42].

Poor and Unequal Comparison Groups

Policy makers and social scientists alike have embraced the notion of "evidence-based practices" [43, 44]. And, as a result, they may understand the importance of comparing families that have experienced an intervention with families that have not. However, policy makers may not understand the importance of having equal comparison groups. Some common comparison groups are divorced families from neighboring states or counties that do not have mandates for the target intervention; comparing families that have divorced under a new law with families that divorced several years earlier under a previous law is another common method of comparison. This method is problematic because often families are not well matched, especially when using comparison groups from neighboring regions. States and counties often have distinct cultural characteristics and judicial procedural characteristics that can be difficult to measure. Using families from a previous time period does not allow a researcher to account for subtle changes that have taken place during the intervening years, such as other changes in social policy, education campaigns, and high-profile media cases of family problems—all of which can help to shape social attitudes and behaviors.

Small Sample Sizes

Many of the studies have small samples sizes. This is especially true for studies that have used mail surveys without implementing multiple mailings. Studies using comparison groups from neighboring counties or states often suffer from especially small comparison groups. It is possible that failure to secure a comparison group during the study design may account for some of the latter problem.

Lack of Context

Most studies fail to discuss the larger context of the social and procedural environment. This point is partially related to the problem of unequal comparison groups. There are likely multiple differences between counties and states with regard to divorce filing procedures, courtroom events and procedures, the "backlog" of the docket affecting the length of time before couples can appear in court, differences in child-support guidelines, judicial appointments, whether a policy is fully or partially implemented, and many other considerations. In other words, there are a multitude of characteristics that may vary between jurisdictions that might influence group differences but be unrelated to the intervention that is being measured. The same can be said of cultural differences, such as local religious differences, school- or community-based interventions or approaches to working with divorced families, "freak cases" that have been featured in the local media, the strength of the local women's or fathers' rights groups, and different political orientations, which might all influence group difference. In such circumstances, the cultural characteristics would be associated with differences between the groups being compared, but the policy intervention would be credited with bringing about the difference. As a researcher who has compared policy approaches between two neighboring states, I appreciate the difficulty of tackling this issue. In short, it is nearly impossible for every possible variable to be measured. Nevertheless, the procedural and cultural context in which divorces occur, and in which policy is made and implemented, must become an integral part of the examination regarding policy effectiveness.

Longitudinal Studies

Most studies on the effectiveness of social policy interventions for families of divorce are not able to follow study participants for very long, if at all. This portion of a study design is expensive. Many local programs, such as a divorce education program, are unable to financially support this piece of a study, and it can be difficult to convince state governments of the importance of following families for years after an intervention is completed. Most policy makers are eager to know about the "success" or "failure" of a program to inform them of whether to fully adopt or abolish a pilot program. The legislative system is not designed to keep policy in limbo waiting for the results of social scientists. Nonetheless, longitudinal studies are important, as oftentimes researchers see that the effectiveness of a program diminishes or disappears after a period of time (such as in the case of Head Start [45]). Thus, results can be informative to policy makers, even if they do not have time to wait for results.

If researchers cannot convince state legislatures to fund longitudinal studies, they can more likely convince granting foundations and government research agencies. The results of such studies can be used to inform future policy or to adapt existing state statutes.

Objective Reporters

Most of the research that examines the effectiveness of divorce interventions asks parents to report about their own feelings and behaviors, as well as their children's behaviors. There are few studies that use reports from objective reporters. There have been no studies that have examined the interactions between parents and children in their discussion of the divorce and the life changes that have resulted from the breakup of the family. This would be one possible way to measure communication styles between children and parents, parents' ability to demonstrate knowledge and display empathy toward their children's point of view, and the level of tension or conflict between children and parents with regard to the divorce. The same is true of parents. There is almost no research that objectively examines hostility or cooperativeness between parents, or their ability to plan and communicate about their children. In order to more effectively study this, parents, or parent-child dyads could be observed over the course of several years, comparing those families that experienced specific interventions with those that did not. Parents could be asked to keep a diary regarding how often they correspond with each other, how often they see their children, and when and how they make decisions about their children. This would likely be more precise than asking parents about their level of conflict or how often they remember communicating with their former spouse about the children. Teachers could also be called upon more frequently to report on children's behavior, and measures of academic achievement could also be used more regularly.

Definitions

Some researchers claim to study divorced families, when they actually study families of broken unions. In other words, researchers sometimes include families with never-married parents or families with separated (but not divorced) parents, with divorced families. This is problematic because people who have children out of wedlock differ in important demographic and social attitudinal ways from people who marry before having children [46]. Moreover, where most often married parents live together and both parents form emotional bonds with their children, it is not clear if this is always the case in families with never-married parents.

Parents who are separated, legally or otherwise, may reconcile their relationship; they may hold spiritual or cultural beliefs that separate them from parents who divorce, or there may be other factors (e.g., financial and emotional reasons) that somehow set them apart from parents who do divorce. Lumping all of these families together and calling them "divorced families" inaccurately portrays all of these families and the challenges that they face.

Recommendations

Research recommendation 1: Increase the rigor of study design. This is a broad recommendation and could apply to many different aspects of a study; specifically, I am speaking of the "nuts and bolts" of a study. Strive for random assignment. (Inherent in this recommendation is one for policy makers: permit random assignment to test the effectiveness of social interventions before making the service widely available to all families.) If one must use comparison groups (as opposed to control groups), match the groups on as many characteristics as possible. Shoot for large sample sizes and methods for retaining study participants for follow-up measures, such as multiple mailings or keeping in touch with study participants even when data are not being collected. If at all possible, conduct a longitudinal study that follows families over the course of several years.

Research recommendation 2: Data collection methods. Consider using techniques that have not been widely used in this field of study. Relying on parental reports of their children's progress and level of functioning is problematic. Parents may be prone to underreport their children's problems. Researchers could consider using a measure of "social desirability bias" to control for these problems. More objective data-collection techniques, as previously discussed, could also be employed. Having parents or children keep a diary, using observational techniques and communication styles of parents or parents and children, and obtaining reports from teachers are other possible methods. Finally, few measures ask children about their emotional state or well-being after divorce. Unlike parents, they would be less likely to have a vested interest in inflating their adjustment to postdivorce life.

Research recommendation 3: Context. Consider the context of the state or county being studied and compared with another. Make sure to consider potential procedural and cultural differences as discussed before. It is especially important to examine policy implementation. Just because a law was passed does not mean that it has been implemented. Consider the political environment surrounding the passage of the law and how this, too, might reflect different cultural, procedural, or political differences between potential comparison groups. It might be necessary to interview professionals or parents who have recently divorced in order to gain a full or even partial understanding of these subtle, but essential, differences. Try to control for this variability through the study measures.

Research recommendation 4: If it's a fork, don't call it a spoon. Researchers purporting to study families of divorce should do just that. If one's sample includes never-married families or parents who are legally separated, either run separate analyses for these different groups of families or eliminate them from the examination of divorced families.

Research recommendation 5: Examine the intersection of different interventions. Families receive a multitude of different services as they move through the legal and social-service system. As researchers examine families of divorce, inquire about all of the possible interventions of which a family may have been a recipient. Control for these differences and examine potential interactions between interventions.

RECOMMENDATIONS TO POLICY MAKERS AND RESEARCHERS

Research and policy recommendation 1: Policy makers and researchers should work together. An important recommendation concerns policy makers and researchers working together. This means that state legislatures should look to the college and university system to provide guidance on how other legislatures have tackled social-policy responses to families of divorce and the successes or failures of those legislative responses. And university researchers should actively seek opportunities to provide their research and conclusions to decision makers in the state.

Research and policy recommendation 2: Seek opportunities to establish prevention programs. The research on prevention programs is promising, and because these programs are potentially most helpful to high-risk families, state legislatures should be working with university researchers to establish such programs in either high-risk or divorce-prone regions. State legislatures could earmark money for "demonstration programs" that target families of divorce, which would be housed at university locations and/or run by university researchers.

Research and policy recommendation 3: Examine the effects of parental relocation. State legislatures will continue to be presented with bills to address the problem of parental relocation. There is little to no empirical evidence about the effect of contested and noncontested cases of parental relocation on the psychological adjustment of children. State legislatures could, and should, make monies available to study this phenomenon in order to provide guidelines for creating sound legislation.

CONCLUSION

In this book, we have traveled through the history of divorce, social-policy responses to changes in family formation, and the success of these interventions. Ultimately, I conclude that social policies appear to have a positive effect on families of divorce and that we should continue to strive to find research-based practices that improve the lives of children and families of divorce.

REFERENCES

1. Kelly, J. B. Family mediation research: Is there empirical support for the field? *Conflict Resolution Quarterly*, 2004, 22(1-2): pp. 3–35.
2. Wallerstein, J., and T. J. Tanke. To move or not to move: Psychological and legal considerations in the relocation of children following divorce. *Family Law Quarterly*, 1996, 30(Summer): pp. 305–32.
3. Furstenberg, F. F., S. P. Morgan, and P. D. Allison. Paternal participation and children's well-being after marital dissolution. *American Sociological Review*, 1987, 52(October): pp. 695–701.
4. Amato, P. R., and B. Keith. Parental divorce and the well-being of children: A meta-analysis. *Psychological Bulletin*, 1991, 110(1): pp. 26–46.
5. Toews, M. L., and P. C. McKenry. Court-related predictors of parental cooperation and conflict after divorce. *Journal of Divorce and Remarriage*, 2001, 35(1): pp. 57–73.
6. Braver, S. H., W. A. Griffin, and J. T. Cookston. Prevention programs for divorced nonresident fathers. *Family Court Review*, 2005, 43(1): pp. 81–96.
7. Wolchik, S. A., et al. Six-year follow-up of preventive interventions for children of divorce. A randomized controlled trial. *Journal of the American Medical Association*, 2002, 288(15): pp. 1874–81.
8. Pruett, M. K., G. Insabella, and K. Gustafson. The Collaborative Divorce Project: A court-based intervention for separating parents with young children. *Family Court Review*, 2005, 43(1): pp. 38–51.
9. Adeyanju, M. Public knowledge, attitudes and behavior toward Kansas mandatory seatbelt use: Implications for public health policy. *Journal of Health and Social Policy*, 1991, 3(2): pp. 117–35.
10. Oskamp, S. Resource conservation and recycling: Behavior and policy. *Journal of Social Issues*, 1995, 51(4): pp. 157–77.
11. Puder, D., and P. Visintainer. A comparison of the effect of different bicycle helmet laws in three New York City suburbs. *American Journal of Public Health*, 1999, 89: pp. 1736–38.
12. Chiu, W.-T., et al. The effect of the Taiwan motorcycle helmet use law on head injuries. *American Journal of Public Health*, 2000, 90, pp. 793–96.
13. Mann, R., et al. Changing drinking-and-driving behavior: The effects of Ontario's administrative driver's license suspension law. *Canadian Medical Association Journal*, 2000, 162: pp. 1141–42.

14. Hernandez, R. A new move to help insure child support. *New York Times*, March 12, 1999, p. 37.

15. Siegel, M., and L. Biener. Evaluating the impact of statewide anti-tobacco compaigns: The Massachusetts and California tobacco control programs. *Journal of Social Issues*, 1997, 53(1): pp. 147–68.

16. Kelley, M. J., and D. C. McCrory. Prevention of lung cancer. *CHEST*, 2003, 123(1): pp. 50S–59S.

17. Frieden, T. R., and D. E. Blakeman. The dirty dozen: 12 myths that undermine tobacco control. *American Journal of Public Health*, 2005, 95(9): pp. 1500–1505.

18. Besharov, D. J., and L. A. Laumann. Child abuse reporting. *Society*, 1996, 33(4): p. 46.

19. Hayes, M., J. Hutchings, and P. Hayes. Reducing unintended pregnancy by increasing access to emergency contraceptive pills. *Maternal and Child Health Journal*, 2000, 4(3): pp. 203–8.

20. Alexander, D. Reducing the risks of SIDS through community partnerships. *American Family Physician*, 2005, 72(2): pp. 228–29.

21. Salazar, L. F., et al. Moving beyond the individual: Examining the effects of domestic violence policies on social norms. *American Journal of Community Psychology*, 2003, 32(3/4): pp. 253–64.

22. Elkin, M. Joint custody: Affirming that parents and families are forever. *Social Work*, 1987, 32(1): pp. 18–24.

23. Maldonado, S. Beyond economic fatherhood: Encouraging divorced fathers to parent. *University of Pennsylvania Law Review*, 2005, 153(January): pp. 921–1009.

24. Kelly, J. B. Parent interaction after divorce: Comparison of mediated and adversarial divorce processes. *Behavioral Sciences and the Law*, 1991, 9: pp. 387–98.

25. Kelly, J. B., and M. A. Duryee. Women's and men's views of mediation in voluntary and mandatory mediation settings. *Family and Conciliation Courts Review*, 1992, 30(1): pp. 34–49.

26. Pearson, J., and N. Thoennes. Custody after divorce: Demographic and attitudinal patterns. *American Journal of Orthopsychiatry*, 1990, 60(2): pp. 233–49.

27. Shrier, D. K., et al. Level of satisfaction of fathers and mothers with joint or sole custody arrangements: Results of a questionnaire. *Journal of Divorce and Remarriage*, 1991, 16(3/4): pp. 163–69.

28. Arditti, J. A., and D. Madden-Derdich. Joint and sole custody mothers: Implications for research and practice. *Families in Society*, 1997, 78(1): pp. 36–45.

29. Seltzer, J. A. Legal custody arrangements and children's economic welfare. *American Journal of Sociology*, 1991, 96(4): pp. 895–929.

30. Arbuthnot, J., et al. Court-sponsored educational programs for divorcing parents: Some guiding thoughts and preliminary data. *Juvenile and Family Court Journal*, 1994, 45: pp. 77–84.

31. Arbuthnot, J., and D. A. Gordon. Does mandatory divorce education for parents work? A six-month outcome evaluation. *Family and Conciliation Courts Review*, 1996, 34(1): pp. 60–81.

32. Blaisure, K. R., and M. J. Geasler. The Divorce Education Intervention Model. *Family and Conciliation Courts Review*, 2000, 38(4): pp. 501–13.

33. Emery, R. E., et al. Child custody mediation and litigation: Custody, contact, and coparenting 12 years after initial dispute resolution. *Journal of Consulting and Clinical Psychology*, 2001, 69(2): pp. 323–32.

34. U.S. Bureau of the Census. *Custodial mothers and fathers and their child support: 2001.* 2003, Washington, DC: U.S. Bureau of the Census.

35. Chien-Chung, H. Pregnancy intention from men's perspectives: Does child support enforcement matter? *Perspectives on Sexual and Reproductive Health*, 2005, 37(3): pp. 119–24.

36. Emery, R. E., F. D. Fincham, and E. M. Cummings. Parenting in context: Systematic thinking about parental conflict and its influence on children. *Journal of Consulting and Clinical Psychology*, 1992, 60(6): pp. 909–12.

37. Emery, R. E., S. G. Matthews, and M. M. Wyer. Child custody mediation and litigation: Further evidence on the differing views of mothers and fathers. *Journal of Consulting and Clinical Psychology*, 1991, 59(3): pp. 410–18.

38. Dillon, P. A., and R. E. Emery. Divorce mediation and resolution of child custody disputes: Long-term effects. *American Journal of Orthopsychiatry*, 1996, 66(1): pp. 131–40.

39. La Vaque, T. J. The ethical use of placebo controls in clinical research: The Declaration of Helsinki. *Applied Psychophysiology and Biofeedback*, 2001, 26(1): pp. 23–37.

40. Epstein, W. M. Randomized controlled trials in the human services. *Social Work Research and Abstracts*, 1992, 29(3): pp. 3–10.

41. Elliott, S. A., and J. S. L. Brown. What are we doing to waiting list controls? *Behaviour Research and Therapy*, 2002, 40(9): pp. 1047–52.

42. DiTomasso, R. A., and P. A. McDermott. Dilemma of the untreated control group in applied research: A proposed solution. *Psychological Reports*, 1981, 49(3): pp. 823–28.

43. Chambers, D. A., H. Ringeisen, and E. E. Hickman. Federal, state and foundation initiatives around evidence-based practices child and adolescent mental health. *Child and Adolescent Psychiatric Clinics of North America*, 2005, 14(2): pp. 307–27.

44. Moser, L. L., N. L. DeLuca, and G. R. Bond. Implementing evidence-based psychosocial practices: Lessons learned from statewide implementation of two practices. *CNS Spectrums*, 2004, 9(12): pp. 926–36.

45. Barnett, W. S., and J. T. Hustedt. Head Start's lasting benefits. *Infants and Young Children: An Interdisciplinary Journal of Special Care Practices*, 2005, 18(1): pp. 16–24.

46. Herrmann, A. 30 percent of new moms in Ill. unmarried: census. *Chicago Sun-Times*, October 13, 2005. http://www.suntimes.com/output/census/cst-nws-marriage13.html.

Appendix

Appendix: Joint-custody Statutes Nationwide, by State, with Family-violence Protections Noted

State	Joint-Custody Provisions				Family-Violence Provisions	
	Statutory Provisions	Statute No.	Terminology	Notes	Protections	Statute No.
Alabama	Permits joint arrangements	§ 30-3-150	Joint custody	Encourages frequent and continuing contact between child and noncustodian.	Rebuttable presumption that domestic violence is not in the best interest of child. Court must take into account the impact, if any, the domestic violence had on child.	§ 30-3-131
Alaska	Permits joint arrangements	§ 25.20.060	Shared custody		Rebuttable presumption that parent with domestic violence history may not be awarded sole legal, sole physical, joint legal, or joint physical custody of child.	§ 25.24.150(g)
Arizona	Permits joint arrangements	A.R.S. § 25-402	Joint custody		Rebuttable presumption that awarding custody is against child's best interest. Not applicable if both parents have committed acts of domestic violence. Court has discretion to use preponderance of the evidence standard.	A.R.S. §§ 25-403(N) and 25-403(E)
Arkansas	Permits joint custody	A.C.A. § 9-13-101	Joint custody	Encourages frequent and continuing contact between child and noncustodian.	Rebuttable presumption with court using preponderance of the evidence standard.	A.C.A. § 9-15-215(c)
California	Presumption for joint custody when parents have agreed	Cal. Fam. Code § 3020	Joint custody	Encourages frequent and continuing contact between child and noncustodian.	Presumption based on findings by court that domestic violence committed within last five years is not in best interest of the child. This presumption is rebuttable by preponderance of the evidence.	Cal. Fam. Code § 3044

Colorado	No specific provisions		Legislature recognized importance of child spending "quality time" with both parents, in most situations.	§ 46b-59b
Connecticut	Presumption for joint legal custody when both parents agree	Conn. Gen. Stat. § 46b-56a	Joint custody	Joint legal custody may be awarded without joint physical custody being awarded.	No mention of domestic violence, but parent guilty of murder may not be awarded visitation rights.	§ 46b-59b
Delaware	Permits joint arrangements	13 Del. C. § 728	Joint custody	Encourages frequent and continuing contact between child and noncustodian.	Rebuttable presumption against awarding of sole or joint custody.	13 Del. C. § 705A(a)
					Rebuttable presumption that no child shall primarily reside with a perpetrator of domestic violence. Presumption may be overcome through completion of certified domestic violence and drug and alcohol counseling programs. The above can be overcome through state-certified counseling programs.	13 Del. C. §705A(b)
District of Columbia	Presumption for joint legal and physical custody	D.C. Code § 16-194	Joint custody	Court may issue order encouraging frequent contact with each parent.	Joint custody in best interest of child, unless an "intrafamily offense" has been committed. This is any act punishable as a criminal offense against blood relative or mutual resident, or current or previous romantic partner.	13 Del. C. § 705A(c) § 16-194(B)\(5)

(continues)

Appendix: *(continued)*

	Joint-Custody Provisions				Family-Violence Provisions	
State	Statutory Provisions	Statute No.	Terminology	Notes	Protections	Statute No.
Florida	Preference for shared custody	Fla. Stat. § 61.13	Parental responsibilities	Public policy to assure frequent and continuing contact with each parent.	Rebuttable presumption for any parent convicted of felony in 3rd degree or higher involving domestic violence.	§ 61.13(2)(b)(2)
Georgia	Permits joint arrangements	O.C.G.A. § 19-9-3	Joint custody	Encourages frequent and continuing contact between child and noncustodian. Right of child 14 or over to select custodial parent, which is controlling unless parent is found to be unfit.	Court may consider domestic violence, but there is no rebuttable presumption.	§ 19-9-3(a)(3)
Hawaii	Permits joint arrangements	H.R.S. § 571-46.1	Joint custody	Best interest of the child is the standard, which may result in awarding custody to neither parent. Child's wish may be considered by the court.	Domestic violence raises a rebuttable presumption regarding sole, joint legal, or joint physical custody.	§ 571-46(9)
Idaho	Presumption for joint custody	Idaho Code § 32-7170	Joint custody	Encourages frequent and continuing contact between child and noncustodian.		
Illinois	Permits joint custody	750 I.L.S. § 5/602	Joint custody	Encourages frequent and continuing contact between child and noncustodian. Joint custody requires		

Indiana	Permits joint custody	Ind. Code Ann. § 31-17-2-21]	Joint custody	parents to submit a Joint Parenting Agreement to the court. This does not mean equal parenting time.	
				Rebuttable presumption regarding noncustodial parent convicted of domestic violence. Visitation must be supervised for at least one year and not more than two years, or until the child becomes emancipated.	§ 31-17-2-8.3
Iowa	Permits joint custody	Iowa Code § 598.1	Joint legal custody; joint physical care	Encourages frequent and continuing contact between child and noncustodian.	
Kansas	Preference for joint legal custody	K.S.A. § 60-1610	Joint legal custody	If parties have entered into a parenting plan, it is presumed to be in the child's best interest.	
				Spousal abuse is a factor considered by the court to determine custody and/or parenting time.	§ 60-1610
Kentucky	Permits joint custody	K.R.S. § 403.270	Joint custody	Domestic violence is a relevant factor considered by the court when determining the child's best interests.	§ 403.270(2)(f)
Louisiana	Permits joint custody	La.R.S. § 9:335	Shared physical custody; domiciliary parent	As much as possible, shared physical custody. Domiciliary parent has decision-making power, unless an implementation order provides otherwise.	

(continues)

Appendix: *(continued)*

		Joint-Custody Provisions			Family-Violence Provisions	
State	Statutory Provisions	Statute No.	Terminology	Notes	Protections	Statute No.
Maine	Permits joint custody	19-A M.R.S.A. § 1653	Parental rights and responsibilities	Encourages frequent and continuing contact between child and both parents.	Domestic abuse between the parents, past or current, is a factor considered by the court. Primary residence is awarded only if in the best interest of the child and adequate safety may be assured.	19-A M.R.S.A § 1653(6)(A)
Maryland	Permits joint custody	Md. Fam. Code Ann. § 5-203	Joint custody		If the court has reasonable grounds to believe child abuse has occurred, it shall determine whether future abuse would occur. Unless the court finds no likelihood of future abuse, the custody or visitations will be denied, except supervised visitation.	§ 9-101
Massachusetts	Permits joint custody	A.L.M. GL ch. 208 § 31	Shared legal custody; shared physical custody	Encourages frequent and continuing contact between child and both parents.	Court's finding that a pattern or serious incident of abuse creates a rebuttable presumption against sole or shared custody.	ch. 208 § 31A
Michigan	Permits joint custody	M.C.L § 722.26	Joint custody; parenting time	Presumed to be in the best interest of child to have a strong relationship with both parents.	Domestic violence, whether toward or witnessed by the child, is factor used by the court to determine best interest of the child.	§ 722.23
Minnesota	Presumption for joint legal custody	Minn. Sta. § 518.17	Joint custody	Encourages frequent and continuing contact between child and both parents.	Court uses rebuttable presumption that joint legal or physical custody is not in the best interest of the child if domestic abuse has occurred between parents.	§ 518.17

State				
Mississippi	Presumption for joint custody when both parents agree.	Miss. Code Ann. § 93-5-24	Joint custody	Rebuttable presumption that it is not in the best interest of the child to be placed in sole, joint legal, or joint physical custody with parent who has a history of perpetrating family violence. May only be rebutted upon preponderance of the evidence.	Miss. Ann. Code § 93-5-24
Missouri	Permits joint custody	R.S.Mo. § 452.375	Joint custody	Encourages frequent, continuing, and meaningful contact between child and both parents.	
				If the court finds that domestic violence or abuse occurred, the court shall make specific findings of fact to show the custody or visitation arrangement best protects the child, parent, or other family member who is the victim of the abuse.	R.S.Mo. § 452.375(13)
Montana	Allows for shared custody via parenting plan	MCA § 40-4-234	Parenting plan	Declares frequent and continuing contact with both parents is in the best interest of the child.	
				Court shall determine the parenting plan using domestic abuse as one of the factors.	§ 40-4-212
Nebraska	Permits joint custody	R.R.S. Neb. § 42-364	Joint custody	Custody and time spent with each parent based on best interest of child and the objective of maintaining the ongoing involvement of both parents.	
				Court shall consider "credible evidence" of abuse as a factor in determining the best interest of the child.	R.R.S. § 42-364(2)(d)
Nevada	Presumption for joint custody if both parents agree	N.R.S. § 125.490	Joint custody	Encourages frequent and continuing contact between child and both parents.	
				Court finds domestic violence based on clear and convincing evidence, then a rebuttable presumption is created that sole or joint custody is not in the best interest of the child.	

(*continues*)

Appendix: (continued)

	Joint-Custody Provisions				Family-Violence Provisions	
State	Statutory Provisions	Statute No.	Terminology	Notes	Protections	Statute No.
New Hampshire	Presumption for joint legal custody	R.S.A. § 458:17	Joint custody		Court shall make custody and visitation orders that best protect the children, spouse, or both where domestic violence has occurred.	R.S.A. § 458: 17(II)(c)
New Jersey	Permits joint custody	N.J. Stat. § 9:2-4	Joint custody	Encourages frequent and continuing contact between child and both parents.	The court considers the history of domestic violence when determining the best interest of the child.	N.J. Stat. § 9:2-4(c)
New Mexico	Presumption for joint legal custody	N.M. Stat. Ann. § 40-4-9.1	Joint custody		When a prior or current judicial adjudication finds person seeking custody has engaged in domestic violence, then custody or visitation order shall adequately protect the child, abused parent, or other household member.	N.M. Stat. Ann. § 40-4-9.1(B)(9)
New York	Permits joint custody	N.Y.C.L.S Dom.Rel. § 75-a	Joint custody			
North Carolina	Permits joint custody	N.C. Gen Stat. § 50-13.2	Joint custody	Joint custody shall be considered upon the request of either parent.	Court shall consider any acts of domestic violence when determining custody.	N.C. Gen Stat. § 50-13.2(a)
North Dakota	No specific provisions			Encourages frequent and continuing contact between child and noncustodian.	If the court finds domestic violence occurred, then only supervised visitation may occur, unless shown by clear and convincing evidence that unsupervised visitation will not endanger the child.	§ 14.05.22(3)

Ohio	Permits joint custody	O.R.C. Ann. § 3109.04	Shared parenting; residential parent; parental rights and responsibilities	Encourages frequent and continuing contact between child and both parents.	The court shall consider current or previous domestic abuse or violence in determining custody and visitation plans.	O.R.C. § 3109.04(F)(1)(h)
Oklahoma	Permits joint custody	43 Okl. St. § 109	Joint custody and joint care	Encourages frequent and continuing contact between child and both parents. Encourages parents to share in the rights and responsibilities of childrearing.	There is a rebuttable presumption that it is not in the child's best interest to have custody granted to a person convicted of a crime listed in the Oklahoma Child Abuse Reporting and Prevention Act.	43 Okl. St. § 112.2(B)(2)
Oregon	Permits joint custody	O.R.S. § 107.169	Joint custody	Encourages frequent and continuing contact between child and both parents and for those parents to share in the rights and responsibilities of raising their children.	Rebuttable presumption against awarding sole or joint custody to parent who committed abuse.	O.R.S. § 107.137(2)
Pennsylvania	Permits joint custody	23 Pa. C.S. § 5302	Shared custody	Encourages frequent and continuing contact between child and both parents.	Court shall consider each parent's present and past violent or abusive conduct when determining custody or visitation and may deny either to protect the child.	23 Pa. C.S. § 20-7-1535
Rhode Island	No specific provision				Court shall consider domestic abuse when determining custody and visitation. A finding of abuse is sufficient cause to deny visitation.	R.I. Gen. Laws § 15-5-16(3)

(*continues*)

Appendix: *(continued)*

	Joint-Custody Provisions				Family-Violence Provisions	
State	Statutory Provisions	Statute No.	Terminology	Notes	Protections	Statute No.
South Carolina	Permits joint custody	S.C. Code Ann. § 20-7-420	Joint or divided custody		Court must consider evidence of domestic violence when determining custody.	S.C. Code Ann. § 20-7-1530
South Dakota	Permits joint custody	S.D. § 25-5-7.1	Joint custody			
Tennessee	Presumption for joint custody if both parents agree	Tenn. Code Ann. § 36-6-101	Joint custody		Court shall consider evidence of physical or emotional abuse to the child, other parent, or to any other person when determining custody.	Tenn. Code Ann. § 36-6-106(8)
Texas	Presumption for joint legal custody	Tex. Fam. Code § 153.133	Conservatorship	Encourages frequent and continuing contact between child and noncustodian.	It is a rebuttable presumption that the appointment of both parents as joint managing conservators is in the child's best interest. A finding of domestic violence removes this presumption.	Tex. Fam. Code § 153.131(b)
Utah	Permits joint custody	Utah Code Ann. § 30-3-10	Joint custody	Encourages frequent and continuing contact between child and noncustodian. In every case, the court shall consider joint custody.	In determining whether the best interest of the child will be served by ordering joint legal or physical custody, the court shall consider any history or potential for child abuse, spouse abuse, or kidnapping.	Utah Code Ann. § 30-3-10.2
Vermont	Presumption for joint custody if parents agree	15 V.S.A. § 666	Parental rights and responsibilities	When the parents cannot agree to divide or share parental rights, the courts shall award parental rights primarily or solely to one parent.	Evidence of abuse is one factor considered by the court when determining custody.	15 V.S.A. § 665(b)(9)

Virginia	Permits joint custody	Va. Code Ann. § 20.124.1	Joint custody		Any history of child abuse shall be considered when determining custody or visitation arrangements.	Va. Code Ann. § 20-124.3(9)
Washington	Permits joint custody	R.C.W. § 26.09.184	Rights and responsibilities physical care; residential time	Encourages frequent and continuing contact between child and both parents. Encourages the parents to meet their responsibilities through a parenting plan rather than judicial intervention.	Residential time with a child shall be limited if a parent has engaged in a history of acts of domestic violence.	R.C.W. § 26.09.191
West Virginia	Presumption for joint legal custody	W.Va. Code § 48-9-207	Joint custody; decision-making responsibility	Encourages frequent and continuing contact with both parents who show ability to act in the child's best interest.	Court may not allocate custodial or decision-making responsibility to a parent who has abused a child, unless the court makes special written findings the child will be safe.	W.Va. Code § 48-9-207(a)(c)
Wisconsin	Presumption for joint legal custody	Wis. Stat. § 767.24	Joint custody	Encourages frequent and continuing contact between child and both parents	Evidence of domestic abuse creates a rebuttable presumption that awarding sole or joint custody is in the child's best interest.	Wis. Stat. § 767.24(2)(d)(1)
Wyoming	Permits joint custody	Wyo. Stat. § 20-2-201	Joint custody	Custody shall be crafted to promote the best interests of the children, and may include any combination of joint, shared, or sole custody.	Court shall consider evidence of spousal abuse or child abuse as being contrary to the best interest of the children and the court shall make arrangements for visitation that best protects the children and the abused spouse from further harm.	Wyo. Stat. § 20-2-201(b)

Index

Adams, Frank G., 164n25
Adeyanju, Matthew, 187n9
Ahrons, Constance R., 88n31; 140n65
Albert, Gerald, 59n28
Alexander, Duane, 188n20
Amato, Paul R., 12nn1–2; 34n3; 63n92; 114nn96–97; 141n67; 141nn69–70; 164n37; 165n38; 187n4
American Bar Association, 125; 140n53; Model Joint Custody Statute, 67
Anderson, J. E., 59n26
Arbuthnot, Jack, 44; 59n19; 60n49; 61n52; 61n58; 63n94; 89n60; 188nn30–31
Arditti, Joyce A., 113n66; 114n91; 188n28
Arendell, Terri J., 94; 110nn22–23
Arizona, 157–59
Arkansas, 157–59
Association for Conflict Resolution, 19; 35n30
Association for Family and Conciliation Courts, 43; 60n35
Atwood, Joan D., 62n70
Austin, William, 163n7
Ayoub, Catherine C., 163n8

Babcock, J., 80
Bacon, Brenda L., 61n53; 61n60
Bahr, Stephen J., 36n51
Bailey, Deborah S., 88n46
Barnes family: divorce education and, 56–57; introduction to, 9–11; joint custody and, 103–4; mediation and, 17–18; presumption for joint custody and, 118
Barnes, Stephanie N., 138n23
Barnett, W. Steven, 189n45
Barry, Margaret Martin, 111nn39–40; 125; 140n54; 140n56
Bauserman, Robert, 107; 114n86
Beck, Connie J.A., 21; 25; 31–33; 36n41; 61n65
Beck, Peggy, 34n9
Bender, William N., 76; 88n42
Besharov, Douglas J., 188n18
Beyond the Best Interests of the Child. See Goldstein, Joseph
Bigelow, M. A., 59n24
Biondi, Eileen D., 44; 60n47
Blades, Joan, 34n2
Blaisure, Karen R., 40; 43–44; 59nn16–17; 60n36; 188n32

203

Bloom, Bernard L., 62n69; 154; 165nn55–56
Blossfeld, Hans-Peter, 35n22
Borenzweig, Herman, 110n21
Boyd, Susan, 111n29
Bradford, Jack, 43; 60n33
Brandt, Elizabeth, 112n56
Brandwein, Ruth A., 110n19
Braver, Sanford L., 59nn13–14; 76; 88n45; 149–50; 153; 165n50; 166n59; 166n64; 187n6
Brindley, Jean, 43; 60n34
Brinig, Margaret F., 167n77
Brody, Gene, 114n98; 139n34; 164n36
Brown, Emily M., 35n31
Brown, T. C., 87n10
Bruch, Carol S., 95
Buchanan, Christy M., 12n3; 107; 113n83; 114n85
Buehler, Cheryl, 59n12; 166n63
Bulow, Janet, 164n29
Bussey, Marian, 62n76

California: mediation, 15; 19; parenting plans, 67
Cancian, Maria, 113n72
Carbone, June R., 111n30; 140n57
Carpenter, Krista, 138n18
Carpenter, Mackenzie, 165n51
Carrington, Christopher, 165n42
Catania, Francis J., 87n19
Census Bureau, 2; 9
Chambers, David A., 189n43
Chesler, Phyllis, 96
Cheung, Siu-kau, 35n26
Chien-Chung, Huang, 189n35
child custody decisions: best interests of the child, 4; tender years doctrine, 2. *See* gender neutral laws
child custody terminology: used in book, 6–9
Children's Rights Council, 114n89; 133; 139n33
Chiu, Wen-Ta, 187n12
Chused, Richard H., 12n9
Clement, Debra A., 45; 60n48
Coates, Christine A., 87n17; 88n47

Cohen, M., 58n3
Cohen, Orna, 35n25
Coller, David R., 112n52
Cook, James A., 112n50; 138n6
Coontz, Stephanie, 12n11
Corcoran, Mary, 110n25
Coren, Ester, 58n7
Cornfield, Leslie Ann, 34n10
Covell, Katherine, 87n26
covenant marriage, 156–62; history of, 157–58; implementation of, 161–62; state statute, 158–59; use of, 159–61
Cowen, Emery L., 115n105
Creswell, Richard W., 13n35
Criddle, Monte N. Jr., 61n61
Crippen, Gary, 139n20
Crosbie-Brunett, Margaret, 113n81
Crosby, Heather, 87n4
Cullen, Francis T., 110n24
Cummins, H. J., 87n11
Czapanskiy, Karen, 87n8

D'Errico, Maria G., 89n53
Danoff, Nancy L., 58n6
Darmstadt, Gary, 58n2
de la Cruz, Bonna M., 89n56
deLusé, Stephanie Raue, 62n80
Depner, Charlene E., 110n9
Devlin, Ann Sloan, 61n55; 165n54
Di Bias, Trecia, 60n39
Dillon, Peter A., 189n38
DiTomasso, Robert A., 189n42
divorce: history of, 1–2
divorce education, 39–58; 170–71; barriers to program adoption, 44–45; for children, 42; 48; 56; effectiveness of, 50–56; family violence and, 41; history of, 43–45; in mediation, 17; 45; problems with research and, 48–50; in state statute, 46–48
divorce laws: gender-neutral laws, 3–4; National Conference of Commissioners on Uniform State Laws, 4; no-fault laws, 2–3
Donnelly, Denise, 105; 113n74; 113n78

Douglas, Emily M., 13n36; 62n81; 89n52; 101; 113n44; 113n67; 134; 138n14; 141n62
Dowd, Nancy E., 110n7
Dunne, John E., 80; 89n51

Elderkin, Patsy, 113n68; 113n69
Elkin, Meyer, 140n43; 178; 188n22
Elliott, S. A., 189n41
Ellis Jane W., 67; 79; 81–82; 87n5; 87n7
Emery, Robert E., 16; 25; 30–31; 33; 34n6; 34n11; 35n32; 36n46; 188n33; 189nn36–37
Epstein, William M., 189n40

Families in Transition, 63n86
Fatherhood Coalition, 140n50
Fathers and Families, 140n51
fathers' rights arguments, 93–95
Feld, Scott L., 166n72
feminist arguments, 95–97
Feng, Pei, 62n74
Ferguson, S., 87n23
Fetzner, William N., 109n3; 139n39
Fields, Lynda Fox, 88n41; 163n2
Fineman, Martha A., 110n8; 111n28
Finley, Gordon E., 163n12
Fischer, Karla, 35n34; 163n9
Fischer, Robert L., 45; 60n50
Florida, 157; 159
Folberg, Jay, 34n19; 112n47; 112n55; 138n5
Foster, Catherine, 13n37; 110n13; 139n40
Foy, Kathy, 35n27
Frazee, Evelyn, 59n22; 88n28
Freely, Maureen, 87n21
Freeman, Rhonda, 87n20
Frieden, Thomas R., 188n17
Frieman, Barry, 60n45
Fuhrmann, Geri S., 41–42; 59n21; 86n3
Furstenberg, Frank F., 113n79; 187n3

Gallagher, Maggie, 166n69
Gallagher, Mary P., 165n46
Garner, Joe, 164n22

Garon, Risa J., 71; 87n18
Gaynor, James K., 117; 138n1
Geasler, Margie J., 40; 42; 44; 55; 59n15; 59n18
Geelhoed, Robyn J., 48; 59n23
gender neutral laws, 3–4
Gentry, Deborah B., 34n4
Glick, Paul C., 12n15; 12n18; 34n12
Glover, Rebecca J., 114n94
Goldstein, Joseph, 34n17; 94–95; 111n27
Goldzband, Melvin G., 112n49
Gomes, Heather, 165n48
Gottfried, Sarah L., 164n20
Green, Maureen, 13n25; 93; 110n17
Groves, E. R., 59n27
Grych, John H., 165n52
Guggenheim, Martin, 109n1
Gunnoe, Marjorie Lindner, 114n84

Hahn, Robert A., 21; 35n36
Halem, L. C., 12n14
Handschu, Barbara E., 164n27
Hans, Jason D., 62n82
Hardcastle, Gerald W., 111n33; 138n4
Hardesty, Jennifer L., 163n6
Hastings, Honey, 13n29; 140n46
Hawkins, Alan J., 167n75
Hawkins, Asher, 164n28
Hawkins, Lois E., 138n8
Hayes, Maxine, 188n19
Haynes, John M., 18; 34n1; 34n18
Heim, Sheila, 111n41
Henry, Ronald K., 121; 137; 138n13
Hernandez, Raymund, 188n14
Herndon, Nancy, 110n16
Herrmann, Andrew, 189n46
Hetherington, E. Mavis, 163n8
Hipke, Kathleen N., 115n106
Holstein, Ned, 140n58
Howe, George, 60n44
Howell, Robert, 13n33
Huang, Chien-Chung, 113n75
Huber, Arlene Brown, 139n21
Hughes, Robert Jr., 36n53
Humphrey, Tom, 89n55; 89n57
Hutchinson, Eliza B., 111n37

Hyden, Margareta, 35n24
Hymowitz, Paul, 88n44

Idaho, 77; 119
Illinois, 157
Indiana, 71; 157
Irvin, Karen K., 34n8

Jacobs, Margaret A., 165n43
Jaffe, Peter G., 163nn10–11
Jekielek, Susan A., 63n91; 141n71
Johnson, Kendall D., 35n29
Johnston, Janet R., 34n7; 63n93; 112n53; 114n95; 135; 141nn72–73; 162n1; 164n34
joint custody, 91–109; 192–201; 171–72; effectiveness of, 104–9; factors associated with, 102–3; history of, 92–98; parental preferences for, 100–1; percentage of families with, 101–2; state statute, 192–201
Jones, Tricia S., 28; 36n58

Kay, Herma Hill, 12n17; 34n14
Keim, David, 89n58
Kellam, Susan, 110n4
Kelley, Michael, 188n16
Kelly, Joan B., 13n26; 21–22; 25; 27; 29–30; 35n39; 36nn44–45; 36n48; 36n56; 71; 88n33; 113n70; 141n63; 187n1; 188nn24–25
Kelly, M., 110n18
Kids' Turn, 63n85
Kim, Walter, 166n74
Kingsbury, Jill S., 165n47
Kisthardt, Mary Kay, 164n26
Kline, Marsha, 63n90; 113n77
Knight, Al, 87n12
Koel, Amy, 88n39
Kramer, Kevin M., 41; 55; 59n20
Kramer, Laurie, 54; 61n59; 62n77; 86n1
Krucoff, Carol, 36n49
Kruk, Edward, 124; 112n57; 140n41; 140n48
Kuehl, Sheila J., 95; 111n35; 126; 138n15

Kuhn, D. Richard, 13n27; 101; 113n63; 140n60
Kurkowski, Kevin P., 62n78

La Vaque, Theodore J., 189n39
Lamb, Michael E., 13n23
Lee, Mo-Yee, 112n60; 139n35; 165n39
Lee, Philip, 13n39
legal professionals: attorneys, mediation and, 26; judges, divorce education programs, 45
Lehner, Larry, 60n43
Leinonen, Jenni A., 115n102
Levy, David, 140n64
Logan, T. K., 163n5
Louisiana: presumption for joint custody, 119–21
Lowery, Carol, 12n6
Lye, Diane B., 81–82; 85; 89n54
Lyon, Eleanor, 60n42

Maccoby, Eleanor E., 13n28; 88n30; 112n51; 114n88; 126; 140n47
Magana, Holly A., 35n35
Maldonado, Solangel, 138n24; 178; 188n23
Mann, Robert E., 187n13
Mannino, Fortune V., 60n32
Martinez, Charles R., 166n65
Marvell, Thomas B., 13n21
Masters, Brooke A., 163n16
Mathis, Richard D., 62n72
Mazur-Hart, Stanley F., 13n20
Mazzoli, Enrico A., 163n15
McClure, Thomas E., 61n62
McElroy, Wendy 163n13; 165n44
McIsaac, Hugh, 34n20; 112n48
McKee, Mike, 165n45
McKenry, Patrick C., 61n63; 112n59
McKenzie, Brad, 62n73
McLanahan, Sara S., 110n20
mediation, 15–33; 169–70; alternative to adversarial system, 15–17; description of, 15–17; effectiveness of, 24–32; family violence and, 20–21; gender and, 21; history of,

18–20; international trends, 19; problems with research on, 31–32; special populations and, 20–22; state statute, 19; 22; 23–24; types of, 22
Medley, Morris L., 36n52
Meierding, Nina R., 36n57
Meislin, Richard J., 163n17
Melton, Brian J., 139n25
Meyers, S. A., 58n9
Missouri, 70
Minnesota, 122
Montana, 76
Moody, Janette, 110n5
Moore, A. A., 58n1
Morrison, Donna Ruane, 63n89
Moser, Lorna L., 189n44
Musetto, Andrew P., 13n34

Nagel, Stuart, 111n26
Nakonezny, Paul A., 34n13
National Center for Health Statistics, 35n28
National Organization for Women, 97; 112n45; 121; California chapter, 121; 139n22; Washington chapter, 111n36
Neubauer, Peter B., 59n29
Nock, Steven L., 159–61; 166nn70–71
Nord, Christine Winquist, 113n65

Ohio, 26
Oklahoma, 77
Oliphant, Emmerentie, 63n87
Oregon, 70; 77
Oskamp, Stuart, 187n10
Owen, M. T., 58n10

Packer, G. M., 59n25
Pagani-Kurtz, L., 114n100
parental conflict, 71; 108
parental relocation, 143–51; history of, 144–48; research and, 149–51; state statute, 148–49
parental rights and responsibilities. *See* joint custody
parenting plans, 65–86; 171; description of, 65–66; 68–75; effectiveness of, 79–85; examples of, 72–75; family violence and, 77; history of, 67–68; international trends, 68; noncompliance with, 75–76; state statute, 77–79
Pearson, Jessica, 34n5; 36n47; 36n55; 58; 113n73; 139n28; 188n26
Pedro-Carroll, JoAnne L., 62n83
Peterman, P. J., 58n5
Petersen, Virginia, 62n71
Peterson, James L., 12n4
Peterson, Richard R., 34nn15–16
Phear, W.P., 113n71
Polikoff, Nancy D., 138n19
Pollak, Gertrude K., 60n30
Pons-Bunney, Jacqueline, 87n14
Ponzetti, J. J., 59n11
Pruett, Marsha Kline, 62n68; 89n50; 114n99; 139nn36–37; 141n68; 152; 164n35; 166n57; 166nn60–62; 187n8
presumption in child custody statute, 117–37; 172; debate over, 122–28; description of, 117–18; family violence and, 121–22; history of, 119–22; legal custody and, 121; parental conflict, 134–36; physical custody and, 119–21; primary caregiver presumption and, 122; state statute, 129–32
prevention programs, 151–56; Collaborative Divorce Project, 152–53; Dads for Life, 153–54; effectiveness of, 152–56; New Beginnings Program, 155–56; Orientation for Divorcing Parents, 153; Parenting for Divorced Fathers, 154
Puder, Douglas R., 187n11
Puente, Maria, 163n14

Rankin, Bill, 164n30
Rankin, Deborah, 110n6
Reihing, Katherine M., 138n16; 163n3
Reilly, Jackie L., 58n8
Reynolds, Suzanne, 112n46
Ricci, Isolina, 35n38

Rigby, Kenneth, 120; 138n7; 138n9
Riley, Glenda, 12n10
Robinson, Holly L., 113n76; 140n42
Roeder-Esser, Carol, 60n38
Roman, Melvin, 13n24; 37n59; 110n10; 111n32; 139nn31–32
Rosier, Katherine Brown, 167n79
Rothberg, Barbara, 114n92
Rotman, Arline S., 164n23
Rotundo, E. Anthony, 13n22; 109n2

Salazar, Laura F., 178; 188n21
Salem, Peter, 60n46
Sanchez, Laura, 166n73; 167n76; 167n78
Saposnek, Donald T., 26; 36n54
Scherer, David G., 115n104
Schleuderer, Claude, 87n16
Schulman, Joanne, 97; 111n38; 126; 140n59
Scott, P. Mars, 87n13
Selleck, Linda R., 138n12
Seltzer, Judith A., 112n62; 114n87; 139nn26–27; 139nn29–30; 188n29
Shapero, Lila, 112n43
shared parenting. *See* joint custody
Shifflett, Kelly, 62n79
Shiller, Virginia F., 114n93
Shrier, Diane K., 114n90; 188n27
Siegel, Michael, 188n15
Silitsky, Daniel, 106; 114n82; 141n66
Slaikeu, Karl A., 36n40
Smart, Laura S., 36n50
social policy: changing social attitudes and, 173; 176–78; effectiveness of, 173; 176–78; for families of divorce problems with research, 181–85; recommendations for policymakers, 178–81; 186; recommendations for research, 185–86; summary, 173; 174–76
Spaht, Katherine Shaw, 140n61
Sprecher, Susan, 12n8
Sprenkel, Douglas H., 60n37
Stamps, Leighton E., 110nn11–12; 138nn10–11

Stearns, Peter N., 12n13
Stern, Marilyn, 139n38
Stewart, Jim, 87n15
Stolberg, Arnold L., 155; 166n68
Stone, Glenn, 62n75; 112n61
Straus, Murray A., 35n37
Surace, Peter Ted, 164n24

Taylor, Raymond J., 61n51
Taylor, Ronald D., 115n103
tender-years doctrine, 2; 92
Tennessee, 69–70; 76; 82–84
Terdal, Leif, 60n31
Thoennes, Nancy, 58; 61n54
Thomas, Amanda McCombs, 115n101
Thompson, Ross A., 138n17
Tjaden, Patricia, 140n52
Toews, Michelle L., 30; 61n57; 187n5; 163n4
Tondo, Carrie-Anne, 34n21
Tschann, Jeanne M., 63n88; 165n40

U.S. Bureau of the Census, 76; 88n40; 101; 113n64; 140n55; 189n34

Vanderkooi, Lois, 22; 36n43
Vestal, Anita, 36n42

Wald, Michael S., 13n30
Walker, David M., 137n3
Wallerstein, Judith, 12n5; 12n7; 146–47; 150; 163n19; 164nn31–33; 187n2
Walton, Lisa, 35n23
Warren, Nancy J., 60n41
Washington, D.C., 121
Washington State, 65–67; 76; 79–82; 157
Weiner, Barbara A., 13n32
Weissman, Herbert N., 164n21
Wells, Kris, 110n15; 140n44
West Virginia, 67–68; 76
Wolchik, Sharlene A., 61nn66–67; 88n43; 106; 113n80; 155; 165n53; 166n58; 166nn66–67; 187n7
Women's Law Center of Maryland, 111n42

Woo, Junda, 87n9
Woodhouse, Barbara Bennett, 12n12; 112n54
Woods, Gloria, 111n34
Wright, Gerald C., 13n19
Whipple, Ellen E., 58n4
Wilcox, Katheryn L., 112n58
Wilgoren, Jodi, 88n34
Wisconsin, 127

Yankeelov, Pamela.A., 53; 61n64
Yenckel, James T., 110n14; 140n45
Young, Cathy, 13n38; 140n49

Zibbell, Robert A., 60n40
Zimmerman, Diane Kircher, 53; 61n56
Zuberbuhler, Jayne, 35n33
Zuckman, Jill, 111n31
Zurcher, Kristina E., 167n80

About the Author

Emily M. Douglas, Ph.D., is an assistant professor at Bridgewater State College in Massachusetts. She completed her doctoral work in public policy in 2002; her primary research interests focus on social and family policies, including divorce, child maltreatment fatalities, statutory provisions regarding religiously-motivated medical neglect, family violence, and refugee resettlement. Dr. Douglas completed a postdoctoral research fellowship at the Family Research Laboratory, at the University of New Hampshire, under the mentorship of Dr. Murray Straus. Dr. Douglas resides in New England with her family where she enjoys reading political biographies, hiking, training for running races, community involvement, and long back-road drives.

```
HQ 834 .D68 2006
Douglas, Emily M., 1973-
Mending broken families
```

AUG 3 0 2006